ABNORMAL PSYCHOLOGY

ABNORMAL PSYCHOLOGY

K.C. Shukla
Tara Chand

Commonwealth

Abnormal Psychology

Edition : 2019

ISBN 81-7169-905-7

Published by :
COMMONWEALTH PUBLISHERS
4831/24, Prahlad Street,
Ansari Road, Darya Ganj,
New Delhi - 110002
Ph. : 23275511, 23257835
e-mail : commonwealthbooks@gmail.com

Typesetting by :
Rishu Computers
Delhi

Printed at :
Divine Digital Press
Delhi

PREFACE

Abnormalcy in behaviour is a great handicap in the smooth development of a society. Psychologists have found that there are various characteristics of abnormal persons, some of them are hereditary and some of them are acquired. Psychologists have tried to devise correctional methods also.

Consider these facts: Schizophrenia is a major social problem of our times. It is very likely that every reader of this book has watched at least one of his school or college classmates become nervous and "queer" and has subsequently heard that this individual has suffered a "nervous breakdown" and has been sent to the "asylum." In many cases no more has been heard from him. The chances are that this individual has developed schizophrenia. Schizophrenia will be dealt with in all its aspects in the course of this book. For the present it will suffice to point out that more hospital beds are occupied by individuals suffering from schizophrenia than by persons suffering from tuberculosis and cancer combined. In the United States over 15,000 new cases of schizophrenia enter the state-supported hospitals each year and these by no means include all the cases in the population. Furthermore, these are mostly people in the first flush of youth. And schizophrenia is not a disease like mumps or chicken pox or even tuberculosis, having a relatively short and definite course. Schizophrenia are among the youngest admitted to the hospitals and have an average hospital life of over sixteen years.

It is believed that the book will prove to lie of immense value to social reformers, planners and educational administrators as well.

K.C. Shukla
Tara Chand

CONTENTS

Preface V

Chapters **Pages**

1. Normality, Abnormality, Personality 1
2. The Historical Development of Psychopathology 26
3. The Psychosomatic Problem 55
4. The Psychoneuroses 79
5. Abnormalities of Sexual Behaviour 99
6. Character Disorders 116
7. Genius or Abnormal 140
8. Toward an Experimental Psychopathology 165
9. Psychoanalysis: Basic Postulates, Theory of Personality Structure 198
10. Psychoanalysis: Theory of Psychosexual Genesis 229
11. Psychoanalysis: Summary, Criticism 264
12. Other Theoretical Approaches 279

1

NORMALITY, ABNORMALITY, PERSONALITY

1. THE SCOPE OF MODERN PSYCHOPATHOLOGY

Consider these facts: Schizophrenia is a major social problem of our times. It is very likely that every reader of this book has watched at least one of his school or college classmates become nervous and "queer" and has subsequently heard that this individual has suffered a "nervous breakdown" and has been sent to the "asylum." In many cases no more has been heard from him. The chances are that this individual has developed schizophrenia. Schizophrenia will be dealt with in all its aspects in the course of this book. For the present it will suffice to point out that more hospital beds are occupied by individuals suffering from schizophrenia than by persons suffering from tuberculosis and cancer combined. In the United States over 15,000 new cases of schizophrenia enter the state-supported hospitals each year and these by no means include all the cases in the population. Furthermore, these are mostly people in the first flush of youth. And schizophrenia is not a disease like mumps or chicken pox or even tuberculosis, having a relatively short and definite course. Schizophrenia are among the youngest admitted to the hospitals and have an average hospital life of over sixteen years.

If schizophrenia is the most frequent of the major mental disorders, it is by no means the only one. Others range from diseases where the symptoms are quite obviously mental to those which the layman would not consider mental at all. A well-known practising physician estimates that the "cause" of 60 per cent of the apparently physical disorders which he sees is "psychological". Other practising physicians would undoubtedly consider this estimate too high, but every alert practising physician today realizes the role of psychological factors in disease. Thus we can definitely state that, besides the cases of mental disorder which are quite obviously within the province of the psychiatrist, a great many cases of apparent physical disease have important psychological aspects. But modern psychopathology is by no means limited to the study of "psychotics" or the severely insane, as the term "mental disease" usually implies. Rather it is concerned with the whole field of personality and behaviour disorders. In recent times the problems of criminal behaviour, sexual perversion, alcoholic and narcotic addiction, and even genius have become realized to be problems for psychopathology. Modern psychopathology deals with at least six main types of personality structure. These are the psychotic, the psychoneurotic, the sexually perverse, the disordered character, the genius, and the normal. Precise definition of these types will be given in the course of this book. Since we shall have to use these concepts for illustrative purposes before such precise definition is possible we may characterize them provisionally as follows. (The *psychotic* is the individual who is so ill mentally that he is no longer sufficiently adjusted to reality to continue active in his social environment. These are the individuals who are legally "insane". The neurotic (or psychoneurotic, the words being used interchangeably) is mentally ill but not nearly so seriously as is the psychotic. The *sexually perverse* individual is one who gains sexual satisfaction only by perverse means or with love objects other than an adult member of the opposite sex. He is popularly looked on as a degenerate or sinner. The *charactero logically disordered* individual shows no "mental" illness in the ordinary meaning of the term but has behavioural difficulties (criminality, alcoholism, etc.) which lead him to be considered antisocial or degenerate or "ornery". The genius is the individual who, motivated by psychological conflicts, produces works of art or science of social value.

The time has come in contemporary medicine where the practitioner should know as much about psychology and psychiatry as he does about physiology and pathology. Unfortunately, such practising physicians are few. Works like those of Dr. Franz Alexander (1936),[1] Dr. Karl Menninger (1938), and Dr. Flanders Dunbar (1935) show us in detail how modern medicine has discovered that every behaviour, whether we consider the behaviour of a sick individual or of a well individual, offers problems to the physiologist and to the psychologist. It is no exaggeration to say that at least half of the medicine of the future will be psychological medicine practised by medical psychologists. The last quarter century has witnessed the most striking advance throughout the field of internal medicine. Many of the physical diseases previously fatal are today treated in a specific fashion. The average duration of the human life has increased about eleven years in the last quarter century. And in the last quarter century the increased life expectancy brought about by better methods of physical hygiene has occurred at a time when the psychological stresses of war, depression, and economic uncertainty have probably made psychological adjustment more difficult.[2] All this makes it most probable that in the future the importance of psychological medicine will outweigh that of physical medicine. These facts should show how important psychology is for the practising physician.

But modern psychopathology is of great importance to the layman too. About 470,000 Americans are confined in hospitals for the care of the insane and in every year 150,000 new patients are admitted. These figures do not include the many individuals in small private sanitaria or under the care of individual physicians. The many mild cases which never come under a physician's care at all are also unrepresented. Although it is hard to get reliable statistics on this problem, it has been estimated that 5 out of every 100 American citizens will at some time or other be confined in a state hospital because of mental illness, and, since many individuals who should be hospitalized are not, it is conservatively estimated that an additional 5 out of every 100 are at some time incapacitated although not hospitalized because of mental disease. Thus 10 per cent of the population at one time or another suffer from the severer types of mental disease. Just as the common cold, which does not require hospitalization, is more frequent than pneumonia, which does, the greater number of mental diseases are not so severe that they require hospitalization. President Angell or Yale estimated that about 15 per cent of the American college undergraduate body at any given time are in need of the services of the mental hygienist. If at any given time 15 per cent are in need of care, one could fairly accurately estimate that at some time nearly the whole population is at least in need of advice. From the author's experiences as a teacher in American universities, he believes that it is almost impossible for any individual to go through four years of the intensely competitive situation of the college campus without at one time or another developing some slight mental abnormality. Consequently, abnormal psychology is of importance to all of us. Thus its study has become recognized to be of the greatest value in studying the so-called "normal personality". We shall emphasize this throughout this book.[3]

Through recorded history until the middle of the nineteenth century, mental abnormality was considered uncommon and terrible. (At times, as we shall see, the mentally abnormal were also looked on as particularly "inspired" or "chosen" individuals.) Mental abnormality meant "losing one's mind". It was usually considered so terrible a misfortune that one hesitated to speak about it. Today we realize that mental abnormality is neither uncommon nor necessarily terrible. Some of the milder and more frequent forms are today much more amenable to treatment than many physical ailments and, as with physical ailments, are today recognized as exaggerations or perversions of normal processes. The chief tenet of modern psychopathology is that *abnormal psychological phenomena are simply exaggerations (i.e., overdevelopments or underdevelopments), or disguised (i.e., perverted) developments of the normal psychological phenomena.* This viewpoint is undoubtedly the most important single contribution of modern psychology to our knowledge of the human being. Before we point out the reasons for its importance and the reasons for which we hold it, we must review briefly the old conception of abnormality and point out why this old view was held forso many centuries.

2. THE CONCEPT OF ABNORMALITY

Until recent times everyone considered mental abnormality uncommon and terrible. This is the case even today with many laymen. When it was not considered terrible, it was often considered comic or amusing. One has only to think of the stage presentation of the lunatic. If a member of one's immediate family "loses his mind," it becomes a great and unspeakable tragedy. If it is someone not so near and dear who becomes "crazy," "nuts," or "haywire," it may be considered screamingly funny. Until very recently the insane, the mentally deficient, and the criminal were considered to from a special group below the normal group, just as the particularly gifted were considered to form a special group

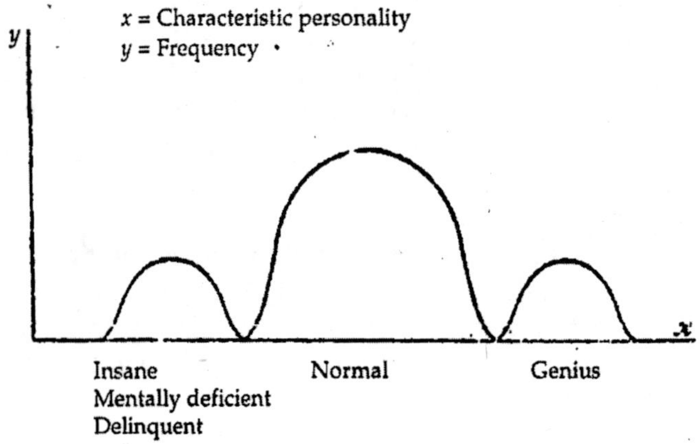

Fig. 1.1 : Showing the distribution of personalities as popularly considered.

above the normal group. The laws governing the behaviour of the insane and delinquent, as well as those governing the behaviour of genius, were considered special laws. The mechanisms underlying the delusions of the insane and the creations of the genius were not the same as the mechanisms governing the behaviour of "the rest of us". The distribution of human personality, popularly considered, is that given in Fig. 1.1. Even today in popular thinking there are three distinct "types" of humans, the unfortunate insane and delinquent, the geniuses, and the normals who make up the "rest of us". Furthermore, in popular thinking there is no continuity between these groupings and no borderline cases. An individual is either definitely "normal" or definitely a "genius" or definitely "insane". While normal behaviour was the result of normal causes, the process of becoming insane or becoming a genius was considered the result of special causes. Those driven insane were being avenged by God for their sins or were suffering through heredity for the sins of their forefathers. These who became geniuses were the recipients of divine inspiration. This viewpoint, which in one form of another was universal, was held until about one hundred years ago even by men of science, and among laymen is still widespread. The author seldom meets for the first time a group of psychology students where there is not at least one individual who considers all the insane syphilitic, or at least one who considers insanity due to masturbation. Similarly, the genius is understood only as the specially chosen or specially gifted.

There are three reasons why such a viewpoint remains so widespread. In the first place, until about one hundred years ago it was the prevalent theory held among even learned men. We must remember that modern science goes back only about four hundred years, and we must remember also that, before science, natural events which were difficult to explain were accounted for on theological grounds. Before we could have a modern psychology, we had to have a modern physics, chemistry, biology, and physiology. The reasons for this will become clear in the next chapter.

In the second place, and this followed from the prevalent theology, there was a decided social stigma in connection with insanity. Insanity was considered possession by the devil or the result of sinning, and even in enlightened circles, where medieval theology had been replaced by modern biology, it was believed to be due to faulty heredity. Consequently, the first discoveries in modern genetics simply pushed the responsibility from the individual as the sinner a little further back onto his sinning ancestry.

In the third place, personality was looked on as constant, bestowed by God or (again, in more advanced circles) by personal heredity. Every individual likes to believe that he has an ego or self, his inner picture of his personality, which remains constant and does not change with the vicissitudes of life, unless, perhaps, he loses it completely. From this arises the popular characterizations of insanity as "losing the mind," "being out of one's self," and the like. The theological belief that man was created in God's image and placed on a world which is the center of things is one which is very flattering and consequently very hard for most of us to give up. The reader has certainly heard something about the great difficulty with which the Copernican astronomy, which rightfully insisted that the sun was the center of the solar system, was established over the Ptolemaic, in which all things revolved about the earth. It is psychologically much easier to give up belief in the earth as the center of things than in personality as a constant, unchangeable, God-given entity. In a few paragraphs we shall develop a modern and very different concept of personality. The popular view, that both the insane and the genius are completely distinct from the normal, must be abandoned for the viewpoint of modern psychology, which sees personality traits as distributed on a continuum. To repeat from above: Abnormal psychological phenomena are simply exaggerations (i.e., overdevelopments or underdevelopments) or disguised (i.e., perverted) developments of the normal psychological phenomena. This viewpoint has several important methodological implications.

In the first place, it overcomes the trichotomy, abnormal, normal, genius. The electricity produced in the laboratory is of the same nature as that produced in the electrical storm. The one law of falling bodies covers such different phenomena as free fall, movement down an inclined plane, the flight of birds, and the movement of the heavenly bodies. The firecracker and the bomb, the electric lamp and the sun obey the same physical laws. Similarly, the productions of the genius, the ravings of the lunatic, and the sentence which you are now reading are produced by mechanisms which vary in degree and not in kind. What we previously considered abnormal, that is, away from the normal and different from the normal, represent simply exaggerations or disguised developments of normal thinking, feeling, willing, and acting.

In the second place, we consider that these abnormal mental phenomena have natural causes and obey the same laws as do the normal mental phenomena. Thus abnormal mental phenomena are not caused by supernatural forces like "punishment by God," or "possession by the devil" or, on the other hand, by "spiritual inspiration" but by ordinary psychological laws. Thus they have a significance or meaning. We believe that just as his logical and coherent thinking has a significance or meaning to the normal individual, so do his "ravings" to the insane individual. Actually through modern psychopathology we can decipher what this significance is when we have considerable knowledge of the individual's past life history and present life situation. Similarly the productions of the genius have a meaning in connection with his life history.

In the third place, we believe that just as normal thinking and willing and doing leads to economical or adaptive results, so does that of the mentally ill if we consider the life history and the present situation.

Thus abnormal phenomena differ from the normal in degree and not in kind. They are caused by the same sort of mechanisms, they have in the biological sense a definite significance or meaning, and with regard to the total life situation they are economical. How each behaviour disorder may be considered as having a cause, a significance, and an economy can only be demonstrated in the course of the book. The modern idea of the continuity between the abnormal, the normal, and the genius is given in Fig. 1.2, which should be compared with Fig. 1.1.

We have already stated that this modern theoretical viewpoint is of the greatest importance. There are three reasons for its importance, one *theoretical, one practical,* and one *cultural.* From the standpoint of *psychological theory,* if it is true that abnormal mental phenomena are simple exaggerations or perversions of the normal phenomena, we can draw conclusions concerning the normal behaviour from the abnormal and concerning abnormality from the normal. Consequently, we may experiment with abnormal subjects

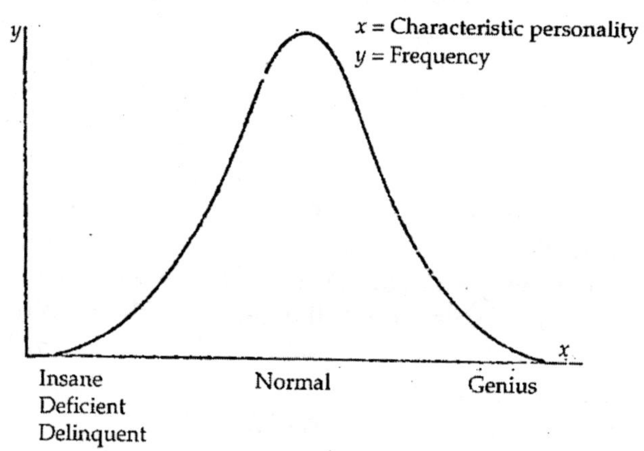

Fig. 1.2 : Showing the scientific view of the distribution of personalities.

and learn something about normality and from experiments on normal subjects learn something about abnormality. For purposes of experimentation, this is of greatest importance, because in some cases the exaggeration or perversion of normal phenomena shown by the abnormal are much easier to study than the less extreme processes of the normal individual. For other problems the inverse of this is true.

Consequently, abnormal psychology may no longer be presented as a domain apart from the normal.

The second reason is *practical*. If abnormality differs from normality in degree rather than in kind, when we understand how this degree difference is brought about the possibility arises of reversing the process. For many cases we can already do this. Not only may we hope to bring many abnormals back to normal, but we may also hope to force an increasing number of normals into the realm previously thought of as that of genius. Until very recently the person who had "lost his mind" was usually considered as lost forever. At the present time many so-called "insanities" are curable, so that the individual returns to a completely normal life, and others who are not yet curable are subject to what we call "social recovery". By social recovery is meant that the individual may come back and take some place in society, although it very often is not the one which he previously held.

The third reason is *cultural*. This viewpoint removes both insanity and genius from the realm of the mystic. If it is possible to speak of human progress at all, progress must be defined in terms of the increase in man's scientific and rational control over nature. The whole history of man's progress has been the history of his slow and not always direct approach to rationalism regarding his place in nature. Although it is very difficult to give up the romance which accrues to mystic explanations, the gains which are to be had from viewing the human personality in both its normal and its abnormal phases from a national viewpoint fully outweigh the consolations of a romantic mysticism.

We have now given the reasons why this modern viewpoint about abnormality is so important, but we have not yet given the reasons why we believe it. These may be given in final form only in the course of the book. It will be worthwhile, however, to point out the nature of these reasons now. In the first place, we believe that personality traits are distributed along the curve of normal probability, as was indicated in Fig. 1.2, for both *theoretical* and *empirical* reasons. *Theoretically* such distribution is given when a great many different causal factors are combined according to the rules of chance. It would take us too far afield to go into probability theory and statistics in a text devoted to abnormal psychology. It can be shown on mathematical grounds that we should expect such a distribution of any personality trait caused by a large number of different causal factors.[4]

Of more immediate interest is our *empirical* reason for so believing. Whenever we measure the heights of a large group of individuals, or their weights, or their intelligence quotients, or their social attitudes, we find a very few who are low in the scale in question and a very few who are high on the scale in question, more who are rather low and rather high, and the *greatest* number tending toward the mean or toward mediocrity. Such a curve as that given in Fig. 1.2 is called the curve of normal probability. Its exact mathematical features may be found in any standard work on statistics. Although F. Allport (1939) has recently shown that the distribution of certain social attitudes, particularly those concerning conformity to social norms (which are undoubtedly important for psychopathology), do not invariably follow the shape of the normal probability curve, we never find dichotomous or trichotomous divisions for personality traits. For example, we do not find any break in the distribution of intelligence between the feeble-minded and the normals, nor between the normals and the geniuses. Similarly, with regard to physical or emotional factors, the extremes do not represent isolated groups but merge gradually into the middle range.

The older concept of the abnormal was taken to mean a special and distinctive group of phenomena which could be divided from the normal. Modern psychopathology theoretically can make no such division. However, for practical purposes we must still set up certain criteria to divide the insane from the sane, the feeble-minded from the normal, and the antisocial from the socially adjusted. Such a division has no theoretical psychological significance, but it is an important applied sociological distinction. As a problem it has considerable sociological, legal, and political significance. Such a problem, however, lies beyond the limits set for this book. At this point we are interested only in the theoretical psychological aspects of the problem.

3. THE CONCEPT OF PERSONALITY

We must next contrast the popular (older) with the scientific (or newer) view regarding personality. The popular view holds personality to be a constant, unchangeable entity given either by God or through the personal heredity. Personality thus is looked on first as a *quantitative* entity. Popularly we still speak of this person as having a great deal of personality and of someone else as having but little. In the modern theory of personality, such a distinction is quite meaningless. Personality is looked on as a *qualitative* rather than a *quantitative* concept. Black or white, rich or poor, stupid or brilliant, beautiful or ugly, every individual is considered to have a personality which distinguishes him from other individuals. It is true that we speak of the structure of personality and the degree of its differentiation, but we do not refer to its amount. Personality is to be considered as a pattern or a configuration or a *Gestalt* rather than a magnitude. The pattern refers to the way which the individual personality traits hang together. In the second place, popular ideas on personality are inclined to be *evaluative.* X has a good, a pleasing, an admirable personality, whereas Y has a bad, displeasing, unadmirable one. To the scientist, of course, such evaluative concepts are not admissible. We are equally interested in the "good" and the "bad" personality. As a matter of fact, it is through study of the "bad" personality that we have learned so much about the "good." In the third place, rather than viewing the personality as *constant,* we know that aspects of the personality are continually changing. Anyone who has seen a well-adjusted individual develop a mental derangement has seen this very clearly. Personality changes when the child becomes adolescent, when the adolescent falls in love, through marriage and through the birth of children, through getting or losing religion, or through changing political faiths. We think of personality then as in a constant flux.

From the modern view personality is a qualitative concept, to be viewed without evaluation and considered as constantly changing. Personality is the pattern or arrangement of the personality traits in an individual. By traits we mean the quantitative variations between individuals which follow generally the normal probability curve. Included in the personality, then, are all the physical characteristics of the individual, all the various individual organs—heart, liver, lungs, genitalia—the individual's existing state of health, his stamina and constitution, his intellect, his emotions, his temperament. By personality, however, we mean not simply the sum total of all these traits but rather *the way in which they are combined to give the individual his individuality*. By the individuality of the person we mean that dynamic organization or configuration of traits which determines the individual's unique adjustments to his environment. It is easy to see that, since all the personality traits may be present in various amounts, an infinite variation in personality is possible. It is often said, although this is a statement which cannot be proved, that no two personalities are exactly alike. Since this is so, some scientists have even despaired to studying the personality and its genesis. However, although no two personalities may be exactly alike, all human beings biologically belong to a species and, in society as it is now constituted, all human beings must meet very similar situations. It is this fact which has enabled a few medical men and psychologists to develop the systematized science of modern psychopathology, to which this book is devoted.

4. THE SOURCES OF PERSONALITY

The theological viewpoint was that the personality was the gift of God. This was a rather easy solution to the complex problem, but one by no means satisfactory to the scientist. In the nineteenth century, when modern biology was established, God was replaced by heredity. In more recent times environment has been stressed as of perhaps even greater importance than heredity. This has led to what is probably the most debated problem in modern biological science, namely, the problem of heredity versus environment in determining personality. The author has expressed his views on this problem in some detail in a previous book, *Psychology and the Social Order*. The following lines attempt to summarize his findings there.

It is true that some personality traits are established through the nature of the human germ plasm and are so to be looked on as hereditary. Many others are established during the lifetime of the individual. It was previously popular to list certain definite traits as due to heredity and certain other traits as due to environment. Modern research has shown that these two important factors may not be separated. There are no hereditary factors which may not be modified by environmental forces, and, similarly, environmental factors can only begin to work on the biologically hereditary organism. The problem of heredity versus environment has received considerable clarification by modern theorists of biology. We can no longer say "heredity versus environment," but must rather say "heredity in environment". We can no longer say "the individual versus his sociopsychological surroundings," but rather "the individual in and as a part of his sociopsychological surrounding". Consequently, modern biological research accepts as axiomatic; "No heredity without environment; no environment without heredity". No longer can we say that certain traits are due to heredity and certain traits to environment. Nor can we even say of any given trait that this trait is 70 per cent hereditary and 30 per cent environmental. A more satisfactory way of expressing the relationship at the present time is by considering the amount of change in behaviour which we can bring about by manipulation of the environment. From this viewpoint it is sensible to look on as definitely hereditary traits those which we have no power of changing during the individual's lifetime and as definitely environmental those which we can completely change. For no single trait have we the complete power of manipulation, nor is there any over which we have no power of manipulation. Consequently, it is best to speak not of hereditary and environmental traits, but of those relatively highly conditioned by heredity and those relatively highly conditioned by environment. In *Psychology and the Social Order* the author made a provisional list of the traits classified on such a basis. This list was as follows:

I. Characteristics of Humans Chiefly Determined by Heredity

*A. **Physique***—The physical characteristics of an individual (height, weight, hair, and eye colour, as well as the general pattern of physical characteristics) are to be considered as relatively determined by heredity. Some of these are, of course, more subject to environmental control than others. The effects of climate and nutrition on height and weight are too well known to require elaboration. Hair and eye colour on the other hand are fairly well established as Mendelian unit traits. Although humans give birth to monsters occasionally, these monsters are, to put it crudely, human monsters, not ape or cow monsters. The species then is completely determined by the germ plasm. But here again it is necessary to point out that no sure set of criteria for the demarcation of species has been established. And the recent work of H.J. Muller and his colleagues has shown that new species may be created by environmental controls. To be sure the species was created by radiation of the eggs of the lowly fruit fly (Drosophila), and the possibilities of similar human manipulation seem far away. But Galileo probably never realized that his discovery of the basic law of mechanics would have the applications we know today. Also the general characteristics or pattern of physique are chiefly determined by "heredity". Thus family resemblances are often so striking that an unknown individual is immediately recognized to be a Smith or a Jones. Thus for immediate practical purposes we may include physique in those factors chiefly determined by "heredity". But even here we must not lose track of the fact that height, weight, stamina, etc., are *modifiable* by *manipulatory* changes in the environmental field.

Physique is, to be sure, one of the most important combined traits in the make-up of the human personality.

Lack of pulchritude in a female or lack of virility in a male may, in extreme cases, completely modify the personality. Dr. Alfred Adler (1917) has in fact attempted to build a whole theory of personality genesis on the idea of "inferiority complexes" developed roughly on such a basis. The Adlerian theory of personality genesis attacks the problem in a somewhat superficial manner, but Adler has succeeded in pointing out that certain embryologically conditioned factors are of great importance in personality genesis.

B. Reaction Tendencies—The properties just spoken of are chiefly structural aspects of the personality. In addition to these must be listed certain functional reaction tendencies which are also primarily determined through "heredity". F. Allport (1924) makes a rather specific list of these tendencies, which he calls without complete justification reflexes. We can best quote his conclusions concerning these:

It is now possible to return with fuller understanding to the problem stated at the beginning of this chapter. Our aim was to give an account of the innate sources of behaviour, and to show how the complexity of human activities is constructed upon these inborn foundations. A certain group of reflexes, either present at birth or involving a later ripening of receptors and effectors, were selected as the origins for which we were searching. These reflexes are classified as (1) the avoiding reactions, such as infantile withdrawing, rejecting, and struggling, and (2) the approach-responses to the stimulations of hunger and of the sensitive and erogenous zones. In the competition with other reflexes for the final common path, these reflexes are prepotent. They are of the highest importance for the welfare of both the individual and the species. And finally, they determine the subsequent acquisition of knowledge and skill by every human being. The intricacies of human conduct are modifications of these simple prepotent responses. [From F.H. Allport, *Social Psychology*, Houghton Mifflin Company, Boston, 1924, p. 79]

Thus Allport classifies as prepotent all reaction tendencies which may be elicited at birth or which mature on a purely biological basis after birth. Here for the sake of completeness we ought to add all the non-voluntary reflexes and in general the reflexes under control of the automatic nervous system. Also we must consider certain voluntary reflexes, like eye movements, grasping, etc. To give a definite list of adequate stimuli for these reflexes would be a misleading procedure, because we know that almost immediately after birth there is learning (conditioning) which elicits these responses to other than the originally adequate stimuli. This conditioning process must be looked on as enviornmental. From certain of the researches of the psychoanalysts we also know that even the non-voluntary reflexes under the control of the automatic nervous system are subject to environmental manipulation. Thus recently the viewpoint has become widespread that also with regard to reaction tendencies no sure line may be drawn between the hereditary and the environmental. The best procedure is to attribute to heredly the reaction tendencies necessary to restore organic equilibrium at birth and to keep the orgarism alive. Consequently nutrition and growth are taken care of and such emotional reaction tendencies are present that the baby is able to "communicate" his needs to the parents through "love," "fear," "rage" reactions. Such original reaction tendencies then are important in the resulting personality pattern of the adult and are to be looked on as relatively fixed in the embryological field. But they too are subjected from the very start to a certain manipulation by the environment. There is no life without the "hereditary" basis for life, but equally no life without what Henderson has called an environment of certain fitness.

We have spoken so far of motor responses. On the sensory side certain perception forms must be considered as laid down in the embryological field. Perception of form, colour, movement, sound, heat, and the other "elements" of perception depend on the peculiar structure and function of the human nervous system. These perceptions, particularly those of outer reality, only arise in an environment, however, and that changes (manipulation) of the environment cause changes in the perceptions is so well known that it is banal to mention it.

We must add a word or two on motor and sensory limitations, which are quite obviously placed on the organism by the embryological field. Large portions of the physical environment are not perceived at all and differences within the environment are perceived only when differences of a definite amount exist in the physical stimuli. I refer here, of course, to the well-known absolute and difference thresholds for sensation and perception. Similarly, reaction times, fatigue-ability, hand-eye coordination depend on factors laid down in the period of gestation. Of course all of these are subject to certain and sometimes very great modification with practice.

II. Characteristics of Humans in Which Heredity and Environment Are Codeterminant

A. Intelligence—We now turn to those personality traits which are decidedly conditioned by heredity but which are highly modifiable by environment. Chief of these is that constellation of traits which psychologists call intelligence. Psychologists have gradually changed from viewing intelligence as a class-determined concept to viewing it as a field-determined one. From the modern standpoint, intelligent behaviour is behaviour which arrives at goals. Until very recently psychologists and biologists always believed that this factor was almost completely determined in the germ plasm. The I.Q. (the intelligence quotient) as a measurement of these correlated traits was considered constant so that one accurate measurement would fix it. Recent researches have indicated quite clearly that very moderate changes in the psychological surrounding field will change the I.Q. by 15 to 20 per cent, and cases of fairly radical changes (through psychoanalytical treatment, for instance) up to 40 per cent. That is to say, subnormal with I.Q.'s around $5 have been brought up to normal, and even some morons. I.Q. = 60, have been made normal through specialized education. Doubtless many normals have been raised equally by a favourable "environment" and certainly many a potential genius has retrogressed through unfavorable surrounding field conditions. The cases reported are usually of subnormal children from households rich enough to allow the employment of the services of specialists.

Thus if comparatively mild chnges in the structure of the environmental field alter the I.Q. by amounts ranging upward to 40 per cent, it is almost certain that very radical changes would alter it even more. Consequently we may be making a fair estimate when we assign equal values to heredity and environment in determining intelligence. There are cases of course where the amentia is so severe that the impressions of the changed environment play no role in the psychological field of the child. Thus in fairness it must be recorded that certain forms of clinical amentia are still to be looked on as hereditary.

All these researches indicate the possibility of changing intelligence through planned manipulation of the environmental field. Those "unplanned manipulations" brought about by poverty, by unemployment, or, on the otherside by great wealth and a favorable environment must affect the I.Q. by like amounts. Early researches on the relative intelligence of different races and different social strata were all misinterpreted. We invariably find the economic or racial underdog averaging lower in intelligence than the racial and economic master. When intelligence was considered purely an hereditary matter, one concluded that these were differences beyond human control. More modern research has changed this viewpoint, so that the old slogan of the poor are poor because they are dumb" must be changed to the "poor are dumb because they are poor".

B. Subtraits Included under the Concept Intelligence—The tests used to measure the I.Q. are made up of a sample of various goal activities. Each of these is to be considered as partially determined by heredity and partially by environment. In actuality, of course, some of the factors such as reaction time are determined almost wholly by heredity. Others like school knowledge are determined almost wholly in the environmental field. Exactly what proportion is to be assigned to each of these fields cannot be known without experiment. The continuation of the work along this line is most important and should enable us to give a more precise answer to this question.

III. Characteristics Chiefly Determined in the Environment

A. Goals—We come finally to the characteristics chiefly determined in the environment. These are most available to manipulation and at the same time are the factors of chief social-psychological importance. First we consider the goals of the individual. What an individual strives for is largely determined by environment. One may accept the "hereditary" determination of some sort of goal-directed activity. In other words the fact that the individual will strive toward goals in general is determined in the embryological field. Furthermore his perception of the goals as such may be likewise considered as determined at birth. Likewise it is true that his striving for self-preservation and his sexual strivings have been laid down embryologically. But his *method* of making a livelihood and the *type* of person he chooses for a love object are conditioned by the social field or psychological surrounding field. Similarly determined are his reactions to his God, to his nation, and to members of different social classes. His attitudes, his ambitions, his aims, and his ideals all depend on "environmental" factors. Here again this determination is limited by certain "hereditary" factors. To become emancipated with regard to religion or to acquire a broad social philosophy requires high intelligence. This we have seen is dependent on factors which may be considered partially "hereditary." But such changes in social attitude as have occurred in Russia since 1917 and in Germany since 1918 are quite obviously almost solely determined in the social field.

B. Emotional Strivings—Finally the emotional strivings of the individual, his loves his fears, and his hates, are never embryologically conditioned but result from his environmental field structures. The ability to strive, believe, and feel, however, depends, as should now be clear, on certain factors conditioned by the embryological field. *What* one believes, strives for, and feels about, are determined in the environmental field. The division we have made is arbitrary and only useful for classification purposes. Even those traits chiefly determined by "heredity" find constant modification in the hands of "environment". And those chiefly determined by "environment" would not exist at all without "heredity." The upshot of the whole matter is that we can really only differentiate operationally between those factors potentially subject to manipulation and those over which at the present we have no manipulatory control. [From J.F. Brown, *Psychology and the Social Order*, McGraw-Hill Book Company, Inc., New York, 1936, pp. 267-73. Some slight changes in nomenclature have been made and some paragraphs omitted in order to make the argument easier to follow.]

Thus the modern viewpoint regards the personality as the resultant of environmental stresses and strains working on an organism which was at one time a hereditary unit. From the very first, however, this biological organism is modified by forces in the environment so that at any given time after birth the individual has in his personality a considerable number of primarily environmentally conditioned traits. Behaviour is to be deduced from the biological organism in a surrounding environment. This relationship may be expressed algebraically in the equation $B = f(P, E)$, which means that the behaviour is always a function of the structure of the person and the environment. This relationship may also be expressed geometrically through the concept of the *psychobiological field*. Figure 1.3 represents such a field, in which person is indicated by *P* and the environment by *E*. Our actual observations are always concerned with such a situation. From the time of the fertilization of the ovum by the sperm to the time of death, the person is never out of some environment. Behaviour consists theoretically of constant change between the relationship of the person so considered and the environment.

In other words the person is constantly doing something in the environment. The person perceives certain objects or

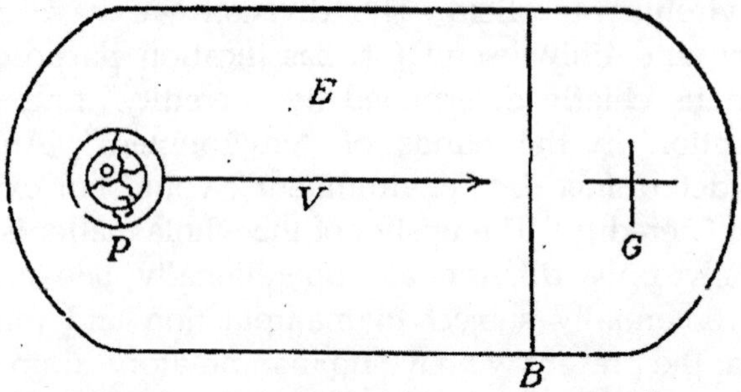

Fig. 1.3 : Showing the structure of the psychobiological field.

situations in the environment as desirable and he strives to attain these. Certain other things he perceives as undesirable and he attempts to avoid these. Such parts of the environment which have a particular positive or negative stimulating value may be mathematically indicated as goals. A goal with such a positive stimulating value is shown by a plus in Fig. 1.3. In order to account for the fact that all life consists of the moving toward some goals and the moving away from others, we must posit some forces within the psychological field. Such positive and negative forces are vectors and one is shown in the diagram by an arrow. The *subject matter of psychology is the study of such goal-directed activity of individuals.* In the diagram the person is shown as having a definite structure or differentiation. This varies from individual to individual and describes what we have called personality.

Life would be comfortable but uninteresting if it were built on the plan that we always arrive at our goals. Many of the goals which we seek we do not arrive at, owing to resistances or frustrations imposed on us by our own biological limitations or by the nature of the physical environment or, perhaps more often, by society. Such frustrations are indicated as barriers. A barrier is also shown in the diagram. To the psychologist particularly interesting are the cases where the arrival at certain goals is frustrated.

Today we believe that it is due to the frustration of drives toward goals that the personality has its development. The blocked-goal situation represents a *conflict*. Conflicts may be resolved by the development of the so-called "enriched" normal personality. The study of such personality is that undertaken by normal psychology. On the other hand, the resolution of conflicts may result in the development of personalities who vary from the normal. Thus psychopathology may be considered the *study of the effect of frustrations on goal-directed activity, where the resolution of the conflict develops abnormal types of personality structures.* Consequently, no strict division may be made between the subject matter of normal and of abnormal psychology. In this book we shall have occasion to speak very frequently of both. Personality has its genesis in the way in which individuals of specific biological constitution meet barriers in the psychological field. This statement is one on which all modern students of psychopathology may agree. It is of the greatest importance, because it means that personality is something which has a genesis and a growth which are largely determined in the psychological field. When we learn the laws of the psychological field, we may change personality. We already have considerable knowledge of some of these laws. In the succeeding chapters we shall go on with the elucidation of this viewpoint. In other to appreciate its significance and many implications we must first devote a chapter to history in order to show why it was so slow in developing.

SUMMARY

For this and those succeeding chapters where it may be helpful we shall give a brief summary of the chief conclusions arrived at in the body of the text. The reader who readily recalls the arguments on which these conclusions were based has mastered the subject matter of this book.

1. Modern psychopathology, to which this book is devoted, is of the greatest importance to medicine because probably one-half of the medicine of the future will be

psychological medicine. It is also of greatest importance to the layman, because over 10 per cent of the total population may expect to become seriously ill psychologically and probably nearly everyone may expect to become mildly ill psychologically in the course of his lifetime.

2. The older (but still popular) concept of abnormality as being uncommon, terrible, a thing apart from normality has been replaced by the newer (or scientific) view which considers abnormal phenomena, as exaggerations or perversions of normal mental phenomena, subject to the same laws, and as having meaning and significance in terms of the total situation. This modern viewpoint is important for theoretical, practical, and cultural reasons.
3. The older (but still popular) concept of personality (constant, quantitative, and evaluative) has been replaced by the newer (or scientific) concept (changing, qualitative, non-evaluative). Personality is defined as the pattern of personality traits which gives the individual his individuality.
4. Personality does not result from a "gift of God," personal heredity, or even personal heredity plus environment. Personality has its genesis in the way in which individuals of specific biological constitution meet barriers in the psychological field. This is a tenet on which all modern students of psychopathology agree and is of great importance because knowledge of the laws of the psychological field allows us to change personality.

NOTES

1. The works of authors mentioned in the text are listed in alphabetical order in the appended bibliography (p. 453). In those cases where several works of a single author are listed the appropriate item is indicated by title or by the date of publication in parenthesis.
2. The number of institutionalized patients has risen with extreme rapidity in the last quarter century. Whether or not this represents a real increase in the more severe types of mental illness is not certain. We shall discuss this problem in detail in Part IV.
3. The statistics given through this section are based primarily on

Bureau of Census Report, issued by the Department of Commerce in January 1938, and on Landis and Page's "Modern Society and Mental Disease." In Part IV we shall return to the problem of incidence of mental abnormality in some detail. At present we simply wish to emphasize the magnitude of the problem.

4. A simple introduction to the mathematics of the normal probability curve may be found in Garrett and a more stringent one in Guilford or Yule.

2

THE HISTORICAL DEVELOPMENT OF PSYCHOPATHOLOGY

A. THE ESTABLISHMENT OF THE SOMATOGENIC VIEWPOINT

We shall best understand the real significance of the modern viewpoint in psychopathology if we trace its slow development and see why this development had to be so slow. Magic, religion, and science are the three chief methods through which man has tried to understand his place in the cosmos and to better it. Sir J.G. Frazer writes in his *Golden Bough*, "The movement of higher thought has been from magic through religion to science." He goes on to point out that recorded history of man's intellectual production could be compared to a web woven of three differently coloured threads, the black thread of magic, the red thread of religion, and the white thread of science. History thus represented would be a long rope beginning almost wholly with black, then changing to black and red with a single white strand or two. Gradually and very slowly we come to modern times, where the black has tapered off and the white becomes predominant. Even today, however, the black of magic is clearly discernible and the red of religion is very striking. The individual sciences also could be illustrated by a similar picture. In modern times, the physical world about us is explained almost wholly scientifically; biological phenomena are explained at least semiscientifically; but we are only at the beginnings of a scientific psychology and sociology. It will be the purpose of this chapter to point out the how and why of this.

Despite the fact that there is a widespread belief that mental disorder is a modern problem, we can be fairly sure that it has always existed. Although social anthropological research shows that among primitive people the psychoses and the psychoneuroses are of a somewhat different sort, and perhaps less frequent than in modern industrialized society, we have no record of primitive tribes completely without mental disorders.[1] Similarly, in the literature of early civilizations we always find descriptions of behaviour which the modern psychopathologist can interpret as psychotic or psychoneurotic, giving, very often, the name of the disease in question. Thus the Old Testament describes the actual insanity of Saul and the feigned or malingered insanity of David.

But the Spirit of the Lord departed from Saul, and an evil spirit from the Lord troubled him.

And Saul's servants said unto him, Behold now, an evil spirit from God troubleth thee.

Let our lord now command thy servants, *which are* before thee, to seek out a man, *who is* a cunning player on an harp: and it shall come to pass, when the evil spirit from God is upon thee, that be shall play with his hand, and thou shalt be well.

And Saul said unto his servants, Provide me now a man that can play well, and bring *him* to me.

Then answered one of the servants, and said, Behold, I have seen a son of Jesse the Beth-lehemite, *that is* cunning in playing, and a mighty valiant man, and a man of war, and prudent in matters, and a comely person, and the Lord *is* with him.

Wherefore Saul sent messengers unto Jesse and said, Send me David thy son, which *is* with the sheep.

And Jesse took as ass *laden* with bread, and a bottle of wine, and a kid, and sent *them* by David his son unto Saul.

And David came to Saul, and stood before him: and he loved him greatly; and he became his armour-bearer.

And Saul sent to Jesse, saying, Let David, I pray thee, stand before me; for he hath found favour in my sight.

And it came to pass, when the *evil* spirit from God was

upon Saul that David took an harp, and played with his hand; so Saul was refreshed, and was well, and the evil spirit departed from him. [I Sam. 16:14-23.]

And David laid up these words in his heart, and was sore afraid of Achish the king of Gath.

And he changed his behaviour before them, and feigned himself in their hands, and scrabbled on the doors of the gate, and let his spittle fall down upon his beard. [I Sam. 21:12-13.]

One can find many examples of this sort. The literature of Persia, Assyria, and Egypt gives countless examples.

Of particular interest in this connection is the detailed psychoanalytic study made first by Abraham (1935b) and later enlarged by Strachey and Freud (1939) of the Egyptian King Amenhotep IV, who reigned as long ago as 330c B.C. Amenhotep was the founder of Egyptain monotheist sun worship. He established one of the greatest periods of Egyptian art. Despite this fact, however, he showed mental aberration of the sort we now call paranoid. From his poems, pictures, and the little historical knowledge we have of his times these scientists have been able to recreate a great deal about his personality problems.

Through the Middle Ages mental disorder was recognized as a common phenomenon. In fact, there are reasons for believing that its incidence then was at times greater than it is now. We know, for instance, that whole monasteries and nunneries and schools would develop group mental illnesses at the same time. In his fascinating *History of the Warfare between Science and Theology,* A.D. White has given us many interesting examples of mental derangement through the Middle Ages.

Finally, in modern times it has become of such magnitude that, as we saw in the last chapter, half of modern medicine is or should be concerned with it.

Only in the last fifty years, however, have we had an understanding of mental health and disease which could be called scientific. Even today magical treatments are by no means infrequent and religious treatments are quite as frequent as are scientific. In some backward countries of

Central Europe exorcism is still openly practised today. Occasionally even in America a case of exorcism is reported. Christian Science, which undoubtedly helps many people with psychological illness, although not for the reasons Christian Scientists give, is one of our most popular religious denominations. The therapeutic value of the Catholic Confessional is undoubtedly also very great in some cases.

In order that a scientific theory of mental disorder should develop it was necessary that we develop a scientific theory of personality and its genesis. By far the greatest part of recorded history has been concerned with overcoming superstition and replacing a supernatural theory of personality with a natural one. The history of psychopathology may be conveniently divided into the period of the gradual overcoming of supernaturalism and superstition and the period of the establishment of a natural scientific viewpoint. We shall deal with both of these periods briefly in this chapter.

1. PRIMITIVE AND PRECIVILIZED IDEAS

In recent times we have learned a great deal about the primitive mind through the endeavors of the social anthropologists. Until fairly recently it was thought that the laws governing the behaviour of primitive thinking were essentially the laws that governed modern civilized thinking, so that the differences in primitive thought were to be accounted for the lack of knowledge and experience. The primitive mind, like the child's mind, was considered simply untutored. Today we realize that the whole structure of the primitive mind is different from the structure of the modern mind.[2] Likewise, we have learned from Piaget (1926) that the mind of the child is like the primitive mind and both of these have similarities with minds of certain of the insane, most notably the schizophrenics. It is possible to distinguish prelogical from logical thinking and to give certain definite characteristics of the primitive mind on this basis. Karin Stephen gives a good summary of these characteristics in her book, *Psychoanalysis and Medicine*.

The first and perhaps the most striking characteristic of primitive thinking is that it is *not hampered by any need for consistency.* While disbelieving and denying, it can also, in the same breath, believe, or it can believe contradictory things simultaneously. Logicians of the unconscious might call this the law of unconscious thought, but it is the exact opposite of the first law of thought in conscious logical mental operations.

The second distinguishing characteristic of primitive thinking is the belief in the *omnipotence of thoughts and wishes.*

The third is the *confusion of fact with fantasy, thinking with doing.*

The fourth is the *small importance, attached to knowing and the all-importance of wishing.*

The fifth is the *complete failure to distinguish from one another things which are somehow emotionally identified.* [From Karin Stephen, *Psychoanalysis and Medicine,* Cambridge University Press, New York, 1935, p. 223.]

Although there is still much argument about the exact nature of the "primitive mind" and many modern anthropologists would prefer not to speak of a separate sort of mind for the primitive, we can distinguish certain characteristics of primitive thinking from scientific thinking. The primitive is inclined to consider all movement to be caused by the spirit or soul. Thus even sticks and stones have souls which move them about. This primitive mode of thinking was carried over with no very great modification to the thinking of the Greeks. There are very good reasons for believing that the modern mind operates differently even from the Greek mind. It is by no means absurd to say that the average intelligent person of today thinks on a different level from even so great a Greek as Aristotle. To the primitive, when things where going well and normally, behaviour was accounted for as being run by the normal spirit and offered no particular problems. Death, dreams, and insanity, however, were terrible things. Consequently, they were given a particular type of explanation. If normal or "good" behaviour was accounted for by the spirit, then when there was abnormal or "bad" behaviour the good spirit must have been replaced by a bad spirit. Thus in death the spirit or ghost or demon left the body permanently, in dreams temporarily, and in insanity or possession the "good" spirit was replaced by a "bad" one. In primitive times all abnormality was explained by the theory of magical animism. This type of theory, with modifications of content but not of form, was the prevalent one until fairly late in the nineteenth century. Insanity was explained on a magical basis (or the beginnings of a religious basis) and never on a scientific basis. Also in primitive societies therapy is attempted, but this therapy in itself always is an application of the theory and is always concerned with enticing the evil spirit to leave the sick individual or enticing the normal, good spirit to come back into the sick individual.

2. THE ANCIENT CIVILIZATIONS

The ancient civilizations, except for occasional scientific insights, continued both the theory of demonic possession and the type of treatment practised by primitive societies. Mention of both is to be found in the oriental sacred literatures. The Assyrian myths in which we find the legends of the creation and the fall from grace and the flood and other early conceptions also contain formulas for driving out the evil spirits which caused disease. As we saw, essentially the same theory and treatment are reported time and time again in Old Testament literature. Even in enlightened Greece the idea recurs in the philosophies of Plato and Socrates. Among some Greek medical men, however, the most notable being Hippocrates (b. 460 B.C.), certain beginnings of scientific knowledge were established. Hippocrates first established the modern view that the brain is the seat of consciousness and that mental abnormality is due to brain pathology. To him and his followers we also owe the first attempts at nosology. The Hippocratan school differentiated mania, melancholia, and dementia. With the exception of Hippocrates, the physicians of the Alexandrian school of medicine and a few Romans like Galen (ca. A.D. 130-200), the scientific view did not prosper in the ancient period. Although many of the views of the Hippocratan school seem quite modern and scientific, even this school was by no means freed from superstition. And the vast majority of Greek medical men continued to support some form of magico-religious demonology. Before the collapse of ancient civilizations some beginning, however slight, was made in the study of abnormal mental phenomena. With the establishment of Christianity as the religion for the Dark Ages and the mediaeval period even these few advances were lost. The magical concepts of the primitive demon were merely replaced by the religious concept of the Christian soul. The beliefs as to the psychological processes governing thought changed in content but the type of theory remained the same. Instead of the spirit guiding normal human behaviour and being replaced by the demon in abnormal human behaviour, the Christian soul guided normal behaviour and abnormality was explained as possession by devils or occasionally as punishment by God. We see, then, that in ancient times not much was accomplished for the theory of personality. In ancient civilizations, however, the prevalent treatments were more humane than those practised in the Middle Ages.

3. THE MIDDLE AGES

With the rise of Christianity, the few positive findings of Greek science were forgotten. The Greek metaphysics of Plato and Aristotle, to be sure, were gradually incorporated in the theological dogma of the Christian church. But from the standpoint of modern science abysmal ignorance was everywhere in western Europe throughout the Middle Ages. Recent historical research led by Thorndike and others has shown that the so-called "Dark Ages" were not periods of abysmal ignorance and chaos of knowledge, but rather the completely consequential application of a philosophy which modern science realizes to be false. The chief dogmas of Christian theology are well enough known that particular illustration is unnecessary. The basic philosophy of interactionistic dualism, where body was governed by soul, became basic to the psychology of the times. When humans acted according to the tenets of the Catholic Church, they were activated by the God-given soul. When they did not, something must have happened to the soul. Since the whole cosmos was simply the battleground for the forces of God versus those of the devil, all that was bad was attributed to the devil and all that was good was attributed to God. Thus, to suppose that mental abnormality was due to possession by devils was entirely consequent and entirely logical, and followed from the cosmology and theology of the Christian church. During that time, even the most learned men held to this theory. Pope Gregory, who was certainly one of the leaders of Scholastic philosophy, personally reported his success with the driving out of devils. White gives the case:

The case of St. Gregory the Great is typical. He was a pope of exceedingly broad mind for his time, and no one will think him unjustly reckoned one of the four Doctors of the Western Church. Yet he solemnly relates that a nun, having eaten some lettuce without making the sign of the cross, swallowed a devil, and that when commanded by a holy man to come forth, the devil replied; "How am I to blame? I was sitting on the lettuce, and this woman, not having made the sign of the cross, ate me along with it." [From A.D. White, *A History of the Warfare of Science with Theology in Christendom,* D. Appleton-Century Company, Inc., New York, 1910, p. 101.]

But mild coaxing like Gregory's was often unsuccessful. If one could not coax the devil out, it followed quite naturally that one might insult him out. The following are some of the exorcistic formulas for dealing with evil forces and insulting the devil.

"If an elf or a goblin come, smear his forehead with this salve, put it on his eyes, cense him with incense, and sign him frequently with the sign of the cross."

"For a fiend sick man: When a devil possesses a man, or controls him from within with disease, a spew-drink of lupin, bishopswort, henbane, garlic. Pound these together, add ale and holy water."

And again: "A drink for a friend-sick man, to be drunk

out of a church bell: Githrife, cynoglossum, yarrow, lupin, flower-de-luce, fennel, lichen, lovage. Work up to a drink with clear ale, sing seven masses over it, add garlic and holy water, and let the possessed sing the Beati maculati; then let him drink the dose out of a church bell, and let the priest sing over him the Domine Sancte Pater Omnipotens."

The devil might be insulted in this way: "Thou lustful and stupid one,. . .thou lean sow, famine-stricken and most impure, . . .thou wrinkled beast, thou mangy beast, thou beast of all beasts the most beastly, . . .thou mad spirit, . . .thou bestial and foolish drunkard, . . .most greedy wolf, . . .most abominable whisperer, . . . thou sooty spirit from Tartarust . . .I cast thee down, O Tartarean boor, into the infernal kitchen! . . .Loathsome cobbler, . . .dingy collier, . . .filthy sow (scrofa stercorata), . . .perfidious boar,. . .envious crocodile, . . .malodorous drudge, . . .wounded basilisk, . . .rust-coloured asp, . . .swollen toad, . . .entangled spider, . . .lousy swine-herd (porcarie pedicose), . . .lowest of the low, cudgelled ass," etc. [From A.D. White, *A History of the Warfare of Science with Theology in Christendom,* D. Appleton-Century Company, Inc., New York, 1910, pp. 102, 107.]

Insulting and cantation sometimes failed, and the treatment then resorted to was to make the body so uncomfortable a place of residence that no self-respecting devil would remain in it. Consequently, torturous treatment by heating, immersion in hot water, immersion in sulphur fumes, and the like were resorted to. It should be quite obvious, even to the uninitiated, that such methods are not conducive to mental health.[3] Thus we have reasons for believing that insanity spread widely during the Middle Ages, not only among individuals but also at times to whole groups.

The only places where the few positive findings of Greek medicine found recognition during the Middle Ages were in Arabia. This occurred through the influence of the Alexandrian school of medicine, and the humane treatment of the Greeks was continued in some of the Arabian asylums.[4] Over the rest of the civilized world the devil theory of demonic possession held sway. This theory took two forms, one of which held that the devil gained possession of a human through some stupidity or failing of this human, so that he was not himself totally to blame. Such individuals were usually treated by exorcism of the sort we have mentioned above. Occasionally, however, the individual was considered to be in league with the devil. In these cases the treatment was even more drastic. Everyone knows something about witchcraft and witchcraft trials. These witches, many of whom were burned to death at the stake or otherwise executed, were really unfortunate psychotics who were victimized by mass hysteria. Hanging for witchcraft occurred late in the seventeenth century even in America, and a legal trial for witchcraft occurred as late as 1793. In backward parts of Europe today exorcism is still widely practised. Even in America there are certain Catholic priests who today report the successful driving out of devils by the old formulas. This is, however, not done with the approval of the Catholic Church.

Even during the Middle Ages and the early modern period there were a few individuals who were relatively free from superstition and who opposed the demonological theories. Among these were Paracelsus (1493-1541), Weyer (1515-87), and Plater (1536-1614). Weyer particularly assumed a scientific viewpoint and has been called the first psychiatrist by Zilboorg. All these men believed in occasional possession but doubted that all insanity was due to possession and supposed some due to natural causes. Such men were rare spirits, however, and the man of the Middle Ages even more than his Greek predecessor held to a magico-religious interpretation of personality in both its normal and its abnormal phases. Throughout the Middle Ages there also existed some asylums where the treatment was, to be sure, spiritualistic rather than medical but not too inhumane.

The advent of Protestantism undoubtedly gave the first impetus to more modern methods. The Lutheran theology was a theology applicable to capitalism and modern science rather than to feudalism and Scholastic philosophy. Of course, today it is generally realized that changes in economic methods of production were the cause of changes in religious attitudes rather than vice versa. By the middle of the seventeenth century the basic principles of modern physics were established and some beginnings of modern biology are recognizable. The leaders of the Reformation themselves did nothing for psychopathology. It is pretty well established today that Luther himself was at one time in his life a paranoiac and was probably suffering from delirium tremens when the threw the ink bottle at the devil. But after the establishment of Protestantism in many countries the Catholic Church saw the absolute power of its cosmology falling away.

4. SOME EARLY SKEPTICS AND HUMANITARIANS

From the bourgeois revolution, the Protestant and Catholic reformations, and the growth of modern science, Catholicism suffered an irreparable loss in world prestige. The Church had to put up with the modern economic system. It was no longer the only church, and its was gradually forced to admit the truth of the modern physical principles which contradicted many of its cosmological dogmas. Educated and intelligent individuals everywhere were being skeptical of Christian metaphysics. By the start of the eighteenth century physics was established. Biology had made promising beginnings, and more than a few individuals were skeptical of the Church's psychology. Some went even so far as to become atheistic, and among these many could look on the theology of demon possession and the therapy of exorcism as only ridiculous. The writings of skeptics like Montaigne at the end of the sixteenth century and of Voltaire at the middle of the eighteenth century forced many individuals to doubt both the theory of personality and the therapy used by the churchmen for the mentally ill. The mentally ill received no better treatment. They were still incarcerated and chained, but at least they were relieved from the conscious tortures of the exorcistic treatment. The age of skepticism, however, resulted simply in a false theory being replaced by no theory at all, which is always a poor thing for the advance of science.

Not long after the time of Voltaire the inhumanity of the treatment of the insane was to be bettered. Since they could no longer consider such individuals as being punished by possession of the devil, many individuals said, "Why not treat them as poor, unfortunate sufferers?" This movement was coincident with the Romantic period in literature and with the equalitarian theory of Rousseau and others in political science. During the French Revolution, Pinel (1745-1826) established the first hospital in which the chains and rags and filth were replaced by what we would call modern hospitalization. Although Pinel can scarcely be called a modern psychopathologist, at least he began to treat the insane people rather than as sinners. He was also interested in the inner psychological mechanisms behind insanity. His successor, Esquirol (1840), continued his good work, and the Salpêtriere Hospital became the first modern hospital for the care of the insane. Esquirol furthermore published a semiscientific text on psychiatry in 1828. But despite this the names of Pinel and Esquirol are to be remembered chiefly not for their contributions to mental science but for their promotion of humanity in the treatment of the mentally sick. The humanitarian position spread to England under the leadership of the Quaker, William Tuke, early in the nineteenth century and was established in all civilized countries by the middle of that century. In America the advances in humanitarian treatment first undertaken on the continent were partially introduced by Benjamin Rush (1745-1813). Half a century later Dorothea Dix (1802-87) campaigned vigorously for the more humane treatment of the mentally ill, and today we can consider her aims accomplished.

5. THE SOMATOGENIC ERA

The stage was finally set for superstition and supernaturalism to be given up completely. Through the early part of the nineteenth century medical men began to look on mental abnormality as a definite sickness. This was the period in which the pathogenic factors of many of the physical diseases were being uncovered. The earlier workers, consequently, expected a definite brain pathology to be discovered for the mental disorders. This viewpoint, which still has many adherents among the psychiatric profession, may be called the somatogenic viewpoint.

Although many physicians on the Continent had incidentally touched upon the problems of mental disorder, scientific psychiatry as a medical specialty can be considered to have been established in the second-half of the nineteenth century. The same Benjamin Rush who did so much toward establishing humane methods of treatment wrote in 1812 a general treatise on mental disease which is a forerunner of modern psychiatric treatments. The German psychiatrist William Griesinger (1817-68) published a textbook in 1845, wherein the somatogenic viewpoint was thoroughly represented for the first time. Griesinger demanded that pathhiratry proceed on a physiological and clinical basis and insisted that psychopathology must be reduced to brain Psychology Kraepelin Griesinger's most important follower, factually be said to have established the somatogenic viewpoint. His textbook of psychiatry and his clinical lectures have both been through many editions and in some circles are still considered standard. Kraepelin developed the scheme of classification and nosology which is even today in many aspects the standard one. He also insisted on the importance of brain pathology. He is further notable because he saw the possibility of cooperative work between experimental psychologists and psychiatrists. Kraepelin's chief contributions were classificatory and descriptive. He saw that certain groups of symptoms occurred together with enough regulative so that one could think of them as disease entities. He saw that certain problems (such as those of drug addiction and other characterological defects), which had not hitherto been realized as insanities, belonged to the province of the psychiatrist. He really accomplished much in the field of classificatory description. Of almost as great importance to the somatogenic viewpoint in Germany was Krafft-Ebing (1840-1902), who wrote an important text and did more than any of his contemporaries to encourage the treatment of sexual perversion as a medical problem.

At the turn of the twentieth century, superstition had been overcome, supernaturalism had been replaced by naturalism. A workable nosological scheme had been set up. Everyone was waiting for the specific brain pathologies of the various psychoses to be discovered and for their specific therapeutic treatments to turn up. But only one side of the problem had been developed. It had been seen that psychological disorders furnished a medical problem. What had not been seen was that these disorders also furnished a psychological problem. The psychology of the nineteenth century was almost as naïve as that of the Middle Ages. In the Middle Ages the idea of "soul" replaced that of spirit or demon. In the nineteenth century the idea of soul was replaced by that of brain. What had been accomplished, and that was a great deal, was the overcoming of superstition.

B. THE ESTABLISHMENT OF THE PSYCHOGENIC VIEWPOINT

In the period between 1880 and 1910 the somatogenic theory was gradually established in all civilized countries. Among the medical profession at least, the insanities came to be looked on as a group of sicknesses, equally as worthy of medical study as the organic sicknesses. A large textbook and journal literature was established about the diagnosis, treatment, and prognosis of the various mental illnesses. For one of them at least, neurosyphilis, a definite brain pathology was discovered and a specific therapy instituted. Besides the great advance in the treatment of neurosyphilis, it was discovered that mental derangement was often correlated with toxic body conditions, and the category of the toxic psychoses was demarcated. Furthermore, the value of certain diets, rest treatments, hydrotherapy, and recreational and occupational therapy became quite obvious. The mentally sick were getting treatment for the first time based on science rather than on religion and superstition. But if about 10 per cent of those sick recovered from treatment, which logically followed from the theory, in about 90 per cent of the cases treatment was ineffectual. Research after research, laboratory examination after laboratory examination, biophysical and biochemical studies, measurement upon measurement failed to establish anything organically wrong in over half of the mental patients. To be sure, these researches showed in many single respects that the mentally sick were different *physiologically* from the mentally well. The ways in which they differed were not, however, absolute, so that one could point to this factor invariably present in mental disease or that one invariably absent. This unfortunate state of affairs created much pessimism amongst practitioners of medical psychology, so that even in modern times most laymen and even many doctors consider the "lost" mind "lost" forever.

During this same period, however, two phenomena which had been known to the medical profession for centuries were investigated as to their true nature and in their relationship to each other. It was through the discovery of the nature of *hypnosis* and of *hysteria* and the discovery that these two phenomena were intimately connected that the psychogenic viewpoint was established shortly before the time of the First World War. A few geniuses, to be sure, realized the importance of psychogenic factors some time before the World War. The war itself, however great a curse it may have been to civilization, produced so many cases of purely psychogenic sickness that, by the time of the Versailles Treaty, psychopathology had gained a new and very valuable viewpoint. From 1920 on, the medical profession as a whole were willing to admit that there were certain cases of real mental disorder brought about by the *psychological* experience of the individual, in which it was apparent that there was no demonstrable brain or nervous pathology. That there was no demonstrable brain pathology is not to be taken to mean that none will ever we discovered. But it was shown, brain pathology or not, that certain mental illnesses only developed in certain experiential situations and that other experiential situations would cause these to disappear. Thus for a period of time psychopathology was characterized by two antithetical viewpoints. One school, the somatogenic, said that all mental sickness was brain sickness and the thing to do was to set about finding the underlying brain pathology. The other school, the psychogenic, said that most, if not all, mental sickness was due to psychological situations and the thing to do was to set about uncovering the psychological laws governing these. For a period of time there was much debate between the adherents of these two viewpoints and sometimes rather ugly antagonism between the leaders of them. The members of the somatogenic school were inclined to look or the psychogenic school as quacks, charlatans, or fakers, but little better that faith healers and mystics. On the other hand the psychogenic schools viewed the adherents of the somatogenic school as over-conservative and strangely backward in investigating very vital problems by methods which had proved sterile. There was undoubtedly right on both sides. Since 1920 the problem has become clarified to the extent that today we can synthesize this antithesis between the organic and functional in the organismic viewpoint, which sees all behaviour problems as having both physiological and psychological aspects. We shall do this in the next chapter, but before we can really understand this synthesis, it is necessary to relate briefly the chief facts about the establishment of the psychogenic viewpoint.

1. THE DEVELOPMENT OF A SCIENTIFIC THEORY OF HYPNOSIS

Everyone has heard something about the phenomenon known as hypnosis. Hypnosis is a state of very deep suggestibility in which the hypnotized individual goes into the so-called "hypnoid" or somnambulistic" state, where he loses immediate consciousness and where, so to speak, his own conscious self is superseded by that of the hypnotist. In other words, the subject in hypnosis can perform the most varying types of tasks, but he does these under the direction of the hypnotist and remembers nothing of what he has done on coming out of the hypnosis. Not only can the individual do in hypnosis the activities which are normal to him, but in it he can also accomplish many things that he cannot do in his normal waking life; for instance, he can recall experiences that he has long since forgotten. Furthermore, under hypnosis the hypnotist can create varying physiological conditions in the individual which are normally outside the individual's control; for instance, anesthesias and paralyses may readily be created through hypnotic suggestion. In hypnosis such deep-lying physiological factors as the rate of excretion of the urine or the rate of excretion of the sweat glands may be affected and even surface lesions, such as burns, may be created. When, for instance, the hypnotist tells a subject that he will lose sensitivity in a certain area of the body, to all intents and purposes this sensitivity is really lost, so that after the suggestion the subjects does not consciously react to a pin prick or a hot needle applied to the surface in question. In this phenomenon of hypnotically induced anesthesia we recognize today something very similar to the hysterically induced anesthesias of which we shall speak in the next paragraphs.

It is not our purpose at this point to go into a discussion of the detailed facts and theories of hypnosis. At present it is our purpose simply to introduce the phenomenon of hypnosis, speak briefly of its history, and show how the combined research on hypnosis and hysteria gave rise to the modern psychogenic theory.

The phenomenon of hypnosis has been known for ages, although not by the name hypnosis. When it occurred in the earliest times, like all abnormal psychological phenomena, it was looked on as being due to some occult power or demon. Frequently the individuals able to hypnotize others were looked on as possessed of supernatural powers or even in some cases as being in league with the devil. The whole history of witchcraft shows us many phenomena which today we would look on as belonging to the field of hypnosis. The early hypnotists, naturally enough, did not understand the sources of their own powers of suggestion and consequently felt themselves to be in some way specially gifted.

The modern scientific study of hypnosis, through which it was finally realized that hypnosis is by no means rare or by no means supernatural, began in the latter half of the eighteenth century. The man to start both the popular and the scientific interest in hypnosis was the Viennese, Anton Mesmer (1733-1815). The word "mesmerism" still can be found in popular speech, and it was used in the early scientific discussions as synonymous with hypnotism. To understand Mesmer's work one must realize the existing state of knowledge of electrical phenomena at that time. The Italian physicist Galvani had discovered a phenomenon, which he called "animal electricity." This discovery was made in connection with operations on the legs of frogs which he was investigating physiologically. The instruments used it contact with the saline solutions built up potential differences which stimulated contractions of the muscles of the frogs' legs. It was not until much later that it was realized that Galvani's medical electricity was actually a case of electric stimulation of the nerves. Galvani held his experiments to be proof of untapped electricity in living matter. Mesmer was an individual who was evidently a first-rate hypnotist. In experimenting with a magnet, which was still a fairly mystical sort of tool to the eighteenth century mind, he found that certain patients felt themselves to be better after contact with the magnet. Today we know that the magnet has nothing to do with such betterment but that the phenomenon is the result of suggestion which is given in connection with the contact of the magnet. Mesmer later learned that patients would receive the same benefits by simply being touched by him. From this he developed his theory that all individuals have within them magnetic forces which when properly controlled can influence other individuals. He carried his discovery and technique all over Europe, and at first his discovery was greeted with attention and many honours. In 1778 he went to Paris and exhibited his technique before the French Academy. There remains some question whether Mesmer himself was deluded by his theory or was consciously faking. At all events he came into disrepute in

Paris because of his refusal to divulge the secret of his many apparent cures. Today there is some doubt if he knew it himself.

Although Mesmer himself did not make much of the deep hypnotic state, it was probably known to him, and it was found that through Mesmer's techniques patients could be made to enter into a state of deep somnambulism. At first these people were considered to be "magnetized," and some of these" "magnetized" individuals showed the responses which we now associate with hypnosis. From this magnetic somnambulism mesmerism became known as the science whereby individuals were put in a state of somnambulism and could be influenced and in some cases cured by suggestion in this state.

The English physician James Braid (1795-1860) was the first individual to realize that the hypnotic séance was a purely subjective phenomenon which could be created without magnets or other physical apparatus and paraphernalia. Braid found that magnets and electrical machinery and *baquets* were not necessary but that having the individual concentrate on a glass stopper or a pencil or even on the hypnotist's fingers alone would induce hypnosis. In a series of investigations Braid was able to show that the physical means used to induce hypnosis are of very small importance and that the phenomenon is one of extreme suggestibility. Hypnosis was widely used as an aid to psychotherapy throughout the early part of the nineteenth century. An Anglo-Indian physician, Esdaile (1808-59) , made considerable use of it as an anesthetic to aid in surgery in the middle part of the nineteenth century. It was rather widely used, also, as an anaesthetic in connection with childbirth. Two things put hypnosis into disrepute with the medical profession in the latter half of the nineteenth century. The first of these was the discovery of the anesthetic properties of ether and chloroform, which, for quite obvious reasons, were far better suited to surgical practice than was hypnosis. The second was the growth of the somatogenic theory in medical psychology. Anything which was not to be understood biochemically or physiologically was considered to be metaphysical rather than medical. Physiological medicine, of course, was making tremendous headway through this period of time. For nearly fifty years hypnosis was neglected by the medical profession and fell into the hands of quacks and charlatans. Some of these individuals undoubtedly were real hypnotists, by more often the hypnotic demonstrations produced in small road shows were fakes in which the supposedly hypnotized subject was a "plant." Hypnotism thus became of interest to the layman, authors of bizarre stories, and the showman, but of little interest to the medical profession.

Some physicians, however, continued to use hypnosis more or less successfully in their medical practice. Undoubtedly one of the most successful of these was the Frenchman Lieubault (1823-1904), who practised at Nancy. Also in Nancy at this time there was a professor of medicine, Bernheim (1840-1919), who became interested in the relationship between hysteria and hypnosis. Bernheim and Liéubault worked together to present the hypothesis that hypnotism and hysteria were related and both were due to suggestion. In this they were opposed by Charcot (1825-93), who was the leading neurologist of his time. In his opposition Charcot was wrong, but the interest in the problem shown by so outstanding a scientist did much to reawaken the interest of the whole medical profession in hypnosis and hysteria and hence laid the basis for the development of psychogenic theory.

2. THE ESTABLISHMENT OF THE CONCEPT OF HYSTERIA

If hypnosis was a fairly well established concept by the eighteenth century, the history of hysteria goes back even farther. Hysteria refers to the development of physical symptoms of both a positive and a negative sort in organs where there is no demonstrable pathology. Thus an individual may lose the sense of touch in an organ, although (for clinical reasons, which will be discussed later) we know that the organ and its nerve supply are intact. Similarly, a person may become blind without any destruction of the retina, the optic nerve, or the optic cortex or may become paralyzed when muscles and nerve supply are structurally perfect. Physicians through the ages have been seeing such cases where they could discover no cause for the defect in question. By the middle of the nineteenth century these became grouped in the disease entity known as "hysteria." In popular usage the noun "hysteria" and the adjective "hysterical" are terms of reproach. We all use them to refer to an emotionally unstable and unbalanced personality. We realize in many cases that a person will "act queer" and then "get over it." We say popularly, "Oh, that person is just acting hysterically." It was not until recent times, however, that the appearance of psychogenically conditioned symptoms was realized to be related to the disease hysteria. It is well known that some people will throw a hysterical tantium to get out of meeting a social obligation or responsibility. Today it is quite obvious to the medical psychologist that the development of the symptoms of the disease hysteria plays similar roles to the temper tantrum. In other words, if the "hysterical tantrum" is a conscious emotional outburst developed to avoid meeting a social responsibility, the disease hysteria is due to an unconscious mechanism. By an unconscious mechanism we mean one present in the mind but not consciously recognized. The exact nature of these mechanisms will be discussed later. In the last chapter we saw that our modern theories of abnormal behaviour required that each such behaviour have a cause, show significance, and be adaptive in terms of the total life situation. Both temper tantrums and hysterical physical illness have a cause (i.e., emotional conflict), both have a significance (and this we can only explain in detail later), and both have an economy (in that they prevent the individual from being forced to do what he does not want to do).

Before this relationship between "hysterical" behaviour and the disease hysteria was discovered, medical men were at a loss to know: how to treat these patients. Even today, in a number of medical circles where the diagnosis is well-known and used, the practitioner very often tells the patients to "forget about it," "buck up and be a man," "go on a trip," "take a rest," "see another doctor." Since nothing organically wrong is found in these people, the practitioner very often simply considers them to be fakers, to be spoiled, irresponsible people, or to be childish. Now it is quite true that the symptoms of hysteria are often faked, and it is equally true that, when they are not *consciously faked*, it makes sense to speak of them as *"unconsciously faked."* But where they are unconsciously faked it does not do the slightest good to ask the patient to "forget about them." The conscious faking of hysteria is called "malingering." The "unconscious faking" represents a real sickness for which we now have a method of treatment which is practically always successful. In this method of treatment neither drugs nor physical manipulations of the body nor surgery have any part. Rather the treatment consists in recreating the psychological situation which caused the individual to develop these symptoms as defense mechanisms and giving him some insight into his development of them. We shall, of course, have more to say about the detail of all this later. With the delineation of hysteria as a disease entity, at least one disease was established for which the cause was purely psychological and experiential. With one such case established, medical men began to look for other, and they found many. In fact, such psychological mechanisms were found to underlie most if not all of those mental disorders for which no organic physical basis had been established by the somatogenic school. Before we go on to the details of this, however, let us sketch briefly the history of hysteria.

The father of medicine, Hippocrates, was the first to realize that such a thing as hysteria existed. Whereas the disease is by no means less frequent in men than in women, it occurs in women in more obvious forms, and for this reason for many years it was considered a disease related to the female. Thus its name comes from the Greek word *hysteron*, meaning "womb"; and the early conception of hysteria was that the womb wandered around in some females and, in trying to displace some other organ, it caused the development of the disease. Later on we shall see that this concept, which to most people seems only ludicrous today, has in it something very close to the truth. Today we know that the womb itself certainly does not wander, but a sexual drive or libido which is normally connected with the womb becomes misplaced. This is our modern idea of the cause of hysteria.

Throughout the Middle Ages hysterical phenomena occurred, as did hypnotic phenomena. These particular abnormal phenomena were not separated from the whole idea of the theories of demon possession and the prevalent theory of the times. Today we realize that many of the saints and holy men of the Middle Ages were actually hysterical individuals or were suffering from self-hypnosis. The modern interest in hysteria, from the standpoint of the medical profession, originated about 1870 in France. Charcot, in 1862, became the director of the leading neuropsychiatrical clinic of the world, the Salpétriére in Paris. Although Charcot was primarily an experimêntal neurologist, persons suffering from what we now know as hysteria came in large numbers to the clinic, and Charcot early became interested in the theories of hysteria. As in the case of hypnosis, Charcot here at first held to a false theoretical interpretation, one more on somatogenic lines. Later in the clash over the nature of hysteria and hypnosis, the modern psychogenic viewpoint was established.

3. THE RFLATIONSHIP BETWEEN HYPNOSIS AND HYSTERIA

Toward the end of the nineteenth century it was realized that hypnosis was a particularly deep form of suggestibility in which the hypnotized person, so to speak, lost his own sense of himself, which we replaced by the hypnotizer. Secondly, came the discovery that in hypnosis the subject could develop symptoms similar to those of hysteria. Thirdly, we learned that the hysterical symptoms themselves could be destroyed by hypnotic suggestion. This line of reasoning obviously led to the conclusion that hysteria was a sort of "self-hypnosis."

The final realization of this took a long time. Although Charcot was interested in hypnosis and hysteria, he held for a long time that there were other factors than those of suggestion in hysteria. And Charcot was the most influential neurologist of his time. The physicians who first represented the view that two things were equivalent became known as the Nancy school. This school was led by Liéubault and Bernheim. In one of the major medical debates of the nineteenth century, with a great deal of keenness and some vituperation on both sides, the viewpoint of the Nancy school was finally established. Hysteria was seen to be a sort of self-hypnosis, where the self was divided, so that part of it played the role of the hypnotist and told the other part to develop this or that symptom.

The realization of one truly psychogenic disease spurred research on into the whole problem of psychogenic mental illness. Charcot himself came around to the new viewpoint and was a leader in the research. After he became convinced of the psychogenic viewpoint he performed very interesting experiments which definitely convinced many more members of the medical profession. It was gradually realized that there were many mental disorders, like multiple personality and morbid anxieties and fears, which on the surface looked very different from hysteria but which had the same sort of underlying dynamics.

Among leaders in the French school to continue this work were Bernheim and Liéubault and, perhaps most important, Pierre Janet (1859-), whose research did much to popularize the psychogenic theory. The French school as a whole, however, continued to use conceptions which were inclined to place an undue weight on constitutional liability and on traumata (emotional shocks) which occurred in adulthood. We realize today that constitution is important and that adult emotional experience do precipitate mental abnormalities, but we believe today that the most important causes of mental abnormalities lie in unconscious experiences. This point the French school was never quite willing to accept, and the center of modern psychopathology hence moved to Germany at the end of the nineteenth century.

About 1900 it was clear that there were mental diseases with a psychogenic etiology as well as those with a somatogenic origin. Just how certain parts of the self became separated or dissociated so that one of these "hypnotized" the other remained vague, however, until the advent of Sigmund Freud (1856-1939).

Freud was a brilliant young Viennese physician who had first specialized in pharmacology and neurology but who, through his work with Breuer, had become interested in hysteria and went to Paris to study with Charcot. While studying there, he came to believe that the inner conflict most often underlying the hysteria was sexual in nature. Thus Freud set up the theory, which will concern us in the greatest detail later, that the conflict which caused one part of the self to hypnotize another part of the self and so develop hysterical symptoms was usually sexual in nature. Freud used sex in a very much broader sense than we are accustomed to think of it in common parlance. To Freud, as we shall see, the sexual urge was the motivating factor behind all intimate relationships. In its very briefest outline form, Freud's theory was that certain sexual drives, being frustrated by society, are forgotten through being forced into the unconscious part of the personality. But they still remain active and try to get into consciousness. Part of the self prevents them from so doing. They are able, however, to disguise themselves and to return into consciousness as symptoms. Thus Freud completed our understanding of the interrelationship between hypnosis and hysteria toward the end of the nineteenth century. His predecessors had shown that shuch a relationship existed. Freud showed the how and the why of it. Interestingly enough, he gave a modern medical meaning to the speculations of Hippocrates, which we saw earlier in this chapter appear so ridiculous on first hearing of them.

Freud and his followers soon began to apply this basic formula to other problems of mental disorder. His particular mode of attack was called "psychoanalysis." After about thirty years psychoanalysis became recognized as the most scientific of various psychogenic schools. In the 1920's the debate between the somatogenic and the psychogenic sch... ...ached its high point. The outcome of this debate will be the subject of the next chapter. What Freud really did was to show that medical psychology could proceed on the basis of psychological understanding, where the somatogenic school insisted on an organic understanding. Freud's work was more important than that of any one individual in showing that abnormal mental phenomena were simply exaggerations or perversions of the normal mental phenomena and that every symptom had a cause, significance, and an economy. These two ideas of Freud are the chief cornerstones on which modern psychopathology rests. Consequently, as we go on, we shall have a great deal more to say about Freud and his theory.

4. THE CONCOMITANT DEVELOPMENT OF MEDICINE

Throughout this chapter we have talked chiefly about the development of psychological theories, shown how psychological factors were at first explained on magical or religious grounds, how later superstition was overcome by the establishment of the somatogenic viewpoint, and how more recently psychology has come into its own as a branch of medical science. A few words about the concomitant development of medicine in general may help clarify the argument.

If the psychological medicine of the Ancients was magical, so was the organic medicine. Consequently, for early times it is not necessary to differentiate between the history of medicine and that of psychiatry. The medical man who drove out the demons at the same time administered the organic medical therapeutic agencies. The relationship between the priest and the medical man is a close one in all primitive societies. This relationship has been studied in detail by many social anthropologists like maddox and Radin. Even the most primitive societies, however, discovered, largely through trial and error, the therapeutic values of certain herbs and grubs. The first branch of medicine to develop was consequently pharmacological chemical therapy. Despite the many insights into other forms of medicine by Hippocrates and the

Alexandrian school, no more than the beginnings even of chemical medicine were made until late in the Christian Era. The first real discoveries in medicine were applications of pharmacological therapeutics in the alimentary canal. Even until modern times all reputable medicine was chemical medicine. This was so because nothing of real importance concerning anatomy was known until the sixteenth century, nothing of importance concerning physiology until the seventeenth century, nothing of importance concerning microscopic life forms until the eighteenth century or of bacteriology until the nineteenth century. The applications of physical science to medicine came gradually from the midwife and the barber, who originally, of course, did not have the prestige of the medical profession. It is interesting to point out that to a certain extent the tooth puller, who during this whole period was in the same category as the midwife and the barber, has not arrived to medical prestige even today. Only in the eighteenth and nineteenth centuries do we have physical medicine developed so that surgery and obstetrics become reputable medical disciplines. And only in the nineteenth century do we have the establishment of bacteriological medicine and immunology. Only at the present time do we have the establishment of psychological medicine. In most advanced medical circles today the importance of psychology is admitted. As Dr. Karl Menninger has written:

'The emphasis on *psychological* factors in disease (and in health) is slowly permeating the entire practice of medicine. No longer the exclusively *chemical* concepts of the Middle Ages and earlier, nor the chemico-*physical* concepts of the nineteenth century, but a concept of interacting physical *and* chemical *and* psychological factors begins, now, to characterize the theory and practice of medicine. Once it was considered ridiculous to record a temperature; later it was considered ridiculous to examine a specimen of urine; and when these procedures became generally accepted it was still considered ridiculous to inquire into the details of a patient's dream. Now we know that dreams and urine and fever may and *must* all be examined if we are to truly and fully understand a patient. No intelligent or informed physician thinks any of these procedures absurd today—even though in practice he may omit one or several of them. For every thoughtful physician knows that psychological factors are as real and as effective as physical or chemical factors. [From K. Menninger, "Psychiatry and Medicine," *Bull Menninger Clin.*, 1: 2, 1936.]

SUMMARY

A1. The primitive mind accounted for all action and behaviour by "spirits." Thus normal behaviour was guided by the normal "spirit" and in abnormal behaviour something (the demon) must have replaced this. Thus arose the theory of demon possession which in one form or another was used to account for abnormal human behaviour until about 100 years ago.

A2. The ancient civilizations acquired some rudimentary scientific knowledge of human behaviour, but this was lost in the Christian Era.

A3. Christian psychology based on Christian theology was only a sophisticated and modified form of the theory of demon (devil) possession.

A4. With the growth of modern science following the Renaissance and Reformation the validity of the devil-possession theory was questioned until it was gradually abandoned. A more humane treatment was accorded the psychologically abnormal and the Humanitarian Era established.

A5. In the nineteenth century superstition was finally replaced by the somatogenic viewpoint, which insisted that all psychopathology was due to brain pathology

B1. Although the scientific validity of the somatogenic viewpoint is unquestionable, the psychological side of the problem remained uninvestigated. The study of hypnosis revealed that unconscious mental processes existed which affected conscious mental and physical processes.

B2. The disease hysteria was realized to be a sort of "self-hypnosis" and the psychogenic theory was established. The psychogenic theory believed certain mental abnormalities had their origin in experience, in such a way that it was unnecessary to postulate any brain pathology.

B3. From the studies of hypnosis and hysteria of the French school, Freud advanced to the position of psychoanalysis which gave us the first modern scientific theory of the nature of psychogenic illness.

B4. Medicine has gradually developed to the point where we today recognize that psychological factors are present in all diseases.

3

THE PSYCHOSOMATIC PROBLEM

1. PHILOSOPHICAL ASPECTS OF THE PROBLEM

In the last chapter we traced the slow development of psychopathological theory. In this one we shall present in some detail our present ideas about the relationship between body and mind. The great Copernican discovery that the earth was not the center of the universe gave the impetus to modern physical science. The Darwinian hypothesis that man's body is animal and natural and a part of the biological continuum became the foundation for nineteenth century biology. The Freudian postulate that man's mind is conditioned by his body in certain definite ways may well be the integrating principle on which a scientific psychology is established. Its importance necessitates a somewhat detailed discussion of the body-mind problem.

In everyday, prescientific, undisciplined thinking all of us make a distinction between body and mind. No matter what philosophers tell us about the problem, and no matter what our considered solution of it is, we still think of the ego or self or soul or mind as directing, at least at times, the movements of our bodies. We still think that even if the body grows old and changes, we have a self or soul or personality that remains essentially the same. We think of a real difference existing on the one hand between the "I," the soul, the self, the mind—in brief, the psychological—and, on the other hand, the body, the physiological organism, the blood and muscle and bones—in brief, the physical. This distinction comes into most of our practical considerations, into our serious literature, even into our popular songs, like "I am yours, body and soul": and "Why not take all of me?" In brief, we are inclined to think of the psychological aspects of our person as being something distinct from our bodies, something immutable, and, if we are religious, something that endures.

Modern science and philosophy are both very critical of this viewpoint. From the last chapter we can see it as a remnant in popular thinking of the once universally held Catholic theological dogma. The metaphysical shortcomings of the popular view of the body-mind problem have influenced innumerable philosophers, metaphysicians, and scientists to set up a better one in its place. The literature of the body-mind problem in philosophy is tremendous. By no means have we any ambition to cover it here. We must, however, speak briefly of some of the chief solutions of this body-mind problem and adopt that one which is methodologically most valid as a basis of our subsequent discussions; this is necessary because medical psychology must be concerned with this troublesome problem of the psychosomatic and psychophysical relationships.

In his excellent book on the problem, Professor C.D. Broad lists some seventeen proposed solutions with regard to the relationship between the body and mind. Of these he finds some ten impossible, some five unlikely, and two possible. We shall not attempt to review all of these, but we can at least point out why the popular viewpoint as we have presented it above is inadequate for science and why some of its alternatives are better starting places for the development of a medical psychology than are others. There are three chief ways of dealing with the body and mind problem: *dualism,* which may be divided into two types, *interactionism* and *parallelism; monism,* which may be divided into two types, *idealism* and *materialism;* and *neutralism*.

The dualistic solution accepts the reality of both mind and matter, spirit and body, psychological phenomena and physical phenomena. This is the doctrine of Christian theology, of course, which supposes that body may work on mind and mind may work on body. The whole problem of

Christian ethics and morality is concerned with strengthening the control of the spirit or soul over the body and seeing that the soul remains pure and, consequently, a candidate for heaven. Let us give an example of interactionistic dualism as it still persists in our popular thinking: "It is a fine summer day. I feel good. I decide to go out for a walk. I feel hungry. I see an apple. I eat it. It is a green apple. I develop a belly-ache. I feel bad." In this brief sequence of events one popularly says: "It is summer. My body is in good shape and I feel good (body on mind). My fine feelings set my body in operation and I go for a walk (mind on body). I feel hungry because of the exercise (body on mind). I spy the apple and eat it (mind on body). I feel sick (body on mind)."

Now this type of explanation, while completely adequate for the needs of daily life, social intercourse, and popular parlance, is scientifically and philosophically quite inadequate. As a strict matter of face, we can reverse the whole reasoning. "It is summer. The fine weather mentally perceived makes me feel good (mind on body). The muscular tonus leads to physiological tensions which make me decide to walk (body on mind). The pleasant perception of the apple initiates feelings of hunger and my salivary glands work (mind on body). The activity of my salivary glands leads to the decision to eat the apple (body on mind). I realize the apple is green and the thought upsets my stomach (mind on body)." Thus we have two exactly opposite series of causal sequence used to explain the same event, and the philosophically minded person is left in hopeless confusion. Further than that, for purposes of medical psychology the solution is impossible. If we can always show the mind affecting the body or the body affecting the mind for the same sequences of events our theoretical considerations and our applications of these will become very much confused. Consequently, all our behaviour may be attributed either to twists of the mind or to the biochemistry of the brain, and we cannot distinguish between these for an actual sequence of events. It is quite easy for the person who has some sophistry in metaphysics to see that interactionistic mixture of these languages can end only in confusion. As Southard pointed out, we may account for behavioural events in either a "mind-twist" type of theory or in a "brain-spot" type of theory, but we must not mix the two. For this reason, therefore, however useful it may be in popular parlance, we shall consider dualistic interactionism a scientifically impossible solution.

Another type of dualism is that called "parallelism." The parallelistic solution also accepts the reality of both body and mind. It says, however, that neither works on the other, but they run along together in correlation exactly as two perfect clocks keep exactly the same time but are both run by their own mechanisms. Thus the apple-eating incident may be accounted for either in a purely psychological language or in a purely physical language. Accounted for in a purely psychological language it would be related something like this: "It is summer. My consciousness of fine weather is correlated with feeling good. My goodness of health leads to a decision to take a walk. The experience of walking in fresh air leads to a consciousness of hunger," and so on to the end. Accounted for in a purely physical language it would be related: "Certain meteorological conditions prevailed. The stimulus of light of certain wavelengths and intensity strikes the agglomerate of cells of certain physical properties and introduces physical changes in some of these," and so on to the end. This parallelistic viewpoint avoids the confusion brought about by the arbitrary admixture of psychological and physiological language. It has one great difficulty, however. It is very hard for the philosophically minded individual to understand how the clocks got so perfectly synchronized. Even the philosophers who have held this position have had to posit God or some other timekeeper to see that one clock did not get ahead of the other. However, this parallelistic position was that most widely held by reputable biological scientists until fairly recently, and it will not lead us into any methodological confusions if we hold to it. Consequently, it is a possible solution for the scientific psychologist, and if the choice is between it and interactionism it is certainly to be preferred.

Neither form of the monistic position, however, is to be considered scientifically. The idealist say that the psychological word alone has reality, while the material world is simply an illusion. The materialist, on the other side, says that the psychological world is an epiphenomenon (i.e., has no real existence but arises as a sort of shadow of the material), and only real matter exists. On first view of these two positions the materialistic is undoubtedly the more tenable. We have every reason to believe that the physical world had a long and real history before psychological phenomena existed at all. Modern research in philosophy, however, has shown that differences of opinion which may not be decided by some experiential criterion are meaningless. To put this viewpoint into a slogan: "A difference which makes no difference is no difference."[1] Let us say that the equally close friend of a materialist and an idealist is run over by a motorcar. Thus the idealist holding that only mental events exist supposes his friend run over by an ideal automobile and dying an ideal death. The materialist, on the other hand, loses a material friend to a material automobile. Since the friend is dead, and we suppose both philosophers kindhearted persons, there is no way of distinguishing the idea of heartache which the idealist attributes to his ideal heart from the *material* physical changes in the viscera of the materialist. In other words, for all practical purposes, whether we are idealists or materialists is inconsequential. We have no real means of deciding whether a purely material individual with an illusory mind suffers a real death by a real automobile, or whether a purely psychological being made up of illusory material suffers an imaginary death by an imaginary automobile. The trouble with the monistic solution of the mind-body problem is that it ducks the real problem by denying it.

Recently some philosophers, most notably the logical positivists (Cf. the works of Feigl and Pratt), have made it possible for us to see in the difference between physical things and psychological things simply a difference of language expression. Psychological things are real. It is only through psychological reality that we know anything. On the other hand, from our psychological experience we have posited the existence of a physical world about which we know a great deal in physical terms or in physical language. Probably the best solution of the mind-body problem for purposes of science is to posit an organismic *neutralism*. This supposes that the world exists as a neutral substance, being neither body nor mind, physical nor psychological, but that the physical and psychological aspects develop as the two faces of a medal. Psychological reality occurs and has its own laws and sequences, which are just as natural and just as subject to investigation by the scientific method as are the physical aspects of reality. Both aspects are so coordinated that any change which we can make in the physical may create reaction in the psychological, and vice versa, just as any change on one side of a medal must influence the configuration of the other side, even if the change is sometimes hard to discern. Consequently, we suppose that all pieces of behaviour have both a mental or psychological and a bodily or physiological aspect. Influencing bodily behaviour as in organic medical practices will directly change only the bodily aspects of behaviour, and our causal sequences here should be expressed in the language of physics. However, with this change will be correlated psychological changes. On the other hand, influencing psychological experience, as in psychological medicine, will directly change only the context of experience, and such sequences should be expressed in psychological language. With this change there will be correlated physiological changes. Actually this viewpoint does not overcome the philosophical difficulties inherent parallelism but it better fits our modern ideas of science.

It may well be that it would be more sensible to talk not about two levels, of physiology and psychology, but rather of four or five levels. Thus every problem of behaviour presents a physical, a physiological, a psychological, a sociological, perhaps even an ethical aspect. In this book we shall be concerned with the psychological aspects of behaviour problems. In many cases, however, we know more about the sociological aspects on the one hand and the physiological aspects on the other than we know of the psychological, and some of this material must be integrated into the work. It is almost impossible occasionally to avoid talking in the popular language of dualistic interactionism. We shall try never to say that a physical state of affairs directly causes a psychological state of affairs. If on occasion we use the popular language it is only because a strict holding to our philosophical position becomes painfully clumsy and circuitous under certain circumstances.

2. THE SOMATOGENIC SOLUTION

We have already seen how at the time of Kraepelin superstition was finally overcome and mental disorder was looked on as solely due to brain pathology. This occurred toward the close of the nineteenth century, a century in which mechanistic materialism was the basic philosophy for all biological sciences. The nineteenth century saw the birth of comparative and experimental physiology and comparative and experimental neurology. Very many of the diseases of the body which had previously been understood only symptomatically were now understood in terms of their specific etiological pathology. It was quite natural that, with physical diseases being understood on the basis of a mechanistic biology and with the rapidly increasing knowledge of the nervous system, the Kraepelinian view should have been established at the time.

The somatogenic viewpoint considered mental disorder as brain disorder. Since the brain was rightly considered the organ responsible for psychological phenomena, it was quite natural that extraordinary psychological phenomena should be explained by extraordinary physiological conditions in the brain. The perfectly consequent argument of this school was, "Since we know there is a different biochemistry and biophysics underlying the sensations of green and red, we may be sure that there is a different biochemistry and biophysics underlying John Smith's correct identification of himself and his identification of himself with Napoleon." From this stand point research done on the problem of mental abnormality in the latter half of the nineteenth century was done from the somatogenic viewpoint. Undoubtedly at some far-distant future time our knowledge of brain physiology will have so increased that the somatogenic viewpoint may again become the prevalent one. We believe that one legitimate aim of all scientific psychology should be toward establishment of a physiological psychology. There is something more tangible about the biophysics and the biochemistry of nervous tissue, which, when we know about it, will enable us to proceed rapidly in the true scientific sense. Not only are the facts of biochemistry and biophysics more tangible and hence better subject to control and manipulation, but it is easier to grasp and teach the principles of organic medical therapy. Even if this does not mean that we shall be able to reduce all psychological facts to physiological facts, as the nineteenth century thinkers believed would be possible; as we get more and more knowledge of the underlying neurophysiology, more and more of the techniques of psychological therapy will be applied in terms of organic medicine. Somatogenic theory represents a very high type of scientific idealism. I think even most adherents of the psychogenic position would be glad to see the aims of the somatogenic school realized. Unfortunately, however, they are not today realizable.The men who set them up and those who still hold to them are thinking in terms of an ideal science. Despite the fact that we postulate that every change in psychological experience is accompanied by a change in the underlying neurophysiology, we unfortunately know very little about the underlying physiology of either normal or abnormal mental states. There are a few mental diseases, as we shall see, where a specific and demonstrable organic pathology is established. These are, however, by no means the most frequent and even these offer many problems of a psychological nature.

3. THE PSYCHOGENIC SOLUTION

The somatogenic theory proved sterile in actual practice. We did not advance rapidly in our knowledge of the neurophysiology underlying behaviour. Had we done so it is quite probable that the psychogenic school would never have arisen. Some fifty years' study of the problem of mental disease from the standpoint of the somatogenic theorists has added little to our knowledge of this subject. For the most frequent psychoses and for all psychoneuroses we do not yet know just how the nervous system works biochemically and biophysically differently during the exacerbation of the disease than it does when the organism is functioning normally. On the other hand, we know quite definitely that such behaviours follow with at least some regularity upon certain psychological experiences. From our experience in the World War, we know that fear disabled almost as many men as did gunpowder. From our study of young people developing schizophrenia, we know that this disease develops almost exclusively in young individuals afraid or unable to take over the consequences of adult sexuality. We know that individuals who have been frustrated in any of their major psycho-emotional strivings are the candidates for mental disease. We even know the causal relationships between many of the frustration types and the disease symptoms. Thus we realize today that mental abnormality may be caused by frustrating situations. Symptoms develop from the way in which the organism meets blockages in the psychological field. For the organism in question the frustration is resolved in an economic fashion. This viewpoint, as we saw in the last chapter followed from the realization that hypnosis was a form of suggestion and hysteria a sort of self-hypnosis. It was developed by many men, most notably Sigmund Freud and his followers.

The realization that many, and perhaps even most, mental diseases developed from experiential factors gave a great impetus to the psychogenic school. Undoubtedly the idea that abnormal psychological phenomena should be studied *psychologically* has advanced our knowledge of mental disease in the last twenty years more than it was advanced in all of history preceding. For a time at least, it looked as if all mental disorder was to be handled by medical psychologists and that in the future the practice of psychiatry would require as equipment only a room in which two people could sit and talk things over alone. This led to a period when among many psychiatrists the emphasis was almost solely on the psychogenic factors of disease. This emphasis was also unbalanced, because, as we shall see, even in those diseases where we understand nearly everything about the psycho-emotional factors involved, problems of organic medicine are constantly arising.

4. THE ORGANISMIC SOLUTION

The somatogenic and psychogenic solutions are both one-sided. We have seen that the best modern philosophical solution to the mind-body problem is that which considers every side. From a viewpoint which stressed only the body we moved to a viewpoint which stressed only the mind. Today we are interested in studying the mind *in* the body, or the psyche *in* the soma.[2] Although the mind is *in* the body and derives many of its properties from the body, psychological phenomena must still be understood in terms of psychological laws. Our problem, then, is that of the integrated organism. The problem may be studied at various levels and in various languages. Half of the confusion and most of the debate about the organic and the functional viewpoints could have been avoided if this problem had been stated from the first as follows. Every piece of human behaviour, whether it be an unconscious physiological act like elimination or circulation, or a semiconscious act like respiration, or a fully conscious act like writing a poem, may be studies by physiologists in physiological language or by psychologists in psychological language. This solution is called the organismic and is basic to the point of view of this book. Actually, there are many sublevels of investigation within these two major groupings. Thus it is perfectly sensible to talk about the physics, the biophysics, the physiology, the psychology, and the sociology of digestion. It is also just as sensible to talk about the physics, the biophysics, the biophysics, physiology, psychology, and sociology of falling in love. The confusion, and it sometimes becomes very great, arises when half of the discourse is in one of the languages and half in another. Now, of course, it is quite obvious to everyone that some problems may be more profitably discussed in some languages than in others. At the present time most physicians can best discuss digestion in the physiological language. This does not mean, however, that for certain individuals to discuss it in the psychological language is by any means unprofitable.[3] Similarly, the delusions of schizophrenics may be most profitably discussed by the majority of physicains in psychological language. This again does not mean that physiological discussion of it is either unnecessary or unprofitable. I think that the time may come when all these problems may be equally well discussed in all the languages. Then we shall use the language which is most economical in its language function. At the present time, however, it is necessary for the psychopathologist to be familiar with the grammars and syntaxes of both. To sum up: *Every behaviour problem is at the same time a physiological, or organic medical, and a psychological, or psychiatric problem.* Since the author of this book is a psychologist, and since the book is addressed primarily to students of psychology, we shall spend most of our time speaking the language of psychology. We shall try, however, not to lose track of the face that the other languages exist.

5. ILLUSTRATIONS OF THE ORGANISMIC SOLUTION

We can best grasp the wide implications of the organismic solution of the mind-body problem by pointing out that definite psychological factors exist in sicknesses which are usually discussed in the physiological language, on the one hand, and that physiological factors exist in problems usually discussed in psychological language, on the other. In introducing actual psychiatric problems at this point it will be necessary to simplify them. Later on in the book these same problems will be treated in detail. We shall begin by discussing a few problems which were thought in the latter part of the nineteenth century to have been solved in terms of organic medicine and show the presence of psychological factors. From these we shall proceed to problems usually considered purely psychological and show the presence of physiological factors.

Acute Alcoholism (Common Drunkenness)—It may surprise the reader to learn that alcoholic intoxication is a mental illness on abnormality. From the standpoint of the modern theory of perosonality genesis, however, the personality of the drinker is so changed by the ingestion of alcohol that his behaviour may be said to undergo a major change. And this is exactly what we mear by mental illness or abnormality in accordance with our modern views. Alcoholic intoxication brings about a radical change in personality and brings about behaviour which may be both antisocial and personally destructive. It is so frequent and well-known that those of the readers who have not personally experiences such behaviour will undoubtedly be familiar with it in their friends or, if they move in completely abstinent circles, from the moving pictures. For this reason it is a good behaviour with which to begin our discussion.

Everyone knows what happens when an individual who has no exceptional tolerance for alcohol drinks ten highballs. After the first two he becomes uninhibited, talkative, more sociable. With two more his inhibitions may disappear almost completely. From an individual previously controlled almost solely by the intellect, he becomes an individual almost completely controlled by his emotions. He becomes very gay or very sad, very loving and amorous or quite ready to pick a quarrel. With the ingestion of six or seven he becomes increasingly powerless to coordinate muscular activity. (The uninhibitedness and emotionality continue with this loss of control over muscular behaviour. He can no longer walk a straight line or talk straight. Rather he staggers and minces his words.) After about nine or ten drinks he usually goes into a state of somnolence popularly described as "passing out."

But before this stage musch abnormal emotional behaviour occours. A friend of the author says that whenever he drinks too much, he becomes first lachrymose, then bellicose, although the lachrymose and bellicose states sometimes become inverted, and, finally, comatose. The author remembers seeing an undergraduate weeping over the death of Shelley. The profound mental thought which occurred to this fellow after too many highballs was that poor Shelley was dead and that he would never get to talk with him.

Occasionally, however, the results of drinking become more serious. There are cases on record where well-meaning friends have taken an acutely intoxicated person bodily along with them and poured further liquor down the individual's throat. In some such cases death has resulted. Every so often there is an account in the papers of lethal alcoholic poisoning, where an individual attempts for a wager to drink a large quantity of strong alcoholic beverage in a limited period of time, such as a quart in an hour. Thus the end state of alcoholic intoxication is death.

We have, then, a graded series of behaviour which usually follows upon alcoholic consumption. Furthermore, we know quite well what happens to the nervous system during such intoxication.

From the work of the neuroanatomists and neurophysiologists we know that certain parts of the brain are primarily responsible for certain behaviours. Just what amount of exact localization of function exists in the brain is by no means certain but we do know that intellectual processes are chiefly mediated by the cerebral cortex, the emotional processes by the midbrain and thalamus, the vegetative processes by the medulla and brain stem. We know further that the higher portions of the brain exert some inhibitory control on the lower and that the higher portions are first affected by poisons. For the reader whose knowledge of brain anatomy is rusty or non-existent Fig. 3.1 gives a diagrammatic sketch of these relationships.

The fibers of the frontal-thalamic tract first become affected by the alcohol. For this reason the individual comes

A= Frontal lobe
AB= Frontal-thalamic tract
B= Thalamus
C= Speech center
(Broccas area)
D= Cerebellum
E= Medulla oblongata
F= Tenth (vagus) nerve

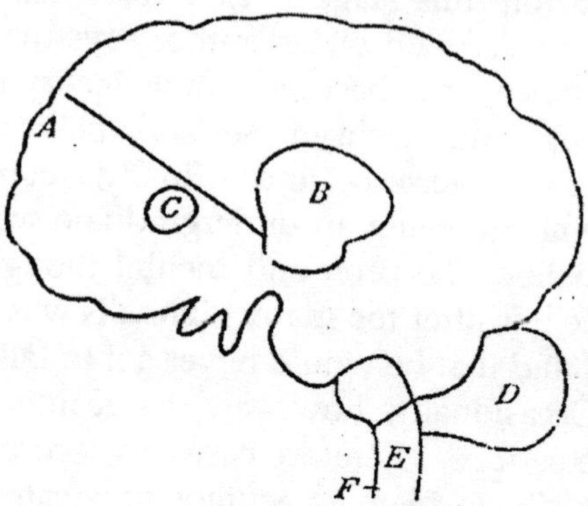

Fig. 3.1. : Showing the relationship between brain anatomy and the sequence of behaviour in alcoholic intoxication.

more under thalamic control and more uninhibited and more emotional. When the cortical control of thalamic function is abolished, the individual is almost completely emotional. Further imbibing leads to partial paralysis of the speech center and so accounts for the slurring alcoholic speech. The alcoholic poisoning next affects the cerebellum, a center for posture coordination, and there is a resulting lack of coordination in muscular movement. In the medulla there is located a center which controls wakeful consciousness. As this is affected the individual "passes out." The tragic cases of lethal alcoholic intoxication are cases where alcohol paralyzes the center of the tenth or vagus nerve, which controls the heart and respiration. From this analysis the somatogenic theorist naturally says, "What could be clearer? The bizarre behaviour of the alcoholic is created by the poisonous effects of alcohol on the nervous system. That's all there is to it."

But there is a great deal more to it. The whole problem of why individuals drink at all is not handled in this explanation. The whole problem of why some individuals drink much more than others is not accounted for. The fact that emotional shock is almost immediately sobering is not accounted for. The problem of why the bellicose behaviour in my friend precedes the lachrymose behaviour in some cases and in others follows it is not explained.

The difference in the use of alcohol as a mild social stimulant and the abuse of alcohol as a psychic analgesic can only be understood in psychological terms. We used to believe that overindulgence in alcohol was simply a matter of habituation. This was the philosophy behind the great American tragicomedy of prohibition. It was believed that by keeping individuals from becoming habituated to alcohol through removing the supply alcoholism would soon disappear. It is well-known that it increased, and probably narcotic drug addiction along with it. Today, while we know just what happens physiologically when an individual drinks too much, we also know that the presence of conflict in the personality, a purely psychological factor, is the cause of the severe and chronic drinking. Thus the alcoholic psychologically is not sick because he drinks, but he drinks because he is sick.[4]

Neurosyphilis—Neurosyphilis is one of the major medical problems of which we have almost complete control. We know-how it is contracted, how the spirochaetes go through the blood stream and affect all the tissues, how occasionally they get into the spinal fluid and affect the nervous tissue. We know-how to kill them in both the blood stream and in the spinal column and brain. The first major psychosis for which we have discovered a specific therapy for some cases is dementia paralytica. There are several forms of neurosyphilis but in this connection we will speak of only one. Dementia paralytica, or ... or general paralysis of the insane, as it is also called, is the most severe mental disorder following from a syphilitic infection. The brain is actually destroyed and the mind is destroyed along with it. In these cases we can arrest the progress of the disease by organic medical therapy, so that its worst ravages are avoided. Psychiatrists can point with great pride to the work of von Jauregg, who first discovered that the human constitution could stand the alternating chills and fevers of malaria while the organisms causing syphilis could not. "Here surely," the adherents of the somatogenic school are accustomed to say, "is a psychosis which is purely an organic medical problem."

To be sure it is an organic medical problem, but it is a psychological problem as well. The paretic develops certain psychological reactions which are enough alike so that we knew the disease as a disease entity before we knew that its cause lies in syphilitic infection. The delusions of these individuals are very similar. One type of delusion is that of bizarre and irrational grandeur. An example of this may be seen in the case of a little East Side Jewish tailor, a hard-working family man, who, in the course of perhaps his only breach of marital vows, contracted syphilis which went into neurosyphilis and ended in paresis. This individual also had a blood syphilis, so that on certain parts of his body, most obviously on his hands and feet, were running sores. This individual was deluded that he was Christ. He interpreted the sores on his hands and feet as being the marks of the nails of the cross. Although we are not sure, it is highly likely that this delusion had an economic significance for the individual. He was possessed by a strong sense of guilt for his sinning. This could be rationalized by supposing himself incapable of sinning. The presence of the sores on his hands and feet gave the necessary stimulus for the form of his delusion. He was Christ: therefore he was not guilty of his sin.

Of the many individuals who contract syphilis, some estimates placing it as high as 8 per cent of the population, only a few develop neurosyphilis. It is interesting that of the syphilitics perhaps 4 or 5 per cent develop mental disorders in connection with the disease. The reader will remember that we pointed out that about 4 or 5 per cent of the population develop some sort of mental sickness serious enough to require confinement at one time or another during their lifetime. The agreement between these percentages is probably no mere coincidence. Neurosyphilis may be simply the invasion by the spirochetes of a nervous system which is in itself unstable for psychological reasons. Although at the present time we have no definite proof of this psychological factor in the disease, it is perhaps the best theory by which we can account for the fact that in the vast majority of syphilitics the syphilis remains a blood disease.

Furthermore, we know that the psychological picture in paresis may be modified by *psychological* therapy. A few years ago the author heard a medical burst into hilarious laughter. The cause of his mirth was that he had heard about a paretic patient being psychoanalyzed. He said, "That shows you how crazy the psychoanalysts themselves are. Here is the one mental disorder about which we know everything and which we can cure, and we find it treated by psychoanalysis." My friend's mirth was unwarranted. No one would undertake the treatment of neurosyphilis by psychoanalysis alone, but psychoanalysis in cooperation with the organic medical therapy, as Ferenczi and Hollos, Grotjahn (1938), and Schilder (1930) have shown, may do a great deal to relieve the acute symptoms of this disease.[5]

Schizophrenia—With schizophrenia we come to a problem in which our psychological language is much more adequate than our physiological language. Schizophrenia is the most frequent as well as the most fascinating of the so-called "functional psychoses." At this point we shall not try to describe its symptoms. The mental behaviour of the schizophrenic, and its accompanying physical behaviour, is very bizarre. There could be no doubt in anyone's mind that a schizophrenic is "crazy." (We shall see later on that many mental disorders are by no means obvious to superficial observation.) Schizophrenia is a disease in which an individual unable to cope with physical and social reality withdraw from it into a mental world of his own. It occurs, as we indicated before, usually in young people at the time when they must assume full social and sexual responsibility. The young person, after his education, is expected by society to support himself, to take a wife or husband, and to start a familial history over again. This means a giving up of the protective atmosphere of one's own parents and taking over parental responsibility oneself. The adolescent period is a sociopsychologically difficult one for everybody, but for some individuals it is so psychologically traumatic that they flee psychological reality entirely, rather than face it. By fleeing reality we mean that the schizophrenic invents through fantasy a dream world of his own in which he can live more comfortably than he can in the world of hard social reality. We see thus psychologically that the symptoms of the disease have a cause and an economy. The cause is social frustration and conflict, and the economy is that the individual can live in his dream world and so exist as a psychobiological organism when the real world becomes so uncomfortable that he cannot stand it. We see also that the symptoms of schizophrenia have a significance, but we can do that only after we are able to talk of them in some detail. Although a great deal remains to be learned about schizophrenia, we know quite a lot about its psychology. But until recently we knew practically nothing about its physiology.

For some time it has been known that schizophrenics get at least temporarily better during and for a short time after any severe physical illness. It has been noticed by psychiatrists in the tropical countries that when an epidemic of any of the severe tropical fevers strikes a hospitalized group of schizophrenics, those who are afflicted by the disease are better psychologically than those who are not.[6] We have reason for believing that many of the alleged cures of mentally ill individuals by exorcism and torture in the Middle Ages were of cases of schizophrenia who responded to the threat of psychobiological destruction with a return to reality. At the time of writing this book it is being claimed in some psychiatric circles that an organic medical cure for schizophrenia now is at hand in the recently adopted insulin shock and metrazol treatments.[7] It is too early to evaluate this treatment finally, but the success which the treatment has already had does indicate that there are definite physiological problems connected with schizophrenia.

Before the insulin shock therapy was so much discussed, the biophysicist Bancroft developed an organic theory of the major psychoses in terms of the biophysics of nervous conduction and the effect of certain drugs upon the nervous system. Space does not permit our developing Bancroft's complete theory, but Bancroft did find that the intravenous administration of sodium amytal brought schizophrenics who had long been out of contact with social reality back to reality to such an extent that communication could be held with them. As first he thought, he had a cure for schizophrenia, but further study by competent psychologists and psychiatrists has shown us that these cures are of little permanent value. For one thing, increasing doses of amytal are required to bring the individual back to reality, and, for another, the individual is simply socialized and not really cured; in other words, even though he reacts socially in a social situation, his psychotic symptoms remain. Consequently, the sodium amytal treatment is not very seriously considered today, although the use of amytal and related drugs opened up a wide field for pharmacological research on psychological theories. Thus in considereation of schizophrenia we see the other side of the picture. Here is a disease which is primarily psychological which offers definite physiological problems.[8]

The Psychoneuroses—By psychoneuroses in general we mean the milder forms of mental abnormality. At this point in our work we shall not attempt to present them in detail. It will suffice to say that the psychoneurotic is an individual suffering from some physical defect which investigation shows to be due to emotional conflict, as in hysteria. Chapter 2, or from some morbid psychological disorder such as fear or anxiety, as in the well-known phobias. Examination after examination by competent physicians shows that there is nothing organically wrong with these individuals. The development of an etiological theory of the psychoneuroses was as great a triumph for the psychogenic school as the etiological theory of paresis was for the somatogenic school. "Here," said the adherents of the psychogenic theory, "is a domain of psychiatry that is predominantly ours. We understand how these things come about and for some of them, most notably hysteria, we have a specific therapy."

But here again the problem is not so simple. It is fairly well-known among physicians that gastric ulcers often develop in periods of nervous agitation. Nearly everyone knows the phrase "nervous indigestion." The loss of appetite suffered by individuals in love or suffered by actors, singers, and lecturers along with their stage fright is a phenomenon which everyone goes through. Long periods of such nervous anxiety which we can best and, in fact, only understand in psychological terminology may lead to the creation of stomach ulcers. Once the ulcer is established, however, the problem becomes a medical one. Similarly with the disease known as "hyperthyroidism." Long periods of nervous agitation where the thyroid gland is hyperactive leads sometimes to hypertrophy of the thyroid glands and they thus become a province for the surgeon. But there again thyroidectomy, that is, excision of part of the thyroid, is by no means a permanent cure unless the psychological precipitating factor is removed. As a matter of fact, as Alexander (1936), Dunbar (1935), and Karl Menninger (1938) believe, today we know that even in many of the organic diseases a psychological factor is also involved.

Some psychoneuroses show no organic involvement whatever. These also furnish physiological problems. Here we include morbid anxieties, obsessions, and compulsions. The obsessional-compulsive neurotic is an individual who has a feeling that such-and-such may occur if he does not do this-and-that. The obsession refers to the idea, such as that his hands are dirty even though he has washed them within the preceding five miunutes. The compulsion refers to the motor act; he must wash his hands. In some cases of this neurosis the carrying out of the compulsion itself creates the necessity for organic medical treatment which may best be couched in the language of physiology. Similarly, feelings of vague anxiety where no specific factor is feared are due to psychological factors. Thus the phenomenon known as free floating fear, where the individual does not know what he is afraid of or is vaguely first anxious about this problem, then afraid to meet this situation, then worried that something will happen to this person, and then doubtful that he can go through with this test or that, is well-known to be caused by psychological factors. Freud first pointed out that the cause of this anxiety was inhibition of sexual impulses. Society, however, forces some individuals to deny their sexual drives. It is socially all-right for them to be timid and anxious and afraid, but they cannot admit that they have sexual urges. The extreme form of this is known privately among psychiatrists as "old maid's neurosis." The standard joke of the old maid looking under her bed at night for fear that some man will be there is recognized everywhere to be a wish perverted into its opposite. The anxiety itself may start a vicious circle so that actual organic changes occur.

6. MEDICINE AND PSYCHOLOGY

Modern medicine is concerned with a sick organism rather than with a sick organ. No longer do we treat the symptom as the sickness, but rather as indicative of a sickness in the personality. Everyone knows this with regard to our modern conceptions of fever. The fever is a symptom of disease processes within the organism and is actually the process of the organ curing itself. What the fever does is destroy the attacking forces. We have seen a good artificial example of this above in connection with the malaria therapy for neurosyphilis.

Similarly, modern psychiatry is concerned also with a sick personality, rather than with the symptoms. The symptoms, as we shall see in the next section, are simply the signs that something is wrong underneath. This something worng is usually of both a psychological and a physiological nature. In every one of the diseases which we discussed we saw both of these factors. What modern medicine does is use every tool it can possibly utilize to further the life of the individual. When organic medical tools are available, they should, of course, be used. All too frequently, however, and that is what creates the problems of psychology, we know of none. Then we have to use psychological tools. Today it is realized that even in the common clinical diseases many psychological factors are involved. The successful practising physician uses suggestion of a psychological nature in his treatment of every disease. Even in organic diseases, such as heart disease, kidney disease, and respiratory disease, the presence or absence of the wish to get well is a well-known and important factor.

Since there are psychological and physiological factors in all diseases, the so-called "organic" ones as well as the so-called "psychological" ones, division of labour is undoubtedly necessary. No one can master all of both aspects of modern medicine. No one can really master either the organic or the psychological aspects alone. Although there is much said, and some of it justly, about the advantages of the private general practitioner, his day in medicine is rapidly coming to a close. The best modern medicine today is clinical medicine, where the various specialists work together on each individual sickness and in cooperation. In treating the sick in the future, pathologists, internists, psychiatrists, psychoanalysts, psychologists must all work together. At a not too far distant time, I believe that the checkup which people quite sensibly are having done by their physicians every year or every other year will also be done in a clinic, and a good share of the examination will be psychiatric. We can only really understand the diseases of the mind as being the diseases of a whole organism according to the organismic viewpoint. We have, to repeat, not body and mind, but mind in body. Future medicine both in its theory and in its diagnosis and practice will more and more be concerned with the biophysical and neurological, the physiological and the psychological aspects of all the diseases. I think there are very good reasons for believing that it will soon have to concern itself more and more with the sociological aspects of disease.

Today we realize that many important phenomena of psychology originate in society. In other words, we realize that the individual's accomplishments, his personality, and finally his adjustment and happiness are not simply functions of his physical body or even of his psychological mind, but depend on the individual's position in the whole social order. We have had this viewpoint thrust upon us very rudely by the threatened collapse of western European industrial civilization. It has been pointed out to us by the first and second world wars; it has been driven home to us by the Great Depression and the fear of new world economic crises. It has been realized, that health and disease both in their mental and in their physical aspects may be distinguished only with reference to norms established by cultural criteria. Not only is the application of medical psychology to the benefit of humanity imperiled by the present economic and political structure of the world, but the constant danger of world financial crisis and world imperialist war is so great that modern medical science seems almost impotent in the face of such threats. In a book on abnormal psychology we may only point out the urgency of these social psychological problems.[9]

In this book, because of limitations of space and because the author's competence lies in psychology rather than in physiology, our treatment will be more concerned with psychological theory and psychological language than with that of organic medicine. We stress, however, even to the point of being tiresomely repetitious, that neither the somatogenic nor the psychogenic solution to the psychosomatic problem is satisfactory. Rather, modern medicine will more and more rely on the organismic solution.

SUMMARY

1. Philosophical analysis indicates that of the various philosophical solutions to the mind-body problem, organismic neutralism is the best starting point for a scientific psychology.

2,3,4. The basic postulates of the somatogenic, the psychogenic, and the organismic solutions of mind body problem are given. The one-sidedness of both the psychogenic and the somatogenic solutions is pointed out. The organismic solution is selected as the basic postulate for this book.

5. A discussion of several types of mental abnormality indicates the presence of psychic factors in those abnormalities usually thought of as purely somatogenic and of organic factors in those usually thought of as purely psychogenic.

6. Modern medicine hence must make increasing use of the discoveries of psychology. The psychology of the

individual, however, depends to a large extent on sociological factors. The medicine of the future will probably be sociological as well as psychological.

NOTES

1. For this slogan I am indebted to Prof. H. Feigl.
2. A similar development has characterized recent social psychology. From the placc where we considered the individual alone, or the group alone, we have come through the position where we considered the individual versus the group, or the individual and the group, to the place where we consider the individual *in* the group. Thus the individual becomes a dependent part of the group and derives many of his characteristics from the group. However, he remains a separate entity in certain respects. *Cf.* Brown (1936c[3c]).
3. *Cf.* the recent valuable work of Alexander and the Psychoanalytic Institute of Chicago on problems of gastric neurosis. This work is reviewed by Karl Menninger (1938), Alexander (1936), and Dunbar (1935).
4. The problem of alcoholic addiction is more fully treated, with references to the literature, in Chap. 6.
5. The problem of neurosyphilis is more fully covered, with references to the literature, in Chap. XV.
6. Personal communication from Dr. James Merriman Lynch, formerly Assistant Superintendent of the State Hospital of the Republic of Panama.
7. The nature of this treatment will be given in Chap. XVI.
8. The problem of schizophrenia is more fully treated with references to the literature, in Chap. XVI.

4

THE PSYCHONEUROSES

1. THE DIFFERENTIAL OF PSYCHONEUROSIS

By psychoneurosis we mean the milder abnormalities of the cognitive, emotional, and motor processes, which usually only partially incapacitate the individual and where the basic symptoms are somehow connected with anxiety. Psychoneurotics are individuals who because of their conscious or unconscious conflicts are prevented from arriving at the accomplishments of a productive sort which would normally be expected of them in consideration of their abilities and culture. Some psychoses are primarily organic. Even in the functional psychoses, organic factors enter into the etiology. The psychoneuroses on the other hand are predominantly socially conditioned. Thus Karen Horney (1937) and others have pointed out that many reactions which we should look on as neurotic in our culture are considered quite normal in other cultures, and behaviour types which we consider quite usual would be considered neurotic at sometimes and in some places. The psychoneurotic, then, is the individual who deviates in his behaviour from the norms accepted by his culture because of anxiety and who feels lonely and inferior because of this deviation. Psychoneuroses may be subdivided into relatively distinct syndromes, and our description of the psychoneurotic as a type is for comparison with the psychotic and normal types we have already described.

There is no sharp break, furthermore, between behaviour which is to be looked on as psychotic and behaviour which is to be looked on as neurotic. The two classifications merge into one another so that it is almost impossible to classify certain diseases definitely in either category, and we must speak of borderline psychotics and borderline neurotics. Let us take one or two examples to illustrate this difficulty. A woman whose daughter had become engaged to a young man of the Protestant faith. This woman previously had not been a particularly religious person and was only an occasional churchgoer. At the time of her daughter's engagement, her whole behaviour changed. She began to go to church very regularly, to go regularly to confession to her own priest, and to become obsessed with the fear that her daughter and her daughter's children would suffer the fires of hell because of the prospective son-in-law's membership in the Protestant church. Her own priest tried to argue her out of this. He pointed out that although a marriage to a Catholic would have been better in his eyes, still in the eyes of God there was no reason why the daughter or the children should really suffer or why the marriage should be unhappy. The woman persisted in this belief and was made very unhappy and anxious and was incapacitated in her functions both as wife and mother because of it. Where the psychiatrist finds difficulty is in classifying such disturbances of the cognitive processes. Are they delusions or are they obsessions? In general, as we saw above, we think of an obsession as a persistent unwelcome belief which the individual realizes is fantastic. A delusion is a persistent false belief. The difficult question of diagnosis in the present case was to say whether the individual was suffering from a psychosis of the paranoid form or from a psychoneurosis of the obsession-compulsion form.

A university professor had always worked in a compulsive fashion. He had been forced by internal conflict of which he was at least partially conscious to turn out not less than ten research papers a year. This meant that he must devote all his spare time during the academic year to research. In addition, he was inhibited from doing any research during his summer holiday. He was neurotic because many times in the school year he would have liked to relax and enjoy himself a little bit, but his anxiety about not getting his programme finished prevented him from so doing. Furthermore, often in the summer he was at a loss to know what to do with himself and very often would like to turn to his professional specialty, but here again anxiety prevented him from so doing. As long as his productive research was of a scholarly, scientific sort, he was to be classified as a compensated neurotic. If, in order to fulfil the demands he made upon himself, he developed irrational beliefs about which he published papers in a field where he had no competence, he would have gone over the borderline into psychosis. Even for the psychiatrist, it is difficult to say at just what time this occurs.

Another example, this time of a fear. Stage fright is a quite normal phenomenon which all of us experience at one time or another in our lives. Normal stage fright may be said to occur when a person makes an appearance in a new role before an unfamiliar audience. Neurotic stage fright is the stage fright from which an individual might suffer in producing familiar material before either a familiar audience or the type of audience with which he has previously had at least moderate success. Psychotic stage fright may be said to occur when the individual is not afraid of failing before the group but is afraid that actually one of the audience is really persecuting him or embarrassing him or may even injure him. It should be quite obvious that it is almost impossible to draw a definite line between psychoses and psychoneuroses.

A psychoneurosis is at the same time a problem of individual psychology because of the anxiety and a problem of sociology because of the deviations in mentality and behaviour from the cultural norm. All psychopathologic behaviours deviate from the cultural norms and any definition of the psychopathologic implies this. Particularly important to psychoneuroses is, besides this deviation, the fact that psychoneurotics do not break with reality (i.e. retain insight) and that they suffer anxiety. In his book, *The Problem of Anxiety* (1936), Freud has pointed out that neurotic anxiety represents a defense against the breakdown of repression and the return of the repressed to consciousness in its original form. The symptoms of psychoneurosis other than anxiety represent a return in disguised form.

The various criteria developed allow us to view psychoneurosis in terms of psychoanalytic theory. In psychoanalytic theory, the psychoses may be differentiated from the psychoneuroses in terms of the amount of ego and libido regression and in terms of the topographical location of the conflict. Thus in psychoses the libidinal regression goes at least as deep as the early anal period (beyond the level of reality testing). Psychosis thus may be considered dynamically as a disorder in which the ego loses much of its contact with reality and aligns itself with the forces of the id. The conflict is that of the ego plus the id versus reality. The psychoneurotic, on the other hand, suffers libidinal regression only to the phallic or late anal period, and his conflict may be considered a struggle between the forces of the id and the ego, in which the ego maintains its anchorage in external reality. The regression is only to the level of reality testing and so the neurotic retains insight and does not deny reality. The borderline cases, such as paranoia (a psychosis) and the obsessional compulsion neurosis (a psychoneurosis), are hence the most difficult to distinguish. The paranoid individual has one part of the ego anchored to reality and another part taking the side of the id. The compulsive neurotic has more of the ego anchored to reality but still has a part which sides with the id. This state of affairs, we shall see, leads to the predominance of delusion in the paranoid individual and to the compulsive element in the abnormality of the compulsive neurotic. As we go down the regression scale from hysteria to schizophrenia (Table 10.1), we find an ever-increasing involvement of the ego on the side of the id. In hysteria, for instance, the ego is relatively intact and unconscious id urges become converted into symptoms of physical disease.—schizophrenia, the ego accepts the disguised id urges almost in toto. The difference between

DIAGRAMMATIC REPRESENTATIONS OF PERSONALITY STRUCTURE

→ ← *Harmonious Balance*

→ ← *Inharmonious Balance*

The Longer Arrows Refer to Relative Balance of Personality as a Whole with the Environment

The Shorter Arrows Refer to the Relative Balance of the Forces Within the Personality

.... *Socially Acceptable Behaviour*

-+-+-+-+ *Unacceptable but Disguised*

-+..-+..-+ *Disguised but Partially Acceptable*

SE-Super-ego

C and M—Respectively, Cognitive and Motor Aspects of the Ego

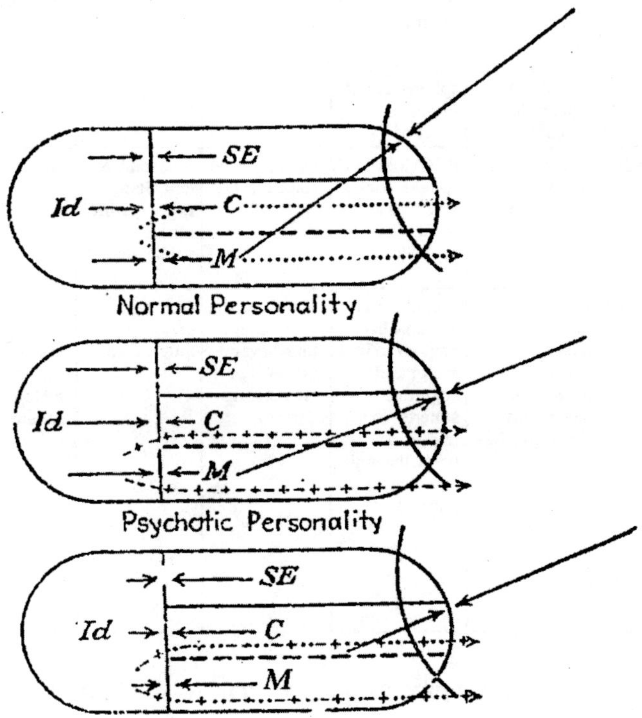

Fig.4.1. : Comparing the neurotic personality with the other types.

psychosis and neurosis is an arbitrary one, but one which must be made for diagnostic and prognostic reasons. Table 4.1 and Fig. 4.1 show the schematic definition of psychoneurosis; to facilitate comparison, the personality structures already discussed are repeated.

TABE 4.1

	Nature of Internal conflict	Social nature of resultant behaviour	Degree of regression	Relation of basic urges to love object	Resolution of conflict results in
Psycho-neurosis	Inharmonious balance in ego, super-ego, id, and reality. Ego in conflict with super-ego and id but ego on side of reality	Behaviour only partially acceptable. Destructive in both motor and congnitive spheres but id impulses checked	To late anal or phallic, thus not beyond the level of reality testing	Ambivalent	Autoplastic symptoms, particularly anxiety
Normal	Harmonious balance between ego, super-ego, id, and outside reality	Behaviour in all spheres constructive and socially acceptable	None, genital stage reached	Postambivalent. Some urges gratified others sublimated	No conflict
Psychosis	Extremely inharmonious balance in ego, super-ego, id, and outside reality. Ego powerless or weak against id and breaks with reality. Super-ego projected or taken over by ego of oversevere	Socially unacceptable behaviour in both motor and cognitive spheres. Id impulses break through in a disguised form	To at least the early anal; thus beyond the level of reality testing.	Objectless or extremely ambivalent	Severe symptom formation in cognitive and motor spheres

2. THE SCOPE OF PSYCHONEUROTIC BEHAVIOUR

It is almost impossible to get statistics on the extent of psychoneurotic disorders. Only about 4 per cent of institutionalized patients in American mental hospitals are classified as psychoneurotic, and this might lead one to believe that psychoneurosis is a comparatively rare form of mental disease. How false this view is should be quite obvious from the differential criteria which we have outlined in the last paragraphs. Psychoneurosis is by no means rare; it is very common. The psychoneuroses are to the psychoses as the minor physical ailments, such as colds, headaches, stomaches, indigestion, and diarrhoea, are to major physical disease. These minor physical ailments do not call for hospitalization. The individual suffering from them often functions at least half efficiently in his economic and social milieu. But we have all had them and we know how thoroughly uncomfortable it is to try to do productive work with a cold or how thoroughly unpleasant it is to attend a social function with a racking headache. We all know how an attack of indigestion will ruin the enjoyment of even the most marvelously prepared meal. It is similar with the psychoneurotic disorders. The individual suffering from them rarely enjoys himself either at work or at play. A morbid fear of meeting new people will do even more to ruin what might be a pleasant social evening than a bad cold. A compulsion to wash one's hands or to urinate frequently may bring a person's professional or business efficiency down much more markedly than a severe headache.

Just as some of the minor physical ailments merge into what one might consider real sicknesses, so some psychoneuroses are much more severe than others. As some colds make life unhappy and force us to bed rather early, others force us to give up attempting to play our role at all in the economic and social world. In this the amount of the physical personality affected determines the depth of a physiological sickness. A common cold makes us simply uncomfortable. A grippe or influenza forces us to bed. A fear of high places might be a very minor thing to a person living in a small town on the plain, while it would be a very major thing to an individual living in the mountains or in a metropolis.

The psychoneuroses, then, rather than being rare, are very common and merge into the normal emotional reaction forms on the one hand and into deep psychoses on the other. Although no definite figures can be given, many psychologically minded general practitioners estimate that up to 50 per cent of their patients are neurotic. Former president Angell of Yale, himself a psychologist, estimates that at any given time 15 per cent of the American undergraduate body is "neurotic." The author believes that the individual who never suffers psychoneurotic maladjustment is quite as rare as the individual who never has had colds. In this chapter we shall give examples of various psychoneuroses, ranging from the obsessional neurosis which borders on psychosis in that the ego is involved on the side of the id to conversion hysteria which borders on normality in that the ego is left relatively intact.

3. THE NOSOLOGY OF PSYCHONEUROSIS

Psychoneurotic symptoms do not appear in such clean-cut syndromes as do the psychoses, so that many mixed neuroses occur. This makes nosological classification difficult. After the realization of the "psychogenic" nature of hysteria gave birth to the modern theories of psychopathology, it soon became obvious that there were many other psychoneurotic reaction forms. Nineteenth century pyschiatry followed the practice of the French school (Janet) in differentiating conversion hysteria, neurasthenia—which included nervousness, fatigability, irritability, and exhaustion without definite conversion symptoms or morbid fears and compulsions—and psychasthenia—which included morbid fears and compulsions—and psychasthenia—which included morbid fears compulsions. Actually the term "neurosis" itself is a misnomer, as it means disease or poisoning of the nerves. "Psychasthenia" means the weakening of the psyche and "neurasthenia," The weakening of the nerves. These terms were all introduced at the time in psychiatry when it was believed that some actual somatic changes or neuropathology would be discovered underlying the neuroses. The terms "psychoneurosis" and "neurosis," which are now used indiscriminately, will undoubtedly (despite their misleading etymological derivation) remain in the scientific language. "Psychasthenia" and "neurasthenia" are so inaccurate that they have been largely given up. Some psychiatric treatises still used them, so the student must be familiar with them.

Freud's work clarifies the genesis of psychoneurosis and gives us a basis for a dynamic classification of the neuroses. The neuroses like the psychoses are classified as to the depth of ego and libidinal regression and the nature of the conflict.

The psychoanalytic nosology divides the psychoneuroses with regard to etiology as well as with regard to regression. Before our detailed discussion of the neuroses on the basis of regression and personality structure, we must deal briefly with these categories.

The True Neuroses and the Psychoneuroses— Freud, in his earlier papers (1924a, Vol. I) distinguished between neuroses which were caused by an existing nervous malfunction and those caused by infantile traumatic experiences. This distinction was made before the introduction of the aggressive or hostile basic urge and both forms of neurosis were considered due to libidinal maladjusment. The true neuroses occurred on the basis of adult sex maladjustment and included neurasthenia, which he attributed to sexual excesses, particularly masturbation, and the anxiety neurosis, which was supposedly due to sexual abstinence. The psycheneuroses include hysteria and the obsessional neuroses and are due to repressed infantile sex experiences, particularly in connection with the Oedipus situation. From Freud's conception of the psychoneuroses has grown the nosology we shall discuss in this chapter. Freud never modified his conception of the true neuroses and he never developed the concept further; in his later writings he spoke of it but occasionally. On the other hand, he has never withdrawn it. The prevalent psychiatric opinion is that, except in rare cases, both sexual excesses and sexual inhibitions are themselves neurotic symptoms and not causes of neurosis. Freud correctly perceived, however, that there are physiological problems even in the neuroses.

The Narcissistic and Transference Neuroses— Psychoanalysts distinguish between narcissistic and transference neuroses. Transference neuroses are those in which the neurotic symptomatology is a disguised form of an originally cathected object relationship. Narcissistic neuroses are those where the libido is turned in. This distinction is important for the prediction of the possible therapeutic success of psychoanalysis. Transference neuroses, like conversion hysteria and anxiety hysteria, are much more easily cured by psychoanalysis. Neuroses like the obsessional neurosis are much less easily cured because of the narcissistic fixation of the libido. The psychoneuroses are characterized in terms of the depth of neurotic regression. Actually, there is considerable overlap between the theoretical stages of the psychoneuroses and their actual symptomatology. Indeed frequent strict diagnosis is almost impossible. It is, for instance, rare to find an obsessional neurotic without compulsions or, for that matter, an anxiety hysteric without obsessions.

As we go from the obsessional neurosis to conversion hysteria, certain differences become quite clear. The obsessional neurotic is obviously mentally ill. In fact in some cases we cannot clearly differentiate between obsession and delusion. The hysteric, on the other hand, is "physically ill". This means that the ego in hysteria is relatively little affected in its contact with reality, while in the obsessional neurosis the ego is deeply involved. The intermediate forms fall between. The deeper the regression, the more obvious the ambivalence of the behaviour and the more infantile the libidinal adjustments. Hysterical individuals are maladjusted chiefly at the phallic level, i.e. the level where ambivalence is becoming overcome, while compulsion neurotics show definite signs of ambivalence and late anal character traits. Thus the more regressed forms approach the psychotic and the less regressed forms approach the normal. This will be clear in a discussion of the symptomatology and etiology of the various neuroses.

The nosology of the psychoneuroses is of recent origin and there are no accurate statistical figures on their incidence. In most cases, psychoanalysis is the therapy of choice. For these reasons, we may shorten our outline and discuss only the sympotmatology and etiology of the neuroses.

4. THE OBSESSIONAL NEUROSES

Symptomatology—In actual practice, the obsessional neuroses cannot be strictly spearated from the compulsion neuroses. Where obsessions predominate, compulsive behaviour is almost always also present, and in compulsion neuroses obsessional fears and doubts are also to be found. To illustrate certain points of theory we shall speak of the obsessional neurosis when obsessions dominate the picture, the obsessional-compulsion neurosis when obsessions and compulsions are balanced and the compulsion neurosis when compulsions dominate. If obsessions predominate, in general the disease is more severe (i.e., more deeply regressive and closer to psychosis) than in case where compulsions predominate. This illustrates an important point about modern psychiatry, which should be clear from the foregoing chapters. The various disease entities represent arbitrary points chosen for diagnostic convenience on a continuum. Mental disease, in general, represents regression and retreat from reality along a continuous scale.

The outstanding symptoms in the obsessional neurosis are the obsessions. These are persistent unwelcome ideas which the patient realizes are morbid but which continue to bother him. These ideas are both self-accusatory and accusatory toward others and may be very close to paranoid delusions. A young mechanic suddenly gets the idea that he is not the father of the eight-year-old daughter he has always adored. This leads to the obsession that his wife is unfaithful. A young matron is obsessed with the idea she will poison her guests and plunge a carving knife into her husband. Another that she will pick up a hideous disease by touching any graniteware surface. Sometimes the obsessions are metaphysical. Religious individuals become obsessed with fear of hell fire or that the world is coming to an end. These obsessions are related to phobias, but in the obsessional neurosis the fear persists constantly. In the phobias of the anxiety hysteria, the fear inhibits the activity and so gives a protection against anxiety.

Almost always with obsessions we find compulsions. These protect the patient against the obsession. The obsessional neurotic who doubts his wife's fidelity becomes compelled to spy on her. The woman who fears that she will poison her guests is compelled to entertain only in restaurants. The more exact nature of these compulsion symptoms will concern us in the next section.

There is usually much conscious anxiety with regard to the obsessions and feelings of inadequacy and helplessness in controlling them. This becomes so great that many obsesssional neurotics finally feel depersonalized and unreal. Besides the secondary anxiety there is usually the so-called "compulsive doubting." This doubting occurs particularly with regard to the fact of the obsession but also covers many everyday decisions.

In severity, the disease ranges from mild obsessional preoccupation, which is but little disabling, to severe obsessional neuroses, which are completely disabling. Usually the disease continues in increasing severity and may end in decompensation into a psychosis. Sometimes, however, obsessions are overcome by causes of which we know nothing. The tendency is for symptoms to become generalized, i.e., to become attached to the most varied stimuli in the environment.

Etiology—Psychoanalysis of numerous obsessional neurotics has shown the following factors in the etiology. The affect connected with a repressed emotional experience is dissociated or isolated and transferred or displaced to some relatively harmless object. This object, of course, has some relation to the primary emotional experience. The source of the patient's obsession of being infected by graniteware may go back to masturbation in a bathtub. The obsession is a transformed self-reproach for some forbidden sexual or aggressive act. The patient who denied the paternity of his daughter and was obsessed by his wife's unfaithfulness had strong unconscious homosexual impulses he could not admit. Actually, he would have welcomed a divorce. Freud has shown in detail how the "isolation" of the affect from its original meaning reduces anxiety. The hairsplitting doubting of obsessional neurotics is derived from the late anal period when ambivalence is very strong. The struggle between hostility and libido and between homosexuality and heterosexuality is strong at this point. There is the constant balancing between the force of the id urges of an anal-sadistic sort and the strongly developed, but not properly integrated, superego in the obsessional neurotic. The compulsive acts which usually follow obsessions serve to neutralize the guilt which the obsession arouses. As the ego becomes more and more involved and at a more regressed level, the whole life of the individual becomes concerned with the typical conflict of childhood, "May I be naughty or must I be good?"

The obsessional neurosis represents a symptomatic protection against repressed conflicts from the late anal level. The mechanisms of doubting, isolation of the emotion from its original situation, and undoing (i.e., performance of the compulsive acts which neutralize the effect of forbidden wishes) enable the individual to reduce some of the anxiety which the threatened reawakening of the conflict arouses. The involvement of the ego and superego is at the pregenital ambivalent level, where ego was relatively weak and superego relatively severe. Earlier theories that the obsessional neurosis is a degenerative disease with neuropathic heredity have been today almost completely abandoned. Thus the obsessional neurosis, like all the psychoneuroses, is primarily psychological in origin.

5. COMPULSION NEUROSIS

Symptomatology—We have already seen that most obsessional neuroses show some compulsive traits. Similarly, most if not all compulsion neurotics exhibit some obsession. When the obsessions are more prominent than the compulsion we speak of obsessional neurosis, and when the compulsions are the more prominent, of compulsion neuroses. Very often both types of symptoms are nicely balanced and we have obsessional-compulsion neurosis.

Compulsions are persistent and irresistible tendencies to engage in meaningless motor acts. These range from simple reactions of relatively segregated muscle groups, which we see in motor tics, to complex integrated motor acts like pyromania, the irresistible impulse to start fires; dipsomania, the irresistible impulse to drink; kleptomania, the irresistible impulse to steal. In both the tics and the monomanias, the obsessional idea connected with the compulsion may be quite repressed.

The most frequent type of compulsion is that where the impulse to perform an act which appears senseless to other observers is very strong and failure to do so creates anxiety. The compulsion, like the obsession, isolates the affect of unconscious conflict by displacing it to an indifferent act or object. Thus, the compulsions to count money, or to memorize railroad timetables, or to touch every paving stone become acts through which the energy connected with repressed and forbidden acts of looking and touching is discharged in a more economical fashion.

Connected with the compulsive acts are always some anxiety and usually much doubting. The compulsion neuroses, like the obsessional, may become chronic. The chronic cases gradually merge into the concept of compulsive character and anal character, on the one hand; and the acute merge into the psychoses, on the other. Actually, as we have seen, many of the ritualistic acts of the schizophrenic are compulsive in origin.

Etiology—Compulsive acts, like phobias, protect against obsessional anxiety and so leave the individual ego more intact. In general, the compulsion represents an undoing of or protection against an id impulse which is not consciously recognizable. The sexual content of the compulsion is recognizable in some cases, such as the compulsion to look at female legs. In others, this is not so clear at first. Compulsions to cleanliness always protect against the guilt feelings connected with infantile sexuality. This is often connected with masturbation. In this case the obsession, "My hands are dirty," based on guilt for masturbation, which is isolated, leads to the compulsion, "I must wash them," which is an example of undoing. The frequent cases of hand-washing mania are thus explained. The compulsion to play cards or "fiddle" with one's hands, gloves, buttons, and so forth is often a displaces masturbation equivalent. It is protective since the genitals themselves are not manipulated. The compulsion neurotic, like the obsessional, is in a continual conflict both between his homosexual and heterosexual strivings and between his love and hate impulses. He can hence neither love nor hate properly. In addition, his weak and vacillating ego is no match for the strong demands of the id on the one hand and the tyrannical superego on the other.

The prevalence of doubting in the compulsion neurotic as in the obsessional neurotic comes from these struggles. In some cases in adolescents the severe doubts which are felt with regard to a choice of the college course and of a career can be traced back to pregenital fixations, i.e., before the time that psychosexuality was definitely established.

Since compulsion and obsessional neurosis represent a regression to pregential sexuality, with an ego regression and with strong homosexual urges, therapy is difficult. Psychoanalysis is the therapy of choice but it is usually a long procedure. The successful treatment of the obsessional and compulsion neurosis by psychoanalysis requires on the average three times as long a period as does the treatment of hysteria.

6. THE ANXIETY NEUROSIS NEURASTHENIA

Symptomatology—Anxiety neurosis and neurasthenia were frequent diagnoses about ten years ago. Today they are seldom made because all neuroses start with anxiety and many of the cases previously diagnosed as anxiety neuroses were early obsessional neuroses on the one hand and anxiety hysterias on the other. Neurasthenia scarcely ever occurs without some marked obsessional or hysterical content.

The symptomatology of the anxiety neurosis is simple. The basic symptom is anxiety of the free floating sort.

Physical symptoms like tachycardia, respiratory upsets, visomotor disturbances, and perspiration often occur. The cause of the anxiety is never known to the patient. It is felt as something inside one's self. It may be displaced on a succession of harmless objects. In addition, there is usually irritability, insomnia, and *pavor nocturnus* (severe anxiety attacks in the night).

Neurasthenic patients often develop paresthesias and hyperesthesias, but the central symptom is an exaggerated feeling of fatigue which is so constant as to diminish capacity to work. The popular idea of the nervous breakdown is involved here. There is irritability, depression, hypochondriasis, insomnia, and various muscular weaknesses, but the central feeling is that of "not being able to go on" with one's work and social obligations.

Etiology—Neurasthenia and anxiety neuroses are the two diseases Freud originally called the true neuroses. As we saw above, neurasthenia was supposed follow on sexual frustration. Although Freud never publicly withdrew this viewpoint, there are reasons to believe that the true neuroses in contradistinction to the psychoneuroses are rare. Freud (1936) later showed that all neurotic anxiety occurs when repressions threaten to breakdown. Anxiety neurosis is probably the early stage of any neurosis. Neurasthenia is probably a hysteroid form of hypochondria in which pregenital factors are at work. The pure forms of both anxiety neurosis and neurasthenia are probably rare. When they do exist, they represent a mixed form of repression between late anal and phallic stages with some aspects of each.

7. ANXIETY HYSTERIA, PHOBIAS

Symptomatology—In earlier psychiatry, anxiety hysteria and the phobias were classified as psychasthenias or as obsessional neuroses. Careful psychoanalysis of many patients has shown this classification to be etiologically inadequate. While it is true that the phobia, which is the chief symptom of anxiety hysteria, is somewhat obsessional in nature, it is easy to show that the sufferers from this disease have neither the depth of regression nor the pregenital conflicts of true obsessional neurotics.

Anxiety hysteria, under which we include all the phobias, has a simple symptomatology. The patient has morbid fears of a situation or object. This may be allayed by not going in the vicinity of the situation or object except under certain circumstances. Secondary symptoms include general anxiety about the phobias, insomnia, and frequent disturbances in the sexual field.

Etiology—The phobias as a protection against a situation which might give rise to primary anxiety. Thus the affect of an unconsciously unacceptable infantile conflict is projected outward to prevent the arousal of anxiety. These conflicts are usually on a phallic level and come from the Oedipus situation. Consequently many phobias in adults are concerned with situations which normally cause fear in children, such as the fear of being shut in, claustrophobia the fear of having to cross the street alone, agoraphobia; and the like. The fear is a reaction formation against temptation because one has an even greater fear of the consequences of temptation.

The etiology of anxiety hysteria is the same as that of conversion bysteria, of which we shall speak next, except that the ego is more involved and there is greater regression and more ambivalence. Both diseases are caused by conflicts at the phallic level, however, and both represent attempts to overcome anxiety which was originally aroused by the Oedipus conflict.

8. CONVERSION HYSTERIA

Symptomatology—Of all the psychoneuroses we know most about conversion hysteria. We have already seen how the nineteenth century interest in conversion hysteria and hypnosis was combined with the realization that the symptoms of conversion hysteria are due to self-induced hypnosis. The hystory of hysteria was important because the study of this disease gave rise to the chief tenets of modern medical psychology. Today the study of hysteroid conditions like those of the pathoneuroses and organ neuroses (cf. the last chapter) is giving rise to psychosomatic medicine. Hysteria refers to those symptoms of "physical" disease which arise on a primarily psychological basis. The symptoms are always connected with organs whose motor or sensory control is mediated by the central nervous system. They are distinguished from the organ neuloses in that the organ neuroses affect organs innervated by the autonomic system. They are distinguished from the pathoneuroses in that their origin is almost exclusively psychological. The psychologically determined hypo-, hyper-, and para-functions of the sense organs and striated musculature are often referred to as stigmata. In addition to the stigmata, there are episodic phenomena of a hysterical nature which range from hysterical "epilepsies" to various mild nauseas and the like. In the concept of hysterical episodes are also included various dream states, somnambulisms, fugues, and personal amnesias. Hysteria, like syphilis, may be called the "great imitator." Hysteria can be confused with nearly every physical and mental disease.

Etiology—Conversion hysteria utilizes chiefly the mechanism of conversion. In conversion, the repressed affect is converted into a symptom in such a way that unconscious conflict is avoided or reduced. This is the so-called *primary gain* of the neuroses. Anxiety is diminished and the ego is left relatively intact. The organ affected has some significance or meaning to the individual and the conversion often follows the principle of *somatic compliance.* By somatic compliance is meant the fact that, although the organ cathected is significant in the life history of the individual, it may be somatically weak through constitutional factors or previous disease. The primary gain comes from the variation of unconscious conflict through the development of symptoms. The sufferer from conversion hysteria also gains sympathy from the family and companions and does not have to face the real life situation. This is called the *secondary gain.*

These conflicts of hysteria usually go back to the Oedipus situation, where there was a conscious attachment at a phallic level to the parent of the opposite sex. The fear of the consequences of the Oedipus attachment leads to the repression and a resultant denial of all sexuality. The physiological sexual ripening at adolescence can find no natural outlet because of the fear of the consequences of all sexuality. Thus sexuality is denied and the libidinal energy is converted into the symptoms of physical disease.

Hysteria, then, is a regression to the phallic level of sexuality. The struggle of the hysteric is always over a conflict between heterosexual urges and a fear of the consequences of these. The sexual elements are genital. The symptoms serve as a denial of the causes of the anxiety.

Conversion hysterics seldom show only "physical" symptoms. The phallic character is clearly seen in the hysteric who develops behaviour problems as well as symptoms. He often shows both curiosity and exhibitionism but denies the sexual significance of these behaviours. There are certain signs of hostility to frustration and there is usually a preoccupation, accompanied at the same time by guilt feelings, with regard to masturbation. The conversion symptoms represent the displacement of repressed genital strivings upward. In this there is an eroticization of the sick organs and distortion as in dreams, while the organ chosen usually has special erotic significance for the individual. There are frequently "hysterical" attacks simulating epilepsy. Freud was able to show that the hysterical episodes always represent a disguised sexual act in which certain psychoanalytic mechanisms like condensation, overcompensation, multiple identification, and reversal of normal time sequences are involved. Thus in the hysterical convulsion, the individual acts out a coitus with his own body, acting both the seducer and the seduced, the male and the female, often beginning with an exaltation similar to orgasm and ending with mimicry of passional attitudes and the like. The attenuated and abbreviated forms of the hysterical episode on analysis are all seen as pantomimic portrayals of sexual activity at the phallic level.

In the following chapters, we have covered the field of mental illness proper. We started with the primarily organic psychoses, developed the primarily functional psychoses, and ended with the psychoneuroses. All these diseases have in common the fact that the symptomatology is somehow concerned with cognitive processes and so are mental diseases in the narrow meaning of the word. Such mental diseases lead to maladjustments which have been called *autoplastic* in that the inner personality structure is changed and mental symptoms result. Modern psychiatry dealt first and most thoroughly with these diseases because all psychology was concerned with the perceptual and cognitive processes.

Our more recent emphasis on behaviour disorders and emotional disorders has developed the modern psychiatric interest in character disorders and sexual maladjustment which will concern us next. The disordered characters show adjustment which has been called *alloplastic* in that the maladjustment works itself out on the environment.

The psychoses and psychoneuroses all have some things in common. They represent regressive forms of behaviour which are exhibited when frustration in adulthood is too severe. Sometimes the regression is to an earlier fixated period. At other times development has been fixated at an earlier period and only gone superficially beyond it. Undoubtedly, biological and constitutional factors enter into determine the depth of the regression. In all these diseases there are medical as well as psychological problems. Disregarding the primarily organic psychoses, we may say that as we come up the regressive scale from schizophrenia to hysteria, psychological factors become more important. Despite the great importance of schizophrenia as a medical problem, the psychoneuroses are much more frequent. Undoubtedly in the psychoses and psychoneuroses there are important sociological problems besides the psychological. Mental disease often occurs as a breakdown in adulthood on the basis of sociological frustration. Sociological frustration, however, probable never causes mental illness alone but only in those cases where a psychological basis is laid down.

5

ABNORMALITIES OF SEXUAL BEHAVIOUR

1. THE RELATIONSHIP BETWEEN PERVERSE SEXUAL BEHAVIOUR AND MENTAL DISEASE

The "normal" layman realizes that there is such a thing as sexual perversion, but he looks at it with horror and considers the pervert either a sinner whose depravity is completely beyond his comprehension or a criminal who should be severely punished by the regular legal procedure. The Victorian taboo on the frank discussion of one of the most important of biological functions applied even to medical men until recently. A few sexologists like Krafft-Ebing and Havelock Ellis (1931b) assembled a great many descriptive data about the abnormalities of sexual behaviour, and about the beginning of the twentieth century the sexual perversions were first seen as psychiatric problems. It remained for Freud, however, to attempt to account for the psychodynamics underlying perverse sexual behaviour in the scientific manner and to relate these behaviour forms to the normal personality on the one hand and the mentally diseased personality on the other hand. Freud's great contribution to this field, *Three Contributions to the Theory of Sex,* appreared in 1905. We have already studied his theory of psychosexual genesis. In this chapter we shall see how perverse sexual behaviours are the result of fixations or regressions to the various stages of infantile sexuality.

Sexual perversions represent behaviour in which release from sexual tension is obtained by practices other than that of normal heterosexual coitus. These practices usually involve contact of the sexual organs with other bodily organs, such as the hand, the mouth, or the anus. In the period of infantile sexuality both the oral and the anal regions have sexual significance in the meaning we gave the word "sex". Since the psychoses and psychoneuroses are looked on as *defences* against returns of repressed infantile material to consciousness Fréud was able to show that the perversions represent fixations at levels of infantile sex adjustment. In psychosis, as we have seen, the ego allies itself with the forces of the id to distort reality and so prevent the unconscious internal conflict from causing continuous anxiety to the individual. In the psychoneuroses the ego struggles with the id and the psychoneurotic symptoms may be looked on as the result of this struggle. In the perversions the ego accepts the pregenital sexual urges, allows them a place in consciousness, and accepts the perverse sexual behaviour forms as natural. In psychoses and psychoneuroses the unconscious infantile strivings appear in a disguised or distorted form and often have little to do with sexuality on the surface. In perversion the infantile means of satisfaction and the infantile sex object are often disguised, but the behaviour is realized and admittedly *sexual* in nature. In other words the behaviour is aimed at the reduction of libidinal tensions. For instance, the homosexual nearly always believes that there are two classes of men or women, the homosexual and the heterosexual, and that he simply belongs to the homosexual class. He considers himself that way "by nature," and, despite the fact that he suffers from social pressure, he believes that he has a right to his own sexuality and that he should fight for that right if necessary. This is one of the reasons why the therapeutic treatment of homosexuality is very difficult. The homosexual, and this is also true for other sexual perversion types, may have no *neurotic* struggle. Since perverse behaviour forms are frequent in neurotics and since many perverts also show neurotic symptoms, this of course does not apply to the borderline cases. Perverts have many conflicts based on the social taboos against perversion and on the fear of being exposed as perverts. Consequently many of them are also neurotic. But some perverts openly admit their perversion.

With this in mind, Fig. 5.1 and Table 5.1, which give the theoretical structure of the perverse personality, may be understood. The theoretical structures of the normal, the psychotic, and the psychoneurotic are again included for comparative purposes.

DIAGRAMMATIC REPRESENTATIONS OF PERSONALITY STRUCTURE

→ ← *Harmonious Balance*

→ ← *Inharmonious Balance*

The Longer Arrows Refer to Relative Balance of Personality as a Whole with the Environment

The Shorter Arrows Refer to the Relative Balance of the Forces Within the Personality

.... *Socially Acceptable Behaviour*

-+-+-+-+ *Unacceptable but Disguised*

-+..-+..-+ *Disguised but Partially Acceptable*

SE-Super-ego

Cand M—Respectively, Cognitive and Motor Aspects of the Ego

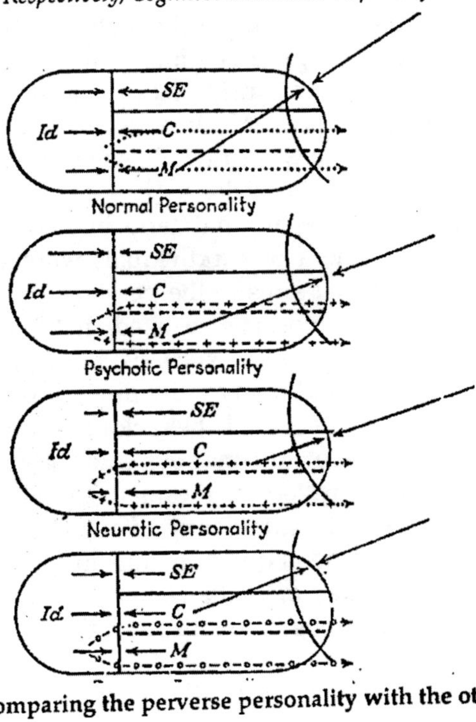

Fig. 5.1 : Comparing the perverse personality with the other types.

Just what it is that makes certain individuals accept fixations at infantile development stages and others develop mental illness is by no means clear. Various theories have been developed on both psychological and biological grounds. Undoubtedly the constitutional and biological factors must be taken into considerations. Some of the passive male homosexuals, for instance, develop the secondary sex characteristics of the female, and many of the female homosexuals develop the secondary sex characteristics of the male; but by far the greatest number of sexual perverts seem to be anatomically quite normal. Psychological and anatomical sexuality are, however, by no means directly correlated. Every individual is psychologically bisexual.

2. WHAT CONSTITUTES PERVERSION IN SEXUAL BEHAVIOUR

Until the introduction of the psychoanalytic concepts of libido and psychosexual genesis into the literature, only heterosexual coitus was considered normal sexual behaviour. The perversions, to be sure, were realized to be sexual in nature, but a strict line was drawn between normal behaviour forms and the sexual perversions. Thus it was considered that most individuals were "normal" and limited in their sexual aims to coitus, while a few individuals were abnormal and limited in their sexual aims to the perverse behaviour forms. To be sure, most individuals realized that certain forms of behaviour with the mouth, such as kissing, were closely related to sexuality, and many individuals realized the sexual significance of certain anal behaviour forms. But those individuals who have no conscious interest in the anus are very often still interested in the anal regions, such as the buttocks. The sexually stimulating effect of the buttocks, for instance, in the female is quite obvious in hula-hula dancing and in certain modes of walking and dancing. The movie actress Mae West has capitalized this with remarkable success.

Today we realize that all behaviour which brings individuals into close physical contact is libidinal or hostile in

TABLE 5.1

	Nature of internal conflict	*Social nature of resultant behaviour*	*Degree of regression*	*Relation of basic urges to love object*	*Resolution of conflict results in*
Sexual perversion	Balance may be either harmonious or inharmonious; no break with reality but with sexual mores	Behaviour socially unacceptable but person "normal" except in sexual sphere	Unless combined with psychosis, neurosis, or genius, there is fixation rather than regression	May be postambivalent in homosexuality. Other cases ambivalent	Perverse sexual practices
Normal	Harmonious balance between ego, superego, id, and outside reality	Behaviour in all spheres constructive and socially acceptable	None. Genital stage reached	Postambivalent. Some urges gratified, others sublimated.	No conflict
Psychosis	Extremely inharmonious balance in ego, superego, id, and outside reality. Ego powerless or weak against id and breaks with reality. Superego projected or taken over by ego or oversevere.	Socially unacceptable behavior in both motor and cognitive spheres. Id impulses break through in a disguised form	To at least the early anal, thus beyond the level of reality testing,	Objectless or extremely ambivalent	Severe symptom formation in cognitive and motor spheres
Psychoneurosis	Inharmonious balance in ego, superego, id, and reality. Ego in conflict with superego and id but ego on side of reality	Behaviour only partially accontable. Destructive in both motor and cognitive spheres but id impulses checked.	To late anal or phallic, thus not beyond the level or reality testing.	Ambivalent	Autoplastic symptoms, particularly anxiety

nature. Thus, as we have seen, close friendships, parent-child love relationships, even platonic love affairs, as well as normal adult heterosexual affairs, are libidinal in nature. Perverse behaviour forms, technically speaking, are the forms of sexual behaviour in which there is orgiastic release of genital tension by other means than coitus or with other objects than an adult sex partner of the opposite sex. Psychiatrists today realize that all possible sex behaviour forms may play a role in leading up to the normal sexual act.

Psychoanalysts have theories as to why this is true. Ferenczi (1938) has written a very stimulating, although speculative, book on the psychological significance of sexual foreplay and coitus.

We further know that the intermixture of the aggressive urges with both homosexual and heterosexual erotic urges occurs in all individuals. Consequently, all individuals exhibit in their normal sexual behaviour some aggression. This is seen in the semisadistic acts of the normal male and the semimasochistic acts of the normal female. The average healthy male often desires to create at least an attenuated form of pain in sexual behaviour. The average healthy normal female enjoys being partly hurt. The sadistic and masochistic elements in sex life become abnormal only when the satisfaction is received solely through the inflicting of or the suffering of pain without the prevalence of concomitant tenderness. When the normal libidinal and aggressive urges are completely lacking or are highly overemphasized, or when the object with which the sexual satisfaction is finally obtained is other than the adult member of the opposite sex, or when the means taken to arrive at sexual satisfaction do not end in coitus, we speak then of sexual perversion.

It is impossible to draw a strict line between perverse sex reaction forms and the normal forms. Even many practising physicians do not know of what the normal sexual act should consist. It is not our purpose in these paragraphs to give a manual on love-making or to set up rules about how to go about the sexual act. There are many such books now available.[1] Rather we are interested in setting up certain criteria for the use of the psychiatrist and psychologist as to when a sexual relationship may be considered normal and satisfactory. The basic criterion of a normal coitus is that both parties should experience the orgasm through coitus and preferably, although it is not of great importance, simultaneously. Such sexual behaviour leads not only to the highest amount of pleasure in itself, but to complete relaxation afterward. The sexual act may be divided into a period of preliminary activity or forepleasure, a period of tumescence called the orgasm, and a period of relaxation or detumescence. The sexual act properly performed should leave both individuals in a state of complete detumescence. It is impossible to set up rules regarding either the length of sexual intercourse or its frequency, but we can say that on its conclusion sexual desire should again arise only after a period of some rebuilding of physiological and psychological tension. Normal sexual relations thus may be relatively frequent and the individual coitus may last a relatively long period of time, or they may quite normally occur relatively infrequently with relatively quick satisfaction. We may, perhaps, given some figures on limits of the normal range. Certainly for individuals living in normal marriage relationships it can be said that coitus occurring only once a month or once in several months is too rare. Likewise we may say that over a period of time coitus occurring as frequently as once or twice a day is too often. It is quite obvious that coitus which lasts only a minute or two or in which the orgasm of the male occurs before penetration—the so-called "ejaculatio praecox"—is not long enough, whereas coitus which lasts an hour or more is too long. It is almost impossible to get accurate statistical figures to set up a statistical norm, and, as we have said, the deviations on each side of such a norm are wide.

In order to arrive at complete sexual satisfactions it is important that the sexual excitation reach a high point. For this reason the preliminary pleasure or the foreplay of the sexual act is very important, particularly for the female. In this category is included all the forms of behaviour which lead up to the actual act of coitus: thus kissing, fondling, stroking are of importance. It is important also to realize that the libidinal urges wax and wane, grow through youth, become strongest probably in the twenties, and gradually diminish as the individual becomes older. Very often there is a recrudescence shortly before the involutional period after which sexuality becomes of less importance. Similarly the libido varies not only through the whole lifetime of the individual, but from year to year, month to month, even from day to day. Individuals who may be said to have a completely normal sexual relationship may undergo, on the one hand, fairly long periods of abstinence such as is necessitated by pregnancy in the woman, and, on the other, periods of heightened sexual activity, such as occurs in the beginning of the normal love affair, the second honeymoon, and at certain times of the year. There may be periods of increased libidinal motivation on vacations or in celebration of important attainments, and there may be decreases in times of disappointment, worry, and frustration or at times when one of the sex partners is forced to engage in heavy work. All these things make it difficult to give definite rules about what is normal in sexual relationships. The psychiatrist sees many individuals who are concerned about or worried about their sexual problems. Individuals are very often worried about a preference for certain types of sexual behaviour or certain positions in the sexual act. Most of these individuals may be helped and reassured by receiving accurate information concerning sexuality.

3. THE A - AND HYPER-FUNCTIONS OF SEXUALITY

We may now turn to the abnormal functions. As in the case of all psychological mechanisms the libido may suffer from being underdeveloped, as in the a - functions, or from being overdeveloped, as in the hyper-functions. On the one hand we have *frigidity* in the female and *lack of libido* in the male. In the male we also have *impotence,* which denotes the presence of conscious libidinal drive without the ability to perform the sexual act through inability to gain an erection. Extreme overdevelopment of libido is called *nymphomania* in the female and *satyriasis* in the male.

Frigidity refers to lack of sexual desire in the female. This may range from the inability to experience the final sexual satisfaction of the orgasm, but with definite pleasure in the sexual act, through lack of conscious desire for sexual behaviour, to outright aversion to the sexual act. The first type, i.e., inability to experience the orgasm, is very frequent so far as we are able to judge from accounts of gynaecologists.

Rosanoff quotes their estimates that 20 per cent of all females never experience an orgasm and that 60 per cent experience once irregularly. In itself such frigidity may not be an abnormality and often comes about from the ineptitude of the male in love-making. This form may be quite frequently cured by proper sex instruction. Undoubtedly, however, it sometimes represents an inhibition where the female through unconscious fear and anxiety is unable to abandon herself in the love relationship. This anxiety often arises from the fear situation in connection with the Oedipus complex and so is related to hysteria. We realize that such forms of sexual maladjustment are closely related to the neuroses because they very frequently occur in the neuroses. In such cases any sexual act becomes an unconscious expression of infantile sexuality and is closely connected with the danger of castration. The fear of castration, which is often present in mild cases of frigidity, may be said to be always present in the more extreme forms. Frigidity is also caused by repressed hostile urges toward men and may indicate a repressed homosexuality. Complete frigidity in the female (i.e., where there is no libidinal desire for heterosexual intercourse) is a more severe form. It is, of course, frequent in overtly homosexual women but may occur with heterosexual libidinal attachments of a tender sort. There are various intermediary forms, frigidity except with certain men or male types, except under certain circumstances or coitus positions, or unless certain acts are performed in the foreplay. A particular form of female frigidity is vaginismus, where the vaginal orifice is so contracted at the moment of intercourse that no penetration is possible. Frigidity of the milder sorts, except where it is based on ineptitude of the male and only instruction is necessary, responds well to psychoanalytic treatment.

In the male there may be *lack of libido* or weakened libido, which corresponds to complete or partial frigidity in the female. This usually arises because of repressed homosexuality and repressed hostility. Considerably more important because very much more frequent are the various forms of psychic importance. Some of the milder of these, undoubtedly like some cases of female frigidity, are brought about by ineptitude on the partner's side, but most have an unconscious psychological etiology. *Psychic impotence* is exceedingly frequent and it has been estimated that all males suffer from it at one time or another. It also has degrees. Complete impotence refers to complete inability to gain an erection. Loss of potency at or just after penetration is another form. *Ejaculatio praecox* refers to ejaculation before or immediately on penetrating the vagina. *Ejaculatio retardata* is the inability to ejaculate after continued intercourse. *Priapism* refers to the failure of the penis to go into a state of detumescence. There are also individuals who superficially perform normal coitus, but experience no true orgastic satisfaction. Nearly every individual suffers some such impotency periodically and, undoubtedly, a fairly high proportion of the male population suffers from such disorders chronically. Statistical figures are hard to obtain, but one may suppose, judging by the wide sale of useless potency nostrums, that a good percentage, perhaps as high as 20 per cent, suffer chronic psychic impotence.

As in the case of females psychic impotence of the milder forms is related to hysteria and comes from unconscious fear of the consequences of sexual activity. There are also hostile urged often toward the sex partner and in some cases deep unconscious homosexuality. Psychoanalysis is the therapy of choice and has had good success with the milder forms. The topic is treated by Menninger (1937b) and in some detail in Bergler's monograph.

The hyper-functions of libidinal urges are just as pathologic as the hypo-functions. They may represent an even greater regression or earlier fixation on infantile stages than do frigidity and impotence. They are perhaps less frequent although statistics are again hard to gather because the individuals suffering from them seldom consult physicians. They are called *nymphomania* in the female and *satyriasis* in the male. The nymphomaniac takes indiscriminately many lovers and/or demands frequent sexual satisfaction (which she rarely attains) from them. The satyriasic individual is the Don Juan or Casanova. In both of these diseases there are obviously strong phallic-narcissistic components. The changing of love partners is like the many "dates" of the adolescent. In addition there are usually strong unconscious homosexual strivings. The person must prove his or her seductive value to the opposite sex and prove his masculinity or her femininity. Hostile wishes toward members of the opposite sex are also present. After the act of seduction, the partner is rejected or punished. The presence of strong oral fixations is indicated also by the predilection of nymphomaniac females for fellatio and satyriasic males for cunnilingus. These people are usually strongly oral dependent types, who feel rejected by the opposite-sexed parent and take revenge on this parent in a series of affairs.

So far we have spoken as if all variation in libido was psychologically conditional. This is certainly not true. Physiological factors enter to make the "normal" range of libidinal energy as large as it is. In the extreme or pathologic cases, however, psychologic factors probably always play a rôle. Thus therapy must to a certain extent always be psychologic in nature.

4. THE PARA-FUNCTIONS OR SEXUALITY

Para-Functions with Regard to the Object—*Homosexuality* is certainly the most frequent and psychiatrically important of the perverse sexual relationships. It has occurred in all ages and in all societies (in some it has even been considered the ethically right love relationship) and affects many individuals who otherwise are normal, productive, and sometimes even geniuses. Despite this fact society, probably rightly, guards against it, and the homosexual is, except in certain definitely homosexual circles, always subject to social and often neurotic conflict. The homosexual hence becomes a subject of definite psychiatric interest.

Homosexuality refers to the choice of a member of one's own sex (biologically and anatomically) as a sex object. It is necessary to stress the biological and anatomical aspects because *psychosexually* the homosexual belongs to the opposite sex. This statement is not quite accurate since today we know that all individuals have both homosexual and heterosexual urges. Individuals are not either homosexual or heterosexual, but bisexual. Heterosexuality merely means that the heterosexual components are strong enough to overshadow the homosexual.

For this reason it is almost impossible to give statistics on the frequency of homosexuality. If we define the homosexual as one whose love object is always of the same sex and who has no libidinal attachments to members of the opposite sex, we may estimate male homosexuals as making up about 2 per cent of the population. Female homosexuality is probably even more frequent. It is these homosexuals who furnish the greatest psychiatric problem, as the lack of ability to control their libidinal urges leads them into socially embarrassing situations. Of the remaining male population Rosanoff believes that 10 per cent should be classified as bisexual, i.e., they enter both homosexual and heterosexual relationships in a society where both are possible. Many other individuals develop homosexuality in social situations like schools, camps, and prisons, where heterosexual sex outlets are impossible. In fact, it is doubtful if there is anyone who has never had a homosexual libidinal attachment, although in many cases these do not lead to overt behaviour and in many others they remain unconscious. Judging by studies of Davis and Hamilton (1920), at least 50 per cent of males and 25 per cent of females have had overt homosexual experiences. In most cases these represent pubescent transition to genital sexuality, which, once obtained, remains the dominant type.

Homosexuals fall into three tpyes. The active males play the male role in intercourse; as do the active females. The mixed types (the most frequent) assume both roles. The passive males play female roles, as do the passive females. Homosexual practices include interfemoral coitus, mutual masturbation, cunnilingus and fellatio, and pederasty. In other words, they include all possible combinations of the genitalia with the oral and anal regions.

The psychological elements in homosexuality are connected with events from the Oedipus situation. In both male and female homosexuality there is a negative Oedipus situation: the body identifies himself with the mother and loves or fears the father, and the girl does the inverse of this. Exactly how this inverse identification occurs is not clear and undoubtedly varies in the individual case. To be sure, everyone makes some identification with both parents. The positive Oedipus situation turns out, however, that the primary identification is with the parent of the same sex. In the negative Oedipus situation the inverse of this is true.

The problem of the choice of the active and passive roles in homosexuality can be partially solved by psychoanalytic theory. All male homosexuals, however, have strong passive components and active male homosexuality is often a reaction formation against these. It becomes a socially conditioned compromise. "I am a woman and hence love men, but as an anatomical man I can't play the complete female role." The exact inverse of this is true for female homosexuals and completely passive female homosexuals are very rare. As we have already pointed out the mixed behaviour is most frequent and probably represents a compromise of the sort, "You play the passive role this time, and I'll play it the next." There are still predominantly active and passive male and female homosexuals. Silverberg has pointed out that the active male homosexual probably starts in a positive Oedipus relationship with the mother but, feeling rejected by her, identifies himself with her through fear of the father and hence consciously wishes to love younger boys the way he unconsciously wishes his mother to love him. The passive male homosexual falls from the first into a negative Oedipus situation, identifies himself with the mother, and, on feeling rejected by the father, wishes to be loved by men consciously as he unconsciously wished the father to love him. In females the relationship is the inverse. In final analysis homosexuality like all the perversions is economical in that it allows some other outlet for sexuality than the feared and repressed genital one.

Homosexuality may arise on a pre-Oedipus basis and the choice of means of homosexual satisfaction indicates always the strong oral and anal elements involved. Hostile impulses are also involved. Helene Deutsch (1925) claims to have found specific pregenital factors in female homosexuality as both she and Karen Horney (1933) find specific factors in female development in general.

Besides the psychological factors in homosexuality, constitutional factors undoubtedly play a role in many cases. There is probably a deep-lying biological basis for human bisexuality. In some cases (hermaphroditism) primary and secondary anatomical sex differences are plainly discernible. Female cells have been found in the interstitial regions of the gonad and male cells in the interstitial regions of the ovaries in some cases. Such cases are primarily constitutional in nature. They account, however, for but a small percentage of the cases of homosexuality. The feminine traits that are quite discernible in the vast majority of male homosexuals are definitely socially conditioned acquired traits. Similarly socially conditioned are the masculine traits in female homosexuals.

Psychoanalysis has had some success in cases of homosexuality where there is a marked bisexual pattern and where a secondary neurosis makes the individual suffer. It is possible in some cases to develop a neurosis and through psychoanalysis of it to effect a cure. The typical "adjusted" homosexual has however, no marked neurotic (ego versus id) conflicts and hence has no desire to be cured. It is asking him to give up his sexuality and he shrinks from this. Let the reader ask himself how he would like some psychoanalyst to turn him into a girl, or vice versa. His horror of the very idea simply goes to show that our sexuality is our most highly prized psychological trait and that Freud was right in paying so much attention to it. The psychoanalytic theory of homosexuality is treated in detail by Stekel (1922), Ferenczi (1916), and Freud (1930).

The other para-functions of sexuality are less frequent and of less psychiatric interest and we shall deal with them more briefly.

Pedophilia refers to the love of small children on either a heterosexual or a homosexual basis. That strong hostile urges are connected with pedophilia is indicated in the many hideous cases of infantile sadistic sex murders in pedophilics. Pedophilia comes again as a distorted solution of the Oedipus situation. The identification is undoubtedly with the parents and the love identified with the self as child. The pedophilic consciously loves and is forced to destroy the child as he consciously wishes his parent would love him and fears his parent will destroy him.

In *bestiality* the love object is a subhuman animal. Bestiality is frequent as a non-pathological sex behaviour in walks of life where human contacts are relatively few. In its pathologic state it represents an unconscious identification of the animal with some human figure. In his basic case histories Freud (1924a) has given several examples of how fear of parents may lead to animal phobias.

In *fetishism* the love object is either a part of the human body (hair, teeth, or feet fetishism) or some piece of human apparel (glove, purse, shoe fetishism). Orgasm only occurs in the presence of the fetish. Although actual coitus sometimes is used to obtain satisfaction the mere looking at or touching of the fetish produces orgasm in some. It is much more frequent in men than in women, and psychoanalysts have shown that the fetish represents the unconscious idea of the imagined female penis. The fetishist is the individual who has been severely traumatized by the discovery of the nature of the female genitalia. He supposes females have been castrated. Only on assuring himself that they have not, i.e., by possession of the penis, is he able to consort with them and overcome his own castration fear.

Para-Functions with Regard to the Means of Satisfaction—Besides perversions with regard to the love object there are perversions with regard to the means of satisfaction. Normal sexuality must end in coitus. Coitus is the union of the genitalia of two adult members of different sex. As sexual satisfaction is perversely obtained with other objects it is also perversely obtained by other means. The object may still be perverse in itself. Thus fellatio may be used in either a homosexual or a heterosexual sex relationship and is considered perverse in both. Besides fellatio, we have already discussed cunnilingus and pederastry in connection with the means of homosexual satisfaction. These may occur as perverse means in other object relationships. They are utilized by individuals who have strong oral and components in their libidos.

Masturbation in infancy and puberty may be considered a universal, and by no means pathological phenomenon. Questionnaire studies (*cf.* Davis) indicate that over 90 per cent of males and over 80 per cent of females remember their adolescent masturbation. In the others there was probably masturbation, the memory for which has been repressed. Masturbation may be considered quite normal in older individuals who have no other sexual outlets. Of course, it remains an infantile and narcissistic sex outlet and is pregenital, but it can be considered pathologic only when there are other outlets for sexuality and these are not utilized. Some individuals do remain fixated on masturbation and prefer it to other sex outlets. These usually are infantile personalities or implicit homosexuals who cannot face homosexuality. In some of the psychoses and psychoneuroses, abnormally frequent masturbation occurs. Although there is a widespread belief that masturbation is etiologic in mental illness, psychiatrists are agreed that it is only symptomatic.

Exhibitionism; Scotophilia—Exhibitionism refers to sexual satisfaction through exhibition of the body, particularly the genitalia, and scotophilia refers to sexual satisfaction through perceiving the body, particularly the genitalia. Mild forms are quite common and all young people go through a curious age and like to show their bodies. There are individuals, however, who gain an orgasm only when they expose their bodies of others. Exhibitionism and scotophilia are both more frequent and severe in men. The burlesque music hall depends almost entirely on scotophilia men. Psychoanalytically exhibitionism represents a denial of castration and an invitation for females to deny castration also. Scotophilia represents the striving to deny feminine castration. Thus they are closely related to fetishism.

Sadism; Masochism—We have already met the hostile and aggressive urges and seen how they are fused with the libidinal urges throughout life. Sadism and masochism represent the sexualization of hostile urges so that sexual gratification comes from hurting in sadism and being hurt in masochism. Here again some sadistic colouring is typical in the male libido and some masochism in the female libido. Sadism and masochism are perverse forms when they are the prevalent and the only means of sexual satisfaction. Sadism always represents regression to or fixation on pregenital levels of infantile sexuality. Although it is not obvious and cannot be demonstrated in this book, both sadism and masochism represent economical solutions to the conflicts of infantile sexuality. Masochism may thus be a regression from Oedipus wishes to the acceptance of punishment as a socially acceptable surrogate. That sadism is economical is more obvious. Sadism allows the male to overcome feminine resistance. The exact methods by which sadism and masochism become separated from constructive libido and become libidinal ends in themselves must be studied in the more detailed treatises.

Psychodynamic theory is beginning to understand the aberrations in sexual behaviour. We finally have the beginnings of a scientific dynamic theory which removes perversion from the field of baffling problems of man's moral degeneracy and gives us some understanding of perversion as a psychobiological problem. Another field in which psychodynamic theory has recently made much headway is that of behaviour disorders. These individuals of whom we shall speak in the next chapter, like the perverse, were considered simply bad and degenerate until the last decades.

NOTE

1. *Cf.* Long, van de Velde, Ellis (1936, 1931) and Buschke and Jacobsohn.

6
CHARACTER DISORDERS

1. THE SCOPE OF THE PROBLEM OF CHARACTER DISORDER

In the category of character disorder we include a great many individuals whom the layman would consider simply queer or mean or unhappy or vicious or wicked. We include other individuals who seem superficially to be quite well adjusted but in whom on closer observation we find some disbalance or lack of proper integration between the various constituent parts of the self. Until recently such individuals were looked on as problems for the clergyman if their character defect was relatively mild or for the police court and the penologist if their character defect was severe. The normal individual is one in whom there is a proper balance between the forces of ego, superego, and id and in whom the ego has a proper relationship to outside physical and social reality. Recently it has been shown that disbalance in these functions, which is not marked or severe enough to create actual psychosis, psychoneurosis, or perversion, creates character disorders or character neurosis. Psychoanalytic characterology, as this branch of the theory is called, is the least systematically developed. There is considerable confusion concerning the terminology which is to be applied to the various character types, with undoubted repetitions under different names of very similar character syndromes. Many points of the theory of character disorder remain to be worked out. However, with its development we may say that the last group of abnormal behaviour typed which previously could not be explained scientifically are beginning to be understood in a scientific manner.

Before we go on to the detail of the psychoanalytic characterology and attempt a systematic classification of the various forms of defective character, it may be well to say something of the history of the problem and to give some examples of character disorders. Although laymen have for years considered such individuals simply as morally degenerate people, or as markedly unhappy people, professional psychiatrists have for some time realized that certain character defects should be studies psychologically. Kraepelin introduced the problem to psychiatry. He used the concepts of "original morbid states" and "psychopathic personalities." The concept of original morbid states has been given up in modern psychiatry. Psychopathic personality, however, became a widely used nosological classification. By such a term Kraepelin referred in general to the individuals we now classify as behaviour problems. In this group he placed the sexually perverse, the unstable, the litigious, alcoholics, narcotic addicts fraudulent people like swindlers, and some criminals. It is easy to see that this included only individuals whom the layman considers morally or ethically degenerate and vicious, or in other words, individuals whose behaviour if mild was treated by moral exhortation and if severe by the criminal court. It was certainly an advance to consider these individuals psychiatrically. Besides Kraepelin's concept of the psychopathic personality other similar concepts like those of "moral imbecile," "moral idiot," and "moral insanity" are found in the literature. The term "psychopath" or "psychopathic personality" is, however, misleading. Etymologically it means "mentally sick," as in the word psychopathological, where actually the sickness of these individuals is usually concerned with alloplastic rather than autoplastic behaviour problems. The disordered character seldom is mentally sick in the sense of being neurotic or psychotic, rather the internal disharmony in his personality is projected into action. He gets drunk and ends in the police court, he forges checks, he repeatedly insults his employers, he cannot tell the truth, or he seduces any girl under any circumstances. He does not have delusions or hallucinations or depressions or phobias. To call these individuals "moral imbeciles" is also misleading, because actually they often have very superior intelligence and insight into their behaviour difficulties. No matter how clearly they foresee the consequences of their behaviour, however, this has but little regulating influence on their actions. Psychoanalysis has shown that there are disordered characters who are in no way "morally degenerate" but who still present psychiatric problems in that they are unhappy or misfits or cannot make friends or hold jobs. By persons with character disorder we consequently mean those individuals whose internal unconscious conflicts lead them to become maladjusted without becoming psychotic, neurotic, or perverse. We have seen that the neurotic and perverse personalities merge gradually into what we must call normal personalities. Between the normal individual and the defective character there is even less of a definite dividing line.

The damage done to the personality of the individual by the character disorders is sometimes even greater than that done by the psychoses. For this reason Bleuler (1924) writes, "Many psychopaths are really only in the social sense not 'insane,' before the forum of natural science they suffer from the same anomalies as many insane, only in a slighter degree. They are paranold, schizoid, latent epileptics, cyclothymic, etc." He might also have added that some of these vary from the perverse only in degree, so that they are related to the sexually perverse. Others are related to the various stages of infantile development and remain infantile. The disordered character is often so near to the layman's ideas of normal, however, that a few examples are in order before we describe the psychoanalytic theory of the structure of the personality of the disordered character.

All of us have known individuals with character disorders. Some years ago the author had occasion to interview a young woman student of eighteen. She had been drinking and going to beer parlors since she was twelve. She had sexual relationships with nearly twenty men. She had two abortions within the last two years. At the time of the interview she was having sexual relationships with two individuals, mutual friends, often in the same evening. She was insulting and sharp-tongued about the house. One might think this young women was child of the gutter, but actually she came from upper-class parents who were well educated and had the highest ethical ideals. Everything had been done for her. Most individuals have met persons of this kind and have considered them simply "bad" or morally irresponsible. To the person trained in modern psychodynamic theory the young woman in question was a neurotic character, who, despite her high intelligence, could not control her underlying erotic and aggressive urges. Psychiatric examination of the girl and her parents indicated that the superficially moral and perfect family life had actually been marred by brutal scenes and lack of affected between parents and child. The young woman was not a "happy sinner" but rather an unhappy individual driven to seek the love she should have had from her father in every man who she met and, similarly, working out the resentment she felt against her father with her aggressive infidelity to her various lovers.

Take the case of the similar type of personality in the male. Mr. X has three times in his career been worth more than a million dollars, has had three beautiful young wives, all of whom have had to divorce him, and, at the age of forty, is drinking himself to death. He is good-looking and intelligent. He used to work hard as an investment banker. He would work hard to get rich, fall in love, marry, and have what to all his friends seemed a perfect economic, social, and emotional adjustment. It was, however, as if he could not stand success. He would begin drinking, become maritally unfaithful, start neglecting his business, and be back where he started, usually considerably scarred in the psychological sense from the rise and fall. His first wife divorced him when he began to bring prostitutes into the home and flaunt his behaviour before both wife and children. His second wife divorced him when in a drunken rage he broke a chair over her back. His third wife divoced him when he began to spend on chorus girls the insurance he was bulding up for his children's education. Most of his friends looked on him as a happy-go-lucky, daredevil sort of a fellow who occasionally fell into bad luck in his business, began to dissipate for that reason, and who as a result, got into marital difficulties. To the psychiatrist he was quite obviously trying to destroy himself.

But not all disordered characters are of the "wild" sort. Many of them seem all too inhibited, too "goody-goody." The author recently interviewed a young man who had been an excellent student of physics and had nearly completed work for a doctor's degree in this subject. Suddenly he began to lose interest and wished to withdraw from the university. In this connection he consulted the writer. One might have thought from his attitude that the young man was going to develop a schizophrenic psychosis, but he showed absolutely no pathology of the cognitive processes. Despite the fact that he was intelligent and really rather handsome, this individual at the time had no friends nor had he ever had any. He was twenty-two years of age and had never had a date with a girl. He was living on a campus where there were some two thousand other young men and he knew none of them intimately. He had neither admiration nor affection for his parents nor for any of his relatives. His only activity outside studies had been reading literature and occasionally going alone to the moving pictures. He spent a great deal of time in daydreaming but not of a psychotic sort. He was perfectly rational about the daydreaming, knew that it was fantasy, and had considerable insight into the role it played in his psychological adaptations. He lost interest in study when it came close to his graduation, i.e., when he might have had to use his knowledge in contact with other individuals. Whereas most of his acquaintances probably thought him shy, backward, a bookworm, to the psychiatrist he was an example of a schizoid personality. Undoubtedly many of our mathematicians and other theoreticians in science are just as shy and withdrawn as this young man, and their scientific activity may be looked on, just as this young man's, as a sublimation. They are, however, engaged in socially useful work and for that reason are not to be looked on as having character disorders. This young man was schizoid in his character because he could not allow himself the possibility of giving away anything of himself, even to society at large in the impersonal form of scientific achievement. The basic emotional pattern of his life was that he loved himself so much he could give love to no one else.

Disordered characters are not only the "wild" and the "queer" ones, but include also the antisocial, the criminals, and the gangsters, and even such anomalies as the chronic practical joker or those who establish queer philanthropies. Many of the bandits and gangsters we are constantly reading of in the newspapers are examples of disordered characters. Dillinger was such a disordered characters; so are Al Capone and the numerous other American gangsters. Don Quixote and Tyl Eulenspiegel and Robin Hood are literary or historical figures that fall in this category.

2. THE PSYCHOANALYTIC THEORY OF CHARACTER DISORDER

According to psychoanalysis the psychopathic personality or character disorder represents a disharmony between the adjustment of the ego, the id, and the superego, and reality, or an inharmonious combination of these factors. The character disorder differs from the psychosis or psychoneurosis in that although external conflict leads to regression and unconscious conflict is worked out on the environment rather than within the self. The symptoms are thus alloplastic. The disordered character differs from the perverse in that the ego will not accept the infantile libidinal and aggressive urges in their original form. It is, of course, impossible to draw any strict dividing line between normality, psychosis, perversion, and the character disorder. Thus the young woman whom we described above as being a neurotic character would have been psychotic had her actual sexual adventures been imagined in the form of schizophrenic delusions. She would have been classified as perverse if the sexual behaviour in which she had indulged had been either homosexual or of a

TABLE 6.1

	Nature of internal conflict	Social nature of resultant behaviour	Degree of regression	Relation of basic urges of love object	Resolution of conflict result in
Character disorder	Extremely inharmonious balance as in psychosis and neurosis. The break with reality is in motor rather than cognitive spheres	Behaviour socially unacceptable. Impulses break through as behaviour problems in a disguised form	Regression to various stages but cognitive ego not regressed.	Ambivalent	Alloplastic symptoms, particularly destructive behaviours
Normal	Harmonious balance between ego, superego, id, and outside reality	Behaviour in all spheres constructive and socially acceptable	None. Genital stage reached	Post-ambivalent. Some urges gratified, others sublimated	No conflict
Psychosis	Extremely inharmonious balance in ego, superego, id, and putside reality. Ego powerless or weak against id and breaks with reality. Superego projected or taken over by ego or oversevere	Socially unacceptable behaviour in both motor and cognitive spheres. Id impulses break through form	To at least the early anal, thus beyond the level of reality testing.	Objectless or extremely ambivalent	Severe symptom formation in cognitive and motor spheres
Psychoneurosis	Inharmonious balance in ego, superego, id, and reality. Ego in conflict with superego and id but ego on side of reality	Behaviour only partially acceptable. Destructive in both motor and cognitive spheres but id impulses checked	To late anal or phallic; thus not beyond the level of reality testing.	Ambivalent	Autoplastic symptom particularly anxiety
Sexual perversion	Balance may be either harmonious or inharmonious; no break with reality, but with sexual mores	Behaviour socially unacceptable but person "normal" except in sexual sphere	Unless combined with psychosis, neurosis, or genius, there is fixation rather than regression.	May be post-ambivalent in homosexuality. Other cases ambivalent	Perverse sexual practices

DIAGRAMMATIC REPRESENTATIONS OF PERSONALITY STRUCTURE

→ ← *Harmonious Balance*

→ ← *Inharmonious Balance*

The Longer Arrows Refer to Relative Balance of Personality as a Whole with the Environment

The Shorter Arrows Refer to the Relative Balance of the Forces Within the Personality

.... *Socially Acceptable Behaviour*

-+-+-+-+ *Unacceptable but Disguised*

-+..-+..-+ *Disguised but Partially Acceptable*

SE-Super-ego

Cand M—Respectively, Cognitive and Motor Aspects of the Ego

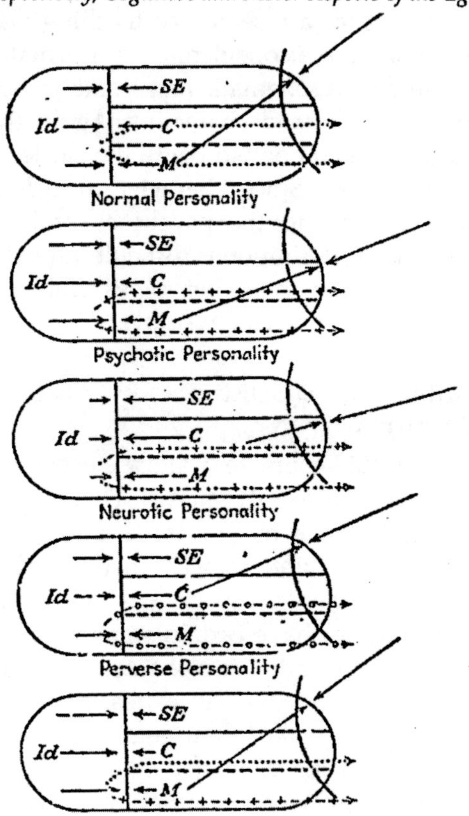

Characterologically Disordered Personality

Fig. 6.1. : Comparing a character disorder with the other personality types.

form other than normal coitus, and we might even have considered her normal if instead of the many love affairs she had had but few. She could, of course, be classified as a nymphomaniac in certain aspects of her behaviour. Similarly, the young physicist would have been a paranoid schizophrenic if he had developed a new and irrational mathematical theory of the universe and had suspected that other people were attempting to steal his inventions. He would have been considered perverse if his narcissistic libidinal urges had forced him to be homosexually seduced by other men or if he had engaged in a great deal of compulsive masturbation. Had he been willing to go on to his degree and accept a research or teaching position in society, we might even have considered him normal. In Table 6.1 and Fig. 6.1, we give a schematic representation of the personality structure in disordered characters. Again these will best be understood by a comparison with the earlier schemata, which are also included. Since character disorders are related to infantile fixations, to the psychoses and neuroses, and to perversion, their definition is difficult in terms of the concepts we have used for the other types. Table 6.1 describe the "neurotic character" as an example.

3. CHARACTER DISORDERS RELATED TO INFANTILE SEXUAL FIXATION

Certain "normal" character traits are established in the earlier period of psychosexual genesis. There of constellations of character traits such as oral, anal, and phallic. The normal character is thus "determined" in the earliest years. We all have similar infantile experiences, and most of us in one respect or another have certain weaknesses of character. The person who technically has a character defect, however, is one who is in need of psychiatric treatment either because his character defect makes him and his family miserable or because through his character defect he comes into conflict with organized society. One might gain the idea from all this that the psychiatrist only considered as "normal" and "well-adjusted" the extremely mediocre personality. This is in a sense true, but, since the psychiatrist is not concerned with moral evaluation but rather with attempting to lead people into socially adjusted personal interrelationships, the accusation loses most of its meaning. Most of the difficult work in the world is, as a matter of fact, done by people who are in some way abnormal in the technical psychiatric sense.

Since the literature on character disorder is so new and also covers such a wide range of behaviour problems, it will be obvious that we cannot deal with it in any detail here. Various nosological schemata have been devised in recent years and each of these has some methodological weakness. We shall attempt a new schema of classification of the character defects,[1] which seems the best we can do at the present time. We shall divide character defects into those primarily related to psychosis and neurosis, and those primarily related to perversion. Table 10.1 (page 258-260) gives the names of the various disordered characters on the basis of the depth of regression and our classificatory scheme. The character disorders primarily related to infantile sexual fixation include those individuals whose sickness consists basically in the fact that, while they have gone through the various phases of nomal development, certain factors in the oral or the anal or the phallic period have been unduly emphasized. Among the character disorders related to psychosis and neurosis belong individuals whose behaviour approaches that of the actually psychotic or psychoneurotic without actually falling into these categories. They will include characters whose individual behaviour approaches mental disease but who still retain cognitive contact with reality. In the character disorders related to perversion we shall be concerned with individuals who have strong perverse sexual impulses, which, however remain unconscious but find an outlet in the antisocial acts of the individual. Of course, since both the perversions and the mental illnesses are in themselves closely connected with infantile. Sexual fixations, this division is rather arbitrary. In general we can think of these character types as individuals who simply exaggerate the normal traits that are in all of us.

We have already seen how many of the normal adult reaction forms are determined respectively in the oral, anal, and phallic periods. The characterological defects primarily related to infantile sexual fixations, those primarily related to psychosis and neurosis, and those primarily related to behaviours. Thus, for instance, individuals who are never "weaned," who are never able to stand on their own feet, who think that the world owes them a living, have an overemphasis in the oral sucking stage so what one may call the early oral or *parasitic character* is evolved. Similarly, individuals whose overdevotion to ideas of duty make them relentlessly severe in carrying out the dictates of conscience, to the extent that their acts become cruel to others and destructive to themselves, may be said to have fixations of the late anal period. In this sense individuals who seek applause and adulation to an abnormal extent have strong fixations at the phallic level. Let us deal with these various types in more detail.

The oral-dependent character type is the individual so dependent that he never stands up for himself. His character is chiefly formed in the preambivalent oral sucking period, and his world outlook is that if the unwearned infant. He is inclined to be happy-go-lucky, optimistic, and emotionally immature in that the serious things of life never affect him. Undoubtedly many of the ne'er-do-wells and many alcoholic addicts belong in this category. The type has also been called the infantile type in that the whole behaviour of the personality is dominated by the pleasure principle and no sense of reality is ever established. Naturally enough a great deal of the real life behaviour of these individuals is at an adult level. Sometimes they are intellectually quite brilliant, but they still drift through life without actually accomplishing much because their basic attitude is more or less that of passive dependence upon the world. Such individuals are in no way mentally disturbed, and the layman is inclined to look on them as either morally deficient or pathologically lazy. The usual treatment of such individuals through punishment and threat avails very little because these oral-dependent characters are actually sick. The concept of the oral-dependent character accounts for the many individuals who go through life without any ambition and fail to obtain the goals their families and friends expect from them.

If the fixation or traumatic experience is connected with the late oral or oral-sadistic stage the personality is quite different. In the late oral stage the sadistic element of oral behaviour develops. And this sadism in place of passive dependence makes the late oral sadistic character in many ways the characterological opposite of the early oral character. The basic reaction is one of pessimistic distrust of the world. The world still owes the individual a living but instead of viewing it optimistically he is inclined to blame the world for everything unpleasant which happens to him. Instead of being easygoing, he is cantankerous, contemptuous, petulant. Instead of feeling that everything is right with the world, he is inclined to find everything wrong with it. Such individuals go through life making enemies instead of friends and constantly blame the other fellow for their shortcomings in accomplishment. Their social attitude is overdemanding and they are emotionally soured with the real world. These individuals are primarily narcissistic and still infantile in their reactions because at the late oral period no sense of social responsibility has been established. They become the perpetually discontented, moody people of unhappy temperament. This they certainly are, but moral exhortation does little for them.

Certain character disorders are determined by a strong fixation at the anal expulsive period. The so-called anal character was the one early (first) studied by Freud (1924a, Vol. II) and his followers, particularly Abraham (1927), and is undoubtedly the one for which we have the clearest theoretical conceptions. Again, anal characters are quite phenotypically different in their behaviour, depending upon whether the fixation is in the anal expulsive period or in the anal whether the fixation is in the anal expulsive period or in the anal retentive period. The character traits of the anal expulsive period are chiefly those of megalomania and suspiciousness, coupled usually with an undue interest in money. The individual who constantly is extremely conceited, very ambitious, and makes unwarranted claims upon his own abilities but who is inclined to attribute his failures to the jealousy of rivals is a personality determined chiefly by fixations in the anal expulsive period. Such individuals are closely related to the paranoid characters, on the one hand, and to homosexual characters, on the other. They are the individuals who develop peculiar theories or peculiar hobbies and who not only bear grudges against other individuals in the field but who also believe that the true reason their real worth is not realized is the jealousy of others. Psychoanalysts derive these character traits from the megalomania connected with early consciousness of sphincter control and from the reaction formation against the homosexuality of this period.

The late anal or anal retentive character is marked usually by over-meticulousness to the extent of hair-splitting pedantry. This usually leads to a devotion to the written line of duty no matter what the cost in personal or social happiness. These individuals are usually petulant, cantankerous, and quick to range, and many of them have an undue interest in collecting things, quite often money, so that they have been called parsimonious. This character comes at about the time of reality testing and these are individuals who are always torn between strong components of the pleasure principle and the emerging components of the superego and reality principle. Their hair-splitting doubting and pedantry come from their inability to mediate between these two types of impulses. These are of course related to the compulsion neurotics. Fenichel has described these individuals as in a constant conflict between, 'I want to be naughty" and "I must be good." The petulance and cantankerousness in their behaviour come from the resentment against the world which had made them give up these infantile modes of sex gratification, and their tendency to hoard comes from their unconscious substitution of money for feces. As examples we find many individuals who are petty tyrants in industry, schoolmasters who are overzealous in their demand on rigid discipline, individuals in all walks of life who must have things done in a very precise way and consequently seem rigid characters to their fellow men. Such individuals are looked on by the layman as queer, unhappy personalities, but to the psychiatrist they are sick. Actually, as the anal expulsive and anal retentive stages overlap, and we seldom find clear-cut anal retentive or anal expulsive characters but rather a mixture of both.

The final stage of psychosexual development is also divided into two phases. The phallic phase is the period of narcissistic sexuality where, as we have already seen, the libidinal relationships are concerned with a sexual partner of the opposite sex but in a narcissistic, selfish fashion. The individual who must be the leader under any circumstances, who must always stand out before any group, who reacts unduly badly in the face of the slightest defeat is the individual with strong phallic fixations. The phallic character thus described is related to the hysteroid character, on the one hand, in that he is inclined to have the temper tantrums of hysteria and may develop certain conversion symptoms and to the neurotic character, on the other, in that he is inclined to demand gratification of his id impulse and may be close to sexual perversion. Such individuals are, of course, so close to normal that their sickness is rarely detected by the layman. To the layman they may be simply overambitious, exhibitionistic braggarts. Usually, however, on closer psychological examination it is found that they, too, are unhappy and sick.

The true genital character need not concern us much because it gives rise to theoretical normal behaviour. It is an ideal personality in actuality seldom encountered.

We seldom find pure character disorders of the types of which we have spoken. Usually there are present in the same individual strong orally determined personality character disorders with less striking anal and phallic-determined ones, or strong anally determined character defects with the others less striking. The transition to perversion or mental illness, on the one hand, and to complete normality, on the other, is also a gradual one. Only in extreme cases is psychiatric treatment indicated for these individuals. Although the world could get along well without the oral-dependent characters, these individuals themselves are often happy. Perhaps the world could not get along without the cranks and petty tyrants and psychological exhibitionists. At all events, the cranks and exhibitionists sometimes really accomplish a great deal, and even if they do not accomplish much they make the world a more colourful place to live in. In the more extreme cases these characterologically disordered individuals are so personally unhappy or make their associates so unhappy or perform such antisocial acts that they should receive psychiatric treatment.

4. CHARACTER DEFECTS RELATED TO PSYCHOSIS AND PSYCHONEUROSIS

We have already seen that schizophrenia is the most frequent and most severe of the major functional psychoses. Many individuals who are not actually schizophrenic are nevertheless so queer, so withdrawn from reality, so isolated from normal libidinal relationships with others that, although their contacts with reality on the surface remain undisturbed, their emotional reactions to real situations are so inadequate that they closely approach schizophrenia. Such individuals we call schizoid characters. Thus, as we have seen, the case of the young physicist who had never had a close friend and who had never had libidinal relationship with a girl is an example of a schizoid character. We do not have to spend a great deal of time in describing the schizoid character because what it amounts to is a mild or attenuated form of schizophrenia. The individual has an emotional schizophrenia without any disturbance in the cognitive and perceptual processes. He may correctly *perceive* the nature of the world but he never correctly *feels* the nature of the social world. The individuals without friends, without normal libidinal and social relationship, without real interest in people may be said to be schizoid characters. Sometimes they breakdown into a real schizophrenia, but otherwise they go through life simply being isolated, queer, and schizoid. They still may accomplish quite a great deal. Many writers, mathematicians, and research workers in science belong in this category. Although some of them make successful adjustments others remain very unhappy. These cases can undoubtedly be helped by psychiatric treatment and psychoanalysis.

By the *cycloid character* we mean those characters who show the emotional symptoms of the manic-depressive psychosis in an attenuated form. Just as the schizoid character was to be looked on as a mild or attenuated from of schizophrenia, the cycloid character represents an attenuated manic-depressive psychosis. All of us to a great or lesser extent have fluctuations in moods of elation or depression, and in but few of us are these fluctuations completely connected with the objective life situation. But the cycloid character suffers fluctuations of mood much more severe than those of the normal individual. He will have periods of time when he is very productive, very gay, very happy, able to work with a great deal of push, when his objective life situation is really quite unfavourable, and he will have other periods when the life situation may be very favourable where he is continually depressed, feels the future has little to offer, feels he can accomplish nothing. We know the cycloid character is related to the manic-depressive psychosis, because in the cycloid character these deviations in mood follow in sequence.

One also finds individuals who are close to paranoia but who do not become psychotic. These are individuals who suffer from *ideas* of grandeur and *ideas* of persecution rather than *delusions* of grandeur and *delusions* of persecutions. In other words, they have a sure belief in their own extreme competence and also a marked hostility toward other individuals, which they project onto the other individuals and rationalize the idea that the others are hostile to them. Perhaps of all the character defects related to psychosis the *paranoid character* is the most frequent, and it is the most difficult to draw the line between the paranoid character and paranoia. We saw that owing to the systematized nature of delusions in paranoia the detection of paranoiacs was a very difficult matter. It is furthermore also hard to draw the line between delusions of grandeur and persecution and ideas of grandeur and persecution. The paranoid character is the person with a pet idea who is unduly suspicious of others. Many paranoid characters are individuals who engage in unnecessary lawsuits, who are inclined to go to court on the slightest provocation. Legal history abounds with cases of individuals who have destroyed their personal fortunes in fighting for crank causes in the courts. Sometimes judges realize the nature of such a psychopathological process, but probably more frequently they do not. The many overly contemptuous individuals, the individuals who are always getting into fights for what are very often minor causes, are paranoid characters. In fact, most of the cranks, most of the faddists, most individuals who are realized to be a little "crazy" about one thing or another on examination are found to be paranoid characters. Undoubtedly from paranoid characters has come much of the systematic research in science and much of the first-rate work in art and literature, and certainly all of them are by no means problems for psychiatry. Insofar as they become antisocial or unhappy, however, they become psychiatric problems.

Individuals suffering from the *compulsive character* are individuals who suffer from a mild form of compulsion neurosis. As in the compulsion neurosis the individual is driven to perform acts and to entertain ideas which he realizes are morbid and out of contact with reality, so the compulsive character is driven to entertain ideas and to perform acts which may or may not be socially useful. When the acts are socially useful we have the very productive workers in the arts, the sciences, and in industry. When the acts are completely meaningless with regard to social reality we have the compulsion neurotic. The compulsive character then covers the range of compulsive behaviour from that of the individual who has to count every fence post on his walks and who has to notice the numbers of every bank note that comes into his hands and who has always to walk in the middle of the street, to the individual who has to work overtime in his position and who consequently makes good. The behaviour similarly ranges from that of the deeply neurotic individual to that of the very successful productive individual. Almost always present in the compulsive character besides the compulsion to do things is the presence of obsessive doubting. Doubts about the correctness of this action, whether he should do this, that, or the other thing at a certain time, etc. This hair-splitting doubt of the compulsive character is related of course to the feeling, "I want to be bad, but I must be good" of the anal character and of the true compulsion neurotic. This obsessive doubting also arises from the ambivalence of the late anal period and from the uncertain sexuality of the late anal period. The inability to decide what activity to undertake is connected with the inability to decide on one's sexuality.

Similarly we have *hysterical characters,* who tend to develop hypochondriasis and infantile behaviour similar to real hysteria, without developing an overt neurosis. If the outstanding symptoms are closer to actual hysteria than to the phallic as we have described it or to the neurotic character which we shall next describe, the individual is to be classified as a hysterical character.

The reader will see that there is no sharp break between the disordered character and the normal character, and perhaps an even less well-defined break between character disorders related to infantile sexual fixation and those related to psychosis and neurosis. For practical purposes the exact diagnosis makes no difference. It should be clear by this time that from the standpoint of modern psychiatry diagnostic categories in general represent differences in degree and not in kind. This is particularly true in the newly developed field of character disorders.

5. CHARACTER DISORDERS RELATED TO PERVERSION

Of particular psychiatric importance is the group of character disorders which seem most closely related to abnormalities of the libidinal and hostile urges. This group most nearly approaches that of the older conception of "psychopathic personality" and most frequently engages in behaviours which are immoral or degenerate from the layman's standpoint. These individuals make wrecks of their own lives and cause great damage to their friends and loved ones and even to society at large. We saw that this group is related to perversion only in the sense that psychoneuroses are related to perversion, namely, that the symptoms of both arise as protections against the consciousness of internal conflict which arises in the pregenital development. This is what led Freud (1930) to define a neurosis as a negation of a perversion.

The concept of the neurotic character as it was first introduced by Alexander is perhaps the one most thoroughly developed in this field. Following examples by Freud (1924a, Vol. IV) and Abraham (1935a), Alexander was able to show how behaviour disorders are closely allied to the neuroses. In the neuroses autoplastic symptoms are developed. In the neurotic character alloplastic behaviour disorders are developed. When Alexander originally set up the concept it was broadly applicable to nearly all character disorders. As generally used today the neurotic character refers to the individuals who "act out" upon the environment the unconscious internal conflicts. Thus the unconscious libidinal impulses tend to seek constant sexual gratification, and the unconscious and introjected hostile impulses lead the individual to indulge in behaviours for which he is punished. Neurotic characters include the two types which we used as examples in beginning this chapter. They also include "people who cannot stand success," those people who always fail after success because the strong sense of guilt in connection with infantile sexuality does not allow them to succeed. In this category fall many "criminals out of a sense of guilt." These individuals perpetrate crimes in order to be punished and thus assuage internal guilt feeling. In some ways these supposedly immoral people are overmoral but, of course, in an irrealistic sense. They sin and commit immoral but, of course, in an irrealistic sense. They sin and commit immoral acts not because they enjoy immorality but because through it they gain revenge and receive punishment. These individuals usually have disordered sexual lives. This makes us believe that they are close to perversion. The neurotic character refers to a large group of individuals whose "neuroses" consist in engaging in antisocial behaviour rather than in neurotic symptoms. The same conflicts, however, underlie both the neuroses and the neurotic characters, namely, conflicts between the ego and id, where regression threatens to breakdown and where behaviour and symptom protect the individual from the anxiety created by unconscious conflict.

Neurotic characters are closely related to criminals, impostors, sexual perverts, alcohci and narcotic addicts, nomads, pathological spenders and liars, and individuals with a mania for gambling. In fact, many of these individuals are neurotic characters and the nature of symptomatic acting out is quite obvious.

Since nuerotic character present such an important psychiatric problem, the question of prognosis and therapy is important. Moral exhortation and punishment are completely unsuccessful. Actually the conflicts which the subject is acting out are *unconscious* conflicts. Psychotherapy is hence indicated. Alexander (1930b) feels that psychoanalysis should be particularly successful here because of the lack of autoplastic neurotic suffering and the ability of the patient to react to reality. Other authorities, for instance, Fenichel, disagree with him rather sharply here. The nature of the individual case is important. There are many good descriptions of neurotic characters in the psychoanalytic literature. Freud (1924a), Abraham (1935a), and Alexander (1930b) are all worth reading on this topic. K. Menninger's book "Man against Himself" gives many good case histories of neurotic characters.

Closely related but not identical to the conception of the neurotic character are the concepts: impulse-ridden character, the fraudulent character, and the inhibited character. An exact description of these would take us beyond the limits set for this book, and the interested reader must go to the original literature which is referred to at the end of this chapter.

6. ALCOHOL ADDICTION

Related to neurotic characters but having also specific etiological factors are the chronic alcohol addicts. In contemporary America these individuals present a particularly challenging psychiatric problem. Of the many alcoholics only a few develop psychoses and get psychiatric care. Still, nearly 5 per cent of all new admissions to state hospitals are individuals suffering a psychosis due to alcoholism and an additional 7 per cent suffer from chronic alcoholism. It is very difficult to get figures on chronic alcohol addiction, but there is no doubt that is a very frequent disease. In some social classes—the upper bourgeois and the lower proletariat—there is small doubt that a very large percentage of the males and a fairly large percentage of the females are alcoholic. Alcoholism leads to both economic and social maladjustments which are so well-known that we need not go into them.

Psychiatrists are not concerned with the social and moderate use of alcohol. For many individuals the moderate use of alcohol is really advisable and for others even its occasional abuse offers a necessary psychological analgesic, nor does the psychiatrist consider everyone who drinks or everyone who drinks too much a psychiatric problem. Some individuals who drink every day lead happy and successful lives. The alcoholic in the psychiatric sense is one who through his drinking creates unhappiness for himself and other individuals and whose drinking is compulsive. In other words, he is an individual who has a conflict as to whether he shall drink or not and sometimes he has to have a drink when his better judgment tells him to refrain. He also tends to use alcohol in increasingly large doses. From his alcoholism or rather with his alcoholism his efficiency in economic and social relationships is diminished. He loses jobs and quarrels with his friends and family.

The alcoholic fits into the general category of neurotic character. The drinking and drunken behaviour is an alloplastic behaviour maladjustment which arises from internal unconscious conflict. There are specific factors in the etiology of alcoholism which have been worked out most precisely by Knight (1937a, b). There are strong oral-demanding character traits. Thus alcohol represents unconsciously the mother's milk. There are definite self-destructive and self-punitive motives in the behaviour. Karl Menninger (1938) has shown how these work. The alcoholic is also related to the sexually perverse in that he has strong unconscious homosexual components in his libido. Actually attenuated forms of homosexuality come out in all stag drinking parties.

Since the use of alcohol is socially permissible in some circles and socially demanded in others, in alcoholism social factors are of great importance. This must be considered in discussion of the prognosis. As long as drinking is considered the thing to do, alcoholics will not look on themselves as sick.

Concerning the prognosis for the psychological treatment of alcoholics, like all neurotic characters, there is much doubt. Durfee claims exceptional results. Knight (1937a, b) is more conservative. Here again the individual case varies greatly, and with some individuals the alcoholism seems to be the basic maladjustment and with others the alcoholism is simply a reaction against other neurotic conflicts. This second group probably responds more favourably to psychoanalytic treatment. For a more extended treatment of alcoholism the reader is referred to Durfee and Knight (1937a b). The existent literature is reviewed by Crowley.

7. CRIMINALITY

Modern psychiatry has recently considered the criminal. Although psychiatrists realize the problem is complicated by both legal and penological factors, they believe the psychology of the criminal furnishes psychiatric problems. To develop adequately the psychiatric theory of criminality would require a separate book. In this section we shall simply point out one or two problems and refer to some of the literature.

That punishment fails to eradicate crime is a banal statement. Recently criminologists have even come to the conclusion that it is the original incarceration that makes the first offender a hardened criminal. Psychoanalysts can understand this. The superego is recriminatory and we all have need for punishment. The punishment, however (cf. The theory of the manic-depressive psychosis), wipes out the guilt and the individual is free to sin again. Refusing to punish them might deter some criminals from further crimes. Even the most adjusted of us, however, harbour criminal—even murderous—impulses. Since we cannot condone them in ourselves, we cannot permit them to others. Consequently, the law becomes the superego of society and we demand law and order. Reform in criminal procedure is of necessity very slow, and perhaps it can never be completely accomplished. Gregory Zillboorg has made important studies in the field of the social psychology of criminal, particularly murder, trials which will be published shortly.

There are undoubtedly occasional crimes committed under economic pressure or for other rational (to the individual) reasons. These criminals are not the concern of the psychiatrist. There are also "normal" criminals—those individuals in whom criminality is a profession of choice, whose fathers were criminals, and whose superego comes from a criminal identification. These are problems for the sociologist. In American cities the gangsters often represent this type.

Probably the majority of criminals are neurotic characters. Crime does not pay economically, at least if one is caught. These individuals repeat crimes as alcoholics repeat sprees and Don Juans repeat seductions. They are criminals out of an unconscious sense of guilt or from unconscious antisocial impulses. This is particularly true of performers of criminal acts against persons (murderes, rapists, etc.) and even of large numbers of crimes against property rights. Menninger,

Alexander and Staub, and Alexander and Healy have written a great deal in this field. Students of sociology will find their works well worth studying.

From the standpoint of modern psychodynamic theory, the genius is not "inspired" but develops in accordance with psychological laws. In our next chapter we shall discuss genius and thus complete the discussion of problems with which modern psychiatry deals.

7

GENIUS OR ABNORMAL

1. SWING AND THE ID

Some readers may take it amiss that we start our discussion of genius with analysis of recent popular dance music of the "swing" variety. "Surely," many will say, "this is not art, and it is not the production of geniuses." From the psychological definition, however, it is art and arises from the same types of psychological conflicts as gave us the Mozart and Brahms symphonies. Our modern theories make no sharp break between "normality" and the psychoneuroses and the psychoses. These represent degree differences rather than kind differences. In the field of genius, the difference between Beethoven's Fifth Symphony and Benny Goodman's "Opus ½" is again one of degree, and not of kind. So for our purposes swing may be considered art. It is a particularly good subject with which to illustrate the theory of genius to students for several reasons. In the first place it is a folk art, so that nearly every reader of this book will be familiar with it. In the second place, the conflicts which are its subject matter are conscious conflicts or lie close to the conscious and are for this reason familiar. In the third place, the phraseology used in the sublimations is easily understandable and is not particularly sophisticated. Thus the analysis of popular songs will be easier than the analysis of Wagner's "Ring." For all these reasons, we start with it. First let us show the nature of the conflicts in few lyrics.

"Fall in love, fall in love, says my heart . . .but each time that I'm almost in your arms, this old schoolteacher brain of mine starts ringing false alarms." Translated into technical language, this is a description of a superego and id conflict. These lines from a recent popular song epitomize a great deal of what this book is about. Personality growth comes about through the modification of basic urges (arising in the id) by social barriers (which become introjected into the person as the superego). Leaving the question open as to whether or not such a song as "Says My Heart" is art on a very high level, its lyric is quite obviously concerned with a basic human conflict. The song writer expressed this thought from his own internal needs and so helped resolve his own conflicts by sublimation. We listen to it or dance to it and reduce our own internal conflicts by identification and sublimation. In some cases undoubtedly the music and dancing lead to love-making and thus are generative of conflict as well as being sublimated resolutions of it.

Freud's (1924a, Vol. III) first published report of the partial analysis of a case of conversion hysteria was the case of Dora. In a varied list of symptoms Dora had a hysterical dyspnea (breathing difficulties) and this was accompanied by an aphonia (loss of voice). Dora did not understand why these symptoms occurred in connection with a certain man, because she was unconsciously rather than consciously in love with him. The lyric of one of the recent popular songs runs, "You leave me breathless, that's all I can say. I can't say more because you take my breath away." The song writer is conscious of his conflict and he sublimates it. The patient remains unconscious of the conflict and has to protect against it by development of conversion symptoms.[1]

The genius is one who finds outlet for unconscious and semiconscious emotional conflicts through sublimation, i.e., through expressing them in a disguised but socially approved form. Such sublimation reduces and partially resolves conflict. We like art, when we are able either consciously or unconsciously to relate it to our own conflicts. The unconscious of the genius is relatively "open." He perceives his own conflicts in such a way that he can present them to others and enrich their lives. The psychoanalytic theory of art thus relates art to life and considers art not related to life to be meaningless. In this way some art productions are closely related to life and conscious strivings, others are related only to the deep unconscious strivings and remain far from life, except for those people who themselves are able to perceive the depths of the unconscious. Of course, a great deal of going to art museums and concert halls comes about not because of the desire for aesthetic experience as a sublimated emotional experience but from a desire for social prestige. But whether one goes for the fun of it or to be seen there, interest in art, like the production of art, is caused by psychological factors.

The basic human urges are, as we have seen, concerned with love and hate objects. No one would call the direct expression of either the basic libidinal or hostile urges, art. "It love——," or "I hate——" are not themselves art, but they are the ground from which art and science grow. These wishes become sublimated (sometimes with a great deal of distortion) in the written words of poets, philosophers, and scientists, in the plastic productions of painters and sculptors, and in the scores of musicians. While the "I love" motive is easy to see in "Says My Heart," it requires considerable analysis to see how it becomes sublimated and distorted in the chorus of Beethoven's Ninth Symphony, but such analysis can discover it and can discover also the projected hostility in many works of art. Shakespeare's *Hamlet* is easily seen to be a dramatization of the Oedipus situation, for Hamlet's struggle is concerned with his attachment to his mother, the memory of his father, and jealousy of his stepfather. All the great madonnas in the European galleries are sublimations of the oral stage of psychosexual development.

Since many of the unconscious conflicts in all of us cannot be admitted by the ego, the process of sublimation in art *distorts* the content of the conflict and expresses it in a derivative form. Thus Shakespeare projects his own conflict onto a Danish prince and expresses this prince's conflictin magnificent poetry. In their sublimated form the expression of psychological conflicts is socially desirable. With sophistication of form and distortion of content comes the need in certain of the arms for *technical competence,* and this develops special performers (musicians and actors) who may only know the artist's conflict in the sublimated form. Thus as art disguises content, uses technically difficult and distorted expression forms, and requires special competence for its performance, it becomes "great" art. In general the more sophisticated the form, the more distorted the content, the more unique the technical competence of the performers, the "greater" the art. If the distortion of content, sophistication of form, and uniqueness of performance become so far removed from life that only very few people can still identify the art work with their own conflicts art becomes very esoteric. Extremes in esoteric art cannot be properly differentiated from psychotic and must be classified as symptoms rather than sublimations. Art thus starts in life and must never become too far removed from it. The real greatness of the really great artist lies in his abilities to keep the sublimations near enough to universal conflict for them to have universal appeal. In this country in swing music we have our *first* indigenous art. Swing combines poetry with music and in it we can see very nicely how mere statements about emotions become art through sublimation. In this music we find the simplest distortion of content, the sophistication of form, and the uniqueness of performance which change mere expression of conflict into art.

An easy way to realize the growing artistry of popular music is to listen to records made in the early twenties and compare these with the latest recording of the same songs. The most striking change is in the sophistication of form, i.e., in the orchestration. The older records usually gave a thinly orchestrated and purely melodic recording of the verse followed by a many *identical* repetitions of the chorus as space would allow. There is a monotony about them which becomes very tiring to the ear. They are only bearable as accompaniments to dancing. The newer recordings are sets of extremely complicated variations on the melodic theme of the chorus. Some of Benny Goodman's and Bob Crosby's and Count Basie's widely swung choruses represent variations as complex as some of Brahms's. With these variations the orchestration becomes enriched so that various subsidiary melodies are integrated and amazing instrumental combinations are accomplished. The musically trained ear while finding too much swing monotonous is able to listen with pleasure to a considerable amount of it. Too much of any music, even Beethoven and particularly Wagner, becomes monotonous. Swing music is making a gradual transition to art in that people are beginning to listen to it for its own sake in swing concerts and recitals and "jam sessions." When it is combined with dancing, the directly sexually stimulating power of the music becomes obvious: heard alone it is more strictly a sublimation.

Parallel with the growing richness of orchestral accompaniment, the sophistication and distortion of content is also mirrored in the lyrics. The lyrics of twenty years ago were inclined to be rather simple statements of an amatory or nostalgic sort like those in "Smiles," "Oh, Give Me the Moonlight," "Jealous," and "Mammie." Today we have such poetically richer images as in the lyrics of "Plenty of Money and You," My Heart Belongs to Daddy," "Thanks for the Memory." The references are more sophisticated. The statement is in a more derivative form.

With both these changes comes the *unique competence of performance* and the requirement of a specific virtuosity as in Goodman's clarinet, Krupa's drums, Teddy Wilson's piano, Louie Armstrong's trumpet, Tommy Dorsay's trombone. Not only is competence demanded of the individual instrumentalist, but the ensemble work becomes more difficult and complicated. Certain of Goodman's and Bob Crosby's recordings indicate an integration of single instruments into complicated harmonic and rhythmic effects which were simply unknown in so-called "aesthetic music" until recently. As in all dance music, the rhythms remain of the greatest importance.

What the future of swing will be one cannot say. As it becomes increasingly sublimated from the love-making of the dance, fewer individuals will be able to follow it directly and it will become more esoteric. At the present, it remains close enough to certain real adolescent conflicts to be very popular with students and so serves as an excellent illustration of the psychological theory of art.

In the lyrics of swing music are to be found illustrations of nearly all the conflict situations we have discussed in this work. In general the conflicts are concerned with heterosexual premarital and hence usually frustrated love. Probably 80 per cent of the titles belong in this category, and so no illustrations are necessary. Other conflictual mechanisms are frequently show, however. The Oedipus situation appears frequently. The love of the child for the parents is enlarged in all the "Mammie" and "Daddy" songs and the love of the parents for the child in all the "Sonny Boy" and "Shirley Temple" songs. The fact that genital heterosexual choices are somewhat determined in the Oedipus situation comes out in songs like, "You Remind Me of My Mother" and incidentally in the appellations of "mama," "baby," "daddy," which occur so frequently in many of the heterosexual love pleas. Song writers for years have intuitively felt the significance of dreams in tides like "You Can't Stop Me from Dreaming," "I'll See You in My Dreams," "I Wake Up Smiling." The overevaluation of the love object appears quite clearly in "What Have You Got That Gets Me" and "Bill," to mention only two titles. The concept of two sorts of love, sacred and profane, which characterizes phallic genitality occurs quite obviously in "Body and Soul" and "Why Not Take All of Me." The lyrics of popular songs thus express the facts of psychoanalytic theory in very slightly sublimated form.

Heterosexual genital love is socially permissible and these songs are folk songs based on conscious or semiconscious conflict. Consequently they are largely concerned with heterosexual genital love. But in a sublimated form homosexuality also appears in songs like "My Buddy" and "That Old Gang of Mine." Hostility occurs openly in popular songs of wartimes, "We'll Hang the Kaiser," and in popular songs about the class struggle. In general however, society represses ingroup hostility and since the popular song is concerned with libidinal social intercourse expression of hostility is rare. If we diverge for a moment from swing we can find plenty of expression of aggression in what are sometimes called America's other two indigenous arts, the comic strip and the animated cartoon. The reader can convince himself of this by watching for the evidences of aggressivity and hostility the next time hc opens the paper to Moon Mullins (or for that matter practically any of the other comic strips) or sees a Walt Disney cartoon (or for that matter any of the other animated cartoons).

We have said nothing about the psychological factors in the playing of swing or the dancing to it. It would be interesting to continue our analysis and show the presence of sublimated erotic and hostile urges in both. Examples are easy to find. "Caressing the keys" and "beating the drum" and "squeezing the trumpet" and "teasing the licorice stick" are vernaculars with regard to playing. "Getting hot" and "burning the carpet" are vernaculars with regard to the dancing. With this much background the reader who is familiar with swing music may work this aspect of the psychology of art out for himself.

Truly great art is often said to be moral. By this is meant that it resolves conflicts through sublimation in such a way that societal ideals are upheld. In other words, the artist sublimates in a socially valuable form and the audience identifies himself in this sublimation. Thus art becomes a powerful ally of the superego in the struggle between biological urges and social frustrations. It often glorifies and celebrates the existing of the developing social mores and social order. Pre-Raphaelite painting is concerned with the celebration of the Christian mediaeval culture while post-Raphaelite painting foresees the development of the Renaissance humanism and the baroque science. The Beethoven symphonies are concerned with individualism and democracy. Thus there are important cultural as well as psychological factors in art. The superego is more heavily weighted with cultural factors that the other constituent parts of the self. In this way great art may be said to be moral so far as it is art with a superego.

In swing music the superego appears in very personal ways in many popular songs. "I'm Sorry I Made You Cry" shows the self-punitive superego at work, and it appears in much the same role in all the "blues" songs. "Cried for You" states the depressed form of a mild manic-depressive cycle where introjected hostility and punitive superego undoubtedly play a role. It is nicely followed by the manic phase, "Now It's Your Turn to Cry Over Me." The superego so designated is quite personal, however. In war songs and in social class songs we have perhaps some more indication of social superego. Most popular songs have little and for this reason many musical critics refuse to call swing art. The author still believes it to be art but an art without superego.

Art without superego may still serve a definite function, particularly in times of cultural crisis such as the present. In his very important essay, *Civilization and Its Discontents* (1930*b*), Freud points out the psychological reasons for our present crisis. The complexity of modern industrial society forces us more and more to renounce basic instinctual urges. The increasing cost of socialization in repression of basis urges hangs together with the complexity of modern life. Swing music allows some sublimated outlet to libidinal urges and in this way makes life in contemporary society more bearable. This is what art has done in all ages and what makes art necessary and defendable.

2. PSYCHOANALYTIC THEORY OF GENIUS

The productions of the genius represent sublimated, i.e. socially acceptable, resolutions of unconscious conflict. Thus in their sources the productions of genius are related to the productions of the normal, the psychotic, the neurotic, and the disordered character. They are similar to all these in that there is a disbalance between the forces of the id, the ego, and the superego, and reality. They are different in that the resulting behaviour is viewed differently by society. We shall see shortly that many genuises have also been neurotic and that the genius is closely related to the neurotic. We shall also see that many contemporary geniuses would be adjudged neurotic or even psychotic in different cultures. In some ways, however, the genius is more like the psychotic. The *sublimation* of unconscious conflict in his productions is a parallel to the symptom formation of the psychotic. The neurotic symptoms protect against the conflicts. The genius is thus outstandng in one very special respect. *His repressions are not severe enough to prevent his being somewhat conscious of the nature of the basic instinctual conflicts.* It is this knowledge which allows him to sublimate (i.e., to distort, to sophisticate, to make unique) his conflicts in a form which allows other individuals to identify their own conflict with the artist's. From this come both the enjoyment and the cathartic effect of art for the audience.

The psychoanalytic theory of genius is not so satisfactory as that of the other categories. However unhappy and neurotic, outstanding geniuses are seldom actually analyzed and the theory has been developed largely through the analysis of documents. Furthermore, there is need for both methodological and factual clarifications of sublimation as the basic mechanism involved in genius. The concept is evaluative and depends on sociological and cultural norms to a greater extent than do many of the other psychoanalytic mechanisms. There is further the factual question of whether actual sublimation of libidinal and aggressive urges in the sense of really discharging libidinal and aggressive energy through socially constructive behaviour is possible. Experiments by Lewin and his students would indicate that substitutive fulfilment of basic needs leads only to a partial resolution of underlying conflict. Freud first developed the idea of sublimation in his *Three Contributions to the Theory of Sex* in 1905. Since he has returned to the idea only occasionally. Other psychoanalysts and psychologists have written about the concept but have not subjected it to basic criticism.[2] Levey has summarized the earlier writings in his paper "A Critique of the Theory of Sublimation," which subjects this concept to its most thorough methodological and factual examination. In this paper he concludes:

Freud's theory of sublimation brought order to the earlier empirical beliefs about the subject. His concept contributed highly valuable generalizations in its description of sublimation as a vicissitude of non-repressed instinct, as an unconscious process, and one helpful in preventing neurosis. Although important features of the concept have remained unverifed and unclarified, it has proved useful as a guide to our thinking and in our therapy.

The proposition presented by this paper is not so much concerned with whether Freud's concept of the process of sublimation achieves standards prescribed by the canons of science as with the facts that the evolutionary character of psychoanalysis as a science has failed to impress itself upon this aspect of the theory, and that Freud's generalizations about sublimation have remained untested and unverified; through not regarding the concept with a perpetual tentativeness, we have neglected to revise it in accordance with metapsychological standards.

One concludes from the literature quoted that the concept of sublimations is an improved racapitulation of empirically known facts, confused, obscure, incomplete, redundant, static, and lacking in objective verification; that the most probable reason for our negligence lies in a subjectivity associated with the difficulty of the problem; and that, though we have maintained a more scientific orientation to the problem than have other schools, our tendency also has been to evade the problem rather than to attack it.

The logical conclusions are that we need to recognize and avoid the evasive techniques described; to approach the problem as one worthy of a primary interest in view of its theoretical, clinical, and social importances; and to adopt, in attempts to reconstruct the concept, the metapsychological standards which have characterized our method of attack upon other problems. [From Harry B. Levey, "A critique of the theory of sublimation," *Psychiatry*, 1939, 2, 269-270.]

In general it seems best to retain the concept of sublimation but to understand by it only the various behaviours and mental symptoms which protect against unconscious anxiety and compensate for unconscious conflict in ways which are not only permissible (as in the case of the

TABLE 7.1

	Nature of Internal conflict	*Social nature of resultant behaviour*	*Degrees of regression*	*Relation of basic urges to love object*	*Resolution of conflict results in*
Genius	Inharmonious balance but no break with reality	Behaviour socially valued. Id impulses break through as art, science, etc.	Regression to various stages but cognitive ego not regressed and behaviour valuable	Ambivalent or postambivalent with some urges sublimated	Works of art, science, etc.
Normal	Harmonious balance between ego, superego, id, and outside reality	Behaviour in all spheres constructive and socially acceptable	None. Genital stage reached	Postambivalent. Some urges gratified, others sublimated	No conflict.
Psychosis	Extremely inharmonious balance in ego, superego, id, and outside reality. Ego powerless or weak against id and breaks with reality. Superego projected or taken over by ego or oversevere	Socially unacceptable behaviour in both motor and cognitive spheres. Id impulses break through	To at least early anal, thus beyond the level of reality testing.	Objectless or extremely ambivalent	Severe symptom formation in cognitive and motor spheres
Psychoneurosis	Inharmonious balance in ego, id, and reality. Ego in conflict with superego and id but ego on side or reality	Behaviour only partially acceptable. Destructive in both motor and cognitive spheres but id impulses checked	To late anal or phallic; thus not beyond the level of reality testing	Ambivalent	Autoplastic symptoms, particularly anxiety
Sexual perversion	Balance may be either harmonious or inharmonious; no break with reality but with sexual mores	Behaviour socially unacceptable but person "normal" except in sexual sphere	Unless combined with psychosis, neurosis, or genius, there is fixation rather than regression	May be postambivalent in homosexuality. Other cases ambivalent	Perverse sexual practices
Character disorders	Extremely inharmonious balance, as in psychosis and neurosis. The break in motor with reality is rather than cognitive spheres	Behaviour socially unacceptable. Id impulses break through as behaviour disguised form	Regression to various stages ego not regressed.	Ambivalent	Alloplastic symptoms particularly destructive behaviours

DIAGRAMMATIC REPRESENTATIONS OF PERSONALITY STRUCTURE

→ ← *Harmonious Balance*

→ ← *Inharmonious Balance*

The Longer Arrows Refer to Relative Balance of Personality as a Whole with the Environment

The Shorter Arrows Refer to the Relative Balance of the Forces Within the Personality

.... *Socially Acceptable Behaviour*

-+-+-+-+ *Unacceptable but Disguised*

-+..-+..-+ *Disguised but Partially Acceptable*

SE-Super-ego

C and M—Respectively, Cognitive and Motor Aspects of the Ego

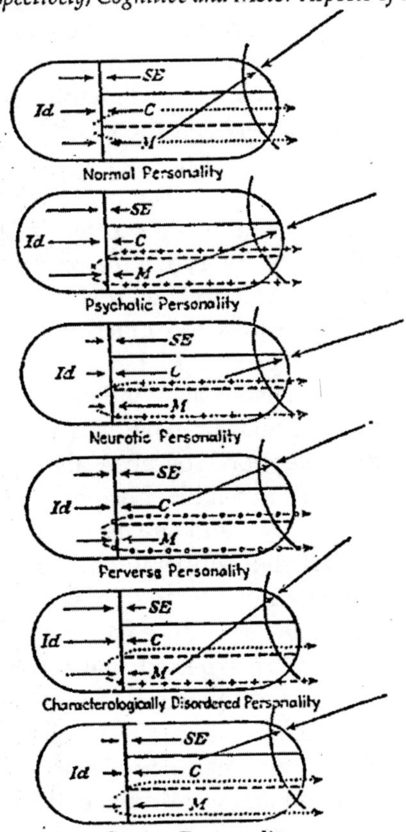

Fig. 7.1. : Comparing the personality structure of the genius with other types.

normal) but also socially valuable. Seen from this viewpoint the genius is differentiated from the neurotic and at times even from the psychotic only on the basis of culturally determined norms. The genius resolves his conflict in a way which others value.

With these points in mind, Fig. 7.1 and Table 7.1 will be quite obvious. For comparative purposes, the other personality structures are again given.

3. THE GENIUS AND THE NEUROTIC

That artists may be very neurotic people is, of course, commonplace knowledge. The neurotic is not able comfortably to comply with the demands of social reality because of the conflicts between the id and the ego. He thus develops symptoms to protect himself against these conflicts. This makes him seem "queer." The artist is also not able to comply and his behaviour is thus often at odds with the demands of social reality. Everyone realizes that many artists are rebels and nonconformers. The artist is a "bohemian," he dresses peculiarly, he drinks too much and eats irregularly, his sexual morals are not too rigid, her retires from the world. Of course, not all artists wear Windsor ties, or drink too much, or starve in garrets, or have series of mistresses, or never answer the telephone because they are producing. Many look and act very much like businessmen and these are often the most productive and greatest artists. But the fact remains that the "artistic temperament" does exist and is closely related to the neurotic temperament.

Since the same conflicts produce works of art and neurotic symptoms it is only to be expected that artists will often be non-productive because of personal or social reasons and hence develop neurotic symptoms. Through his life the artist may also not be able to sublimate completely and consequently may always suffer neurosis. We have already seen that neurosis, psychosis, perversion, and disordered character are all related so that the behaviour of the artist may have earmarks of all these behaviours. A little later we shall try to show how science and philosophy are related to art and so these remarks also refer to scientists and philosophers. In the following paragraphs we shall give examples of the various forms of psychopathological behaviour in some recognized geniuses.

Many geniuses have shown signs of having character disorders for all or some of their lives. Edgar Allan Poe was certainly a chronic alcoholic, unable to make "proper marital success with any woman." Christopher Marlowe died of dissolute living at a very early age. Most of Francois Villon's best poetry is about his own life, which was that of a roisterer and "tosspot" and he too died before thirty. Goethe speaks of his days of *Wusstes Dasein* (dissolute living) before his journey to Italy. In our own recent literature the poet Hart Crane and the novelist Thomas Wolfe were both severely alcoholic. Poets and wine are a familiar combination. Verlaine and Baudelaire, Swinburne and Ernest Dowson and many others all found drink a problem. Many painters suffer likewise. Toulouse Lautrec and Paul Gauguin had alcoholic episodes. Nor is alcoholism infrequent in musicians. Haydn was said to be sober but infrequently and Brahms often disappeared for days in low saloons and houses of prostitution. The only personal papers was have of Galileo are notes from a tavern. Everyone knows the widespread taste of swing musicians for alcohol. It would be easy to give many other examples of geniuses with this type of disordered character from all the arts and sciences.

Newton, who was probably the world's greatest scientific genius, was a schizoid character. Charles Darwin had definite schizoid characteristics, also. The great natural scientist Robert Julius Mayer was a cycloid character who actually developed a manic-depressive psychosis. Neurotic characters in the arts and the sciences are likewise very frequent. The great American economist Thorstein Veblen was a mild neurotic character, poets like Poe and Lord Byron were relatively severe types. Mozart's life was made up of a series of tragedies in which the neurotic elements of his character undoubtedly figured.

Undoubtedly sexual perversion is very frequent among geniuses. This does not mean that all the sexually perverse are genial by any means, nor are all the genial sexually perverse. Tschaikowsky was homosexual, Wagner was markedly bisexual, neither Beethoven nor Brahms ever married. Brahms we know could establish sexual relationships only with prostitutes. There is good evidence that Leonardo da Vinci was, if not an overt homosexual, at least an implicit one. Proust is also in this category. Oscar Wilde's homosexuality was, of course, the great scandal of British literary circles in the 1890's. Walt Whitman's bisexuality appears on nearly every page of his work. There is a great deal of evidence that both Carlisle and Ruskin were chronically impotent.

Many geniuses have suffered periods of psychosis and severe neurosis. Nietzsche died of paresis. Robert Schumann had a severe depression with schizophrenic coloring. The Scandinavian playwright Strindberg was psychotic. Van Gogh suffered a severe schizophrenia and died in an asylum. The popular surrealist painter Dali is an admitted paranoiac and has written entertainingly although superficially about the theory of paranoid art.

It would be easy to give many other examples even among contemporaries from all the fields of art and science. To mention contemporaries is, of course, impossible. If the reader keeps his eyes open among his aquaintances who are "geniuses" or "gifted" he will see many examples of neurotic behaviour in them.

4. THE PRODUCT OF THE ARTIST: PSYCHODYNAMIC ASPECTS OF FORM AND CONTENT

The form and content of art products represent the sublimation of unconscious or semiconscious conflicts. This we have already seen with regard to popular music. The following lines will demonstrate the propositions stated there for the other arts. Most of our examples will be chosen from literature, but enough examples from the plastic arts will be given to illustrate the same mechanisms are at work there too. That the Oedipus situation has been important in motivating great works of literature is of course commonplace knowledge. The technical name Oedipus situation itself is adapted from the Greek tragedy *Oedipus Rex* by Sophocles. This tragedy, considered the greatest of all antiquity, is concerned with the unwitting murder of Laius, his father, by Oedipus and his marriage to his mother, Jocasta. On finding about his patricide and incest, Oedipus tears his eyes out and the gods are appeased. The distortions in this great tragedy are few. Oedipus is made the unknowing patricide, i.e., his incestuous and patricidal wishes are attributed to fate and his eyes (testes symbols) are torn out rather than an actual castration occurring. The playwright also, of course, attributes the incestuous thoughts to another and consequently uses the sublimation to reduce his own castration fears. The incest motive of the Oedipus situation is probably the most discussed theme in great literature. It occurs in the literature of all countries. The tragedy is repeated in numerous adoptions and treatments throughout the history of literature. The daughter-father Oedipus situation occurs also in another great Greek tragedy, the *Elektra* of Aeschylus. Shakespeare's *Hamlet* is, as we have already seen, based upon an Oedipus situation. Balzac's Pére *Goriot,* as Milton Miller has shown, is based on psychoanalytic mechanisms. Stendhal writes specifically in *Le Rough et le noir,* that he, as a child, wished to kill his father and marry his mother. Much of the first part of Proust's *Swann's Way* is concerned with his infantile attachment to his mother. Many contemporary theater goers have seen the theme in Eugence O'Neill's play, *Mourning Becomes Electra.* Such a piling up of examples, however, is not necessary to establish the thesis.

The greatest epic of German literature, Goethe's Faust, has its basic theme in the struggle between the constituent parts of the self. Faust early decides, "Zwei Seelen wohnen ach in meiner Brust" and "In jedem Kleide werd" ich wohl dic Pein des engen Erdenelbens fühlen; ich bin zu jung um ohne Lust zu sein, zu alt um nur zu spielen."[3] Thus it is concerned with a struggle between the forces of the id and the restraining powers of the superego. Faust sells his soul to the devil in the hope of really enjoying the fleeting moment, i.e., in the hope of being able to indulge in basic urge behaviour without a struggle with his conscience. As everyone knows he finds that it cannot be done. Goethe himself led a very similar life and the story of Faust and Margaret parallels his own early love affair with Fredrica Brion. Reik (1929) has written a psychoanalytic account of this affair.

Possibly the greatest modern novel is Proust's *Remembrance of Things Past*. It is concerned psychologically with the thesis that past and relatively unconscious experiences determine present reactions. This is very nicely stated in *Swann's Way* in the following lines:

And so it is with our own past. It is a labour in vain to attempt to recapture it: all the efforts of our intellect must prove futile. The past is hidden somewhere outside the realm, beyond the reach of intellect in some material object (in the sensation which that material object will give us) which we do not suspect. And as for that object, it depends on chance whether we come upon it or not before we ourselves must die.

Many years had elapsed during which nothing of Combray, save what was comprised in the theatre and the drama of my going to bed there, had any existence for me, when one day in winter, as I came home, my mother, seeing that I was cold, offered me some tea, a thing that I did not ordinarily take. I declined at first, and then, for no particular reason, changed my mind. She sent out for one of those short, plump little cakes called "petites madeleines," which look as though they had been moulded in a fluted scallop of a pilgrim's shell. And soon, mechanically, weary after a dull day with the prospect of a depressing morrow, I raised to my lips a spoonful of the tea in which I had soaked a morsel of the cake. No sooner had the warm liquid, and the crumbs with it, touched my palate than a shudder ran through my whole body, and I stopped, intent upon the extraordinary changes that were taking place. An exquisite pleasure had invaded my senses, but individual, detached, with no suggestion of its origin. And at once the vicissitudes of life had become indifferent to me, its disasters innocuous, its brevity illusory—this new sensation having had on me the effect which love has of filling me with a precious essence; or rather this essence was not in me, it was myself. I had ceased now to feel mediocre, accidental, mortal. Whence could it have come to me, this all-powerful joy? I was conscious that it was connected with the taste of the tea and cake, but that it infinitely transcended those savours, could not, indeed, be of the same nature as theirs. Whence did it come? What did it signify? How could I seize upon and define it?

I drink a second mouthful, in which I find nothing more than in the first, a third, which gives me rather less than the second. It is time to stop; the potion is losing its magic. It is plain that the object of my quest, the truth, lies not in the cup but in myself. The tea has called up in me, but does not itself understand, and can only repeat indefinitely, with a gradual loss of strength, the same testimony; which I, too, cannot interpret, though I hope at least to be able to call upon the tea for it again and to find it there presently, intact and at my disposal, for my final enlightenment. I put down my cup and examine my own mind. It is for it to discover the truth. But how? What an abyss of uncertainty whenever the mind feels that some part of it has strayed beyond its own borders; when it, the seeker, is at once the dark region through which it must go seeking, where all its equipment will avail it nothing. Seek? More than that: create. It is face to face with something which does not so far exist, to which it alone can give reality and substance, which it alone can bring into the light of day.

And I begin again to ask myself what it could have been, this unremembered state which brought with it no logical proof of its existence, but only the sense that it was a happy one, that it was a real state in whose presence other states of consciousness melted and vanished. I decide to attempt to make it reappear. I retrace my thoughts to the moment at which I drank the first spoonful of tea. I find again that same state, illuminated by no fresh light. I compel my mind to make one further efforts, to follow and recapture once again the fleeting senastion. And that nothing may interrupt it in its course, I shut out every obstacle, every extraneous idea, I stop my ears and inhibit all attention to the sounds which come from the next room. And then, feeling that my mind is growing fatigued without having any success to report, I compel it for a change to enjoy that distraction which I have just denied it, to think of other things, to rest and refresh itself before the supreme attempt. And then for the second time I clear an empty space in front of it. I place in position before my mind's eye the still recent taste of the first mouthful and I feel something start within me, something that leaves its resting place and attempts to rise, something which has been embedded like an anchor at a great depth; I do not know yet what it is, but I can feel it mounting slowly; I can measure the resistance, I can hear the echo of great spaces traversed.

Undoubtedly what is thus palpitating in the depths of my being must be the image, the visual memory which, being linked to that taste has tried to follow it into my conscious mind. But its struggles are too far off, too much confused; scarcely can I perceive the colourless reflection in which are blended the uncapturable whirling medley of radiant hues, and I cannot distinguish its form, cannot invite it, as the one possible interpreter, to translate to me the evidence of its contemporary, its inseparable paramour, the taste of cake soaked in tea; cannot ask it to inform me what special circumstance is in question, of what period in my past life..

Will it ultimately reach the clear surface of my consciousness, this memory, this old, dead moment which the magnetism of an identical moment has travelled so far to importune, to disturb, to raise up out of the very depths of my being? I cannot tell. Now that I feel nothing, it has stopped, has perhaps gone down again into its darkness, from which who can say whether it will ever rise? Ten times over I must essay the task, must lean down over the abyss. And each time the natural laziness which deters us from every difficult enterprise, every work of importance, has urged me to leave the thing alone, to drink my tea and to think merely of the worries of today and of my hopes for tomorrow, which let themselves be pondered over without effort or distress of mind.

And suddenly the memory returns. The taste was that of the little crumb of madeleine which on Sunday mornings at Combray (because on those mornings I did not go out before church time), when I went to say good day to her in her bedroom, my aunt Leonie used to give me, dipping it first in her own cup of real or of lime-flower tea. The sight of the little madeleine had recalled nothing to my mind before I tasted it; perhaps because I had so often seen such things in the interval, without tasting them, on the trays in pastry cooks' windows, that their image had dissociated itself from those Combray days to take its place among others more recent; perhaps because of those memories, so long abandoned and put out of mind, nothing now survived, everything was scattered; the forms of things, including that of the little scallop-shell of pastry, so richly sensual under its severe, religious folds, were either obliterated or had been so long dormant as to have lost the power of expansion which would have allowed them to resume their place in my consciousness. But when from a long-distant past nothing subsists, after the people are dead, after the things are broken and scattered, still, alone, more fragile, but with more ...more unsubstantial, more persistent, more faithful, the smell and taste of things remain poised a long time, like souls, ready to remind us, waiting and hoping for their moment, amid the ruins of all the rest; and bear unfaltering, in the tiny and almost impalpable drop of their essence, the vast structure of recollection.

And once I had recognized the taste of the crumb of madeleine soaked in her decoction of lime flower which my aunt used to give me (although I did not yet know and must long postpone the discovery of why this memory made me so happy) immediately the old grey house upon the street, where her room was, rose up like the scenery of a theatre to attach itself to the little pavilion, opening on the garden, which had been built out behind it for my parents (the isolated panel which until that moment had been all that I could see); and with the house the town, from morning to night and in all weathers, and the Square where I was sent before luncheon, the streets along which I used to run errands, the country roads we took when it was fine. And just as the Japanese amuse themselves by filling a porcelain bowl with water and steeping in it little crumbs of paper which until then are without character or form, but, the moment they become wet, stretch themselves and bend, take on colour and distinctive shape, become flowers or houses or people, permanent and recognizable, so in that moment all the flowers in our garden and in M. Swann's park, and the water-lilies on the Vivonne and the good folk of the village and their little dwellings and the parish church and the whole of Combray and of its surroundings, taking their proper shapes and growing solid, sprang into being, town and gardens alike from my cup of tea. [From Marcel Proust, *Swann's Way,* Modern Library, Inc., New York, 1928, pp. 54-58.]

The content of much literature can be seen to be concerned with the struggle between the basic urges and their modification through social reality and with conflicts between the constituent parts of the self. This is not to be taken to mean that cultural factors are not important. We have already seen that the superego is heavily culturally determined. Insofar as the superego always plays a role and since great art is moral are cultural determination is, of course, of the greatest importance both for the understanding of art and for aesthetic criticism. Its discussion however lies beyond the limits of this book.

The form of literature is also determined by psychological factors. Sophistication of form, like distortion of content, allows the sublimation of unconscious conflicts. In poetry, the rhythmic elements like those of music may be a sublimated form of masturbatory and coitus movements. Similarly, the dance may be a sublimated form of intercourse and has its origins in sexual play and preparation for aggression. Havelock Ellis (1923) has devoted one of his best books to this theme. In recent times, the stream of consciousness style of writing approximates the free association of psychoanalysis. Both James Joyce's *Ulysses* and Proust's *Remembrance of Things* Past show this quite clearly. In fact, since both of these works have followed the discoveries of psychoanalysis, they have either been influenced by analysis or represent an artistic parallel of Freud's great scientific discoveries.

Uniqueness of performance is the third characteristic of great art. In the field of literature, the drama alone requires performers and the chief performer is the actor. We have already pointed out that most actors are phallic characters. Phallic characters were able to identify themselves easily with other people and understand the emotions of other people better than their own. Thus, the requirement of being able to identify oneself with the character, which is the essence of good acting, is explained psychologically.

We have space for only the briefest discussion of the plastic arts. Insofar as painting and sculpture tell stories about people, what we have already said about literature applies to them. The madonna theme and the Venus and Cupid theme are the most frequent in the great classical plastic productions. Landscape and still life offer other problems. "Mother Earth," "Mother Sea," and "Old Man River" gives us clues to the psychological factors involved. The love of *fatherland* and the *mother* country are to be sure poetic expressions, but they are images based on very early identifications. The original environment of all of us was the mother's womb.

5. THE AUDIENCE

The artist projects his internal conflicts into the art product in somewhat distorted form and hence reduces them. The audience introjects the distorted form or identifies himself with the protagonists and resolves in this way similar conflicts of his own. The universality of art is in the universality of conflict. Art appreciation thus makes life more bearable and enriches it.

As swing music was well adapted for illustration of the nature of art production, the movies may be taken to illustrate the effect of art on the audience. The movies are concerned chiefly with heterosexual, but again with premarital and so frustrated, genital conflicts. These conflicts are resolved by marriage or engagement in life and the happy ending is nearly always at the marriage altar. Naturally, of course, the Oedipus situation and hostility play definite roles. The moviegoer identifies himself with the hero and projects his own hostilities on to the villain. This is so obvious that it scarcely needs demonstration. Even such creations art as the drinking song and the dirty limerick indicate the role of unconscious libidinal and aggressive urges. La Barre has made a special study of this literature from the psychoanalytic standpoint.

The audience for great art is more limited for the same reasons that the productions of great art are more limited. The greater the distortion, sophistication, and uniqueness in the art work, the more rarely may the individual make the required identifications and projections. As we have already seen, extremely esoteric art is understood by very few and thus loses its social value.

6. THE MOTIVATION OF SCIENCE AND PHILOSOPHY

It is no accident that Immanuel Kant both postulated the categorical imperative and was one of the most compulsive characters of all times. The central point of Kant's ethics is that morality is governed by an innate conscience which as a part of the practical reason dictates the necessity of behaving ethically. Of course, we know now that the conscience really is made up of the introjected prohibitions and demands of the parents in the form of the superego. We have seen in the compulsion neurotic has a particularly severe conscience or superego and that his neurotic struggle is between this and his unconscious infantile wishes, which come chiefly from the late anal stage. Kant's life was made up of a series of extreme prohibitions and compulsions. He must have had a very strong superego. That Kant's life was made up of a series of extreme prohibitions and compulsions. He must have had a very strong superego. That Kant's philosophy stems from this neurosis does not in any way distract from the validity of his philosophy for his time and culture. Even psychoanalysts are motivated by unconscious conflicts. Freud himself was the son of an old father and a young mother and must have undergone a fairly severe Oedipus conflict and it may be this which enabled him to formulate his theory in later days. We have already mentioned Newton's schizoid character: Newton also had many compulsive traits. Karl Marx showed signs of definite anal-sadism in his polemical writings. Friedrich Engels was unable to enter into a sex relationship with a woman of his own class and undoubtedly suffered from an unresolved Oedipus conflict. His identification with the proletariat, being as he was the son of a wealthy industrialist, represents his hostility toward his father, his fear of constituted authority, and his unconscious feeling of being the downtrodden one.

Not only are the "facts" which scientists uncover in themselves psychologically determined but also the choice of field in the science. Karl Menninger (1940) will soon publish an interesting paper on the choice of specialties among the medical profession. Helmholtz was an asthmatic who left physics to work in psychology. Darwin, a semiinvalid, spent his life in biology. Surgery is one way in which sadism may be socially sublimated. Psychologists themselves are often people with a large amount of neurotic conflict whose interest in psychology is simply a projection of their interests in themselves.

In art, the content of unconscious conflicts is distorted, through a sophistication of form and in such a way that the repressed wishes may be realized. Science varies in only one respect from art. Sophistication occurs in elegant theories and uniqueness in precise experiments, but the "distortion" represents an adaptation of the wishes to reality. "Reality" itself, however, is determined psychologically and through experience. The scientist expresses his "unconscious conflicts" in a way that is true, i.e., which can be verified experimentally. The artist expresses his in a way which is beautiful. Science consists of propositions about experience to which the universal assent of competent observers may be obtained. Art consists in expressing experience in a way that certain observers realize to be beautiful. But an elegant mathematical deduction has something of beauty about it and a great epic poem something of truth, so even this distinction is a relative one. As soon as the propositions of a science cannot be adapted to reality, the science suffers. But as soon as art becomes esoteric, it suffers too.

In this chapter, we have completed our survey of the ways in which unconscious conflict is resolved. The genius, like the psychotic, the neurotic, the pervert, and the disordered character, differs from the "normal" in that there is a lack of harmonious balance between the constituent parts of the self. This lack of harmony arises largely from the failure to resolve unconscious conflicts. Understanding genius scientifically does not lead us to underestimate the worth or importance of the genius. All life and growth are processes of adjustment of the biological organism to the physical and social environment. Not only do we owe the richness and complexity of modern life to the genius, but without him we should probably all succumb in the struggle. The works of the genius not only make life richer and happier, they make it possible.

NOTES

1. In both of these actual cases we have no way of knowing, of course, about actual conflicts in the song writers. The writer may really consciously be something of a psychologist and perceive their frequency in others without being subject to identical conflict himself.
2. Cf. the summary in Levey's paper.
3. Freely translated: "Two souls dwell in my breast." "In any clothing I shall feel the pain of an earth-bound life; I am too young to be without desire, too old merely to play."

8

TOWARD AN EXPERIMENTAL PSYCHOPATHOLOGY

1. THE PRESENT STATUS OF PSYCHODYNAMICS

We have come to the end of our presentation of psychodynamic theory. In this chapter, we shall evaluate its prsent contribution and try to foresee its future development.

Our most important single conclusion must be that in recent times psychopathology has become a systematized science. A systematized science is one in which an integrated theory attempts to deduce all the phenomenal data in such a way that its deductions may be experimentally or empirically tested. In this sense, physics is the most thoroughly systematized of sciences and sociology probably the least. Psychopathology is, to be sure, much nearer sociology than it is physics on the scale of systematization. So although we cannot yet speak of a completely systematized science of psychopathology, certainly the framework on which it must be built has been laid down in the last half century. We have seen that the possibility of developing this framework has largely been accomplished through the work of Sigmund Freud and his followers.

Besides becoming systematized in the last half century, psychodynamics has made other methodological advances. These give it a particular significance for contemporary culture. Psychodynamic theory overcomes the necessity for mystical or theological or romantic interpretations of the human personality in any of its manifestations. Before the development of psychopathology, academic psychology attempted to account for the behaviour of the "normal" in terms of dynamic principles. But as long as the genius was looked on as "inspired" and the mentally ill as "possessed" and the characterologically defective as "ornery," much of human behaviour remained outside the scope of scientific psychology. Modern psychopathology not only allows us to see that the pathological forms of behaviour are strictly determined and have a significance and an economy but also allows us to relate these to the common or normal forms. Although it is hard for some individuals with an interest in the mystic and the romantic to accept this advance toward scientific determinism, the advance can be looked on only as an increase in rationalism. With the scientific understanding of the personality there is no reason that it should become any less valued or that ethical and cultural ideals should suffer. The history of human progress can be measured only in the growth of rationalism. Finally, psychodynamic theory uses a dynamic-genotypical approach rather than a static-phenotypical one. Class theory is being replaced by field theory, and as this occurs psychodynamic theory approaches the methodological adequacy of the older established sciences.

The advances along theoretical lines have enlarged the possibilities for practical application of psychodynamics, particularly in psychotherapy. There is undoubtedly a gradual improvement in the prognosis for treated cases. Of this the modern psychiatrist is quite understandably proud. Not only are we able to understand the abnormal personality theoretically and extend the field of human endeavour in which rationalism holds sway, but for many individuals we are able to make life richer, longer, and happier. In the pragmatic sense, this alone would be justification enough for the study of modern psychopathology. So much for what has been accomplished by modern psychodynamic theory. We may now ask what remains to be accomplished in order that psychodynamic theory fulfil the promise of the present status?

Although we understand the general principles of personality growth and genesis, much about the detailed principles remains to be discovered. For instance, we understand how frustration leads to personality disorder, but our ideas about the specific etiology of the various specific personality disorders are rather vague. A great deal of work remains to be accomplished on the specific etiology of the functional psychoses, the psychoneuroses, the sexual perversions, and the character defects. The problem of the "choice" of mental illness is very important. We do not know, for instance, in advance of the sickness, why one individual becomes perverse and another neurotic, or why one individual becomes psychotic and another develops character disorders. After a complete psychoanalysis, it is often possible to reconstruct the sequence of events leading to the definite sickness. Undoubtedly, constitutional factors play an important role here, and we may expect considerable advance in the problem of precise etiology through the collaboration of internists, psychologists, and psychoanalysts.

In the second place, we need more precise definitions of our theoretical concepts. In our criticism of psychoanalytic theory, we saw that despite the very great genius of Freud and many of his followers, many of the concepts were ambiguous and not at the present time capable of either scientific definition or experimental evaluation. It is to be hoped that the collaboration of psychoanalysts and academically trained psychologists will bring about a sounder methodological background for psychopathology.

In the third place, we need studies to indicate the effect of given amounts of frustration or thwartings on various types of personality. We have seen that, when there is too much frustration for the given personality, mental abnormality ensues. On the other hand, a certain amount of frustration is necessary to develop the civilized individual at all. We must not lose track of the fact that frustration, while leading to mental illness on the one hand, leads to the highest accomplishments of human genius on the other. If we had ways of ascertaining just how much thwarting would lead to the development of highly diversified but still well-integrated personalities, we could improve the average individual psychologically within a very few generations in much the same way modern organic medicine and physical hygiene has improved him physically. This is a particularly important need if psychopathology properly applied is to help us overcome the present cultural crisis. In his very considered essay, *Civilization and Its Discontents,* Freud discusses this cultural crisis in a rather pessimistic tone, but not all psychoanalysts foresee the future so darkly.

In the fourth place, we have so far done very little along the lines of prevention of mental disorders. Because of the economic costs of psychotherapy, it is easy to see that psychotherapy is not applicable to the vast majority of humans, at least under the present economic setup. The mental hygiene movement has undoubtedly established some good beginnings in this directions. The mere knowledge of the mechanisms underlying human behaviour in itself undoubtedly does a great deal toward the preventing of all mental disorder. On the other hand, the subject matter is not easy and the outlooks for public education along mental hygiene lines are not so bright as they might be. Furthermore, although the theoretical potentialities of a manipulation of barriers in the psychological field seem unlimited, for practical purposes many barriers are definitely established. This is quite obviously so of the barriers which arise in connection with economic goals. Furthermore, there is a real antithesis between some religious goals and those of the psychotherapist. This leads to clashes between the ideals of the mental hygienist and the ideals of the church. Although some individuals believe that we are moving to a society in which the scientific world outlook will completely replace the religious world outlook, others are much more pessimistic about this advance. There is indeed much in psychodynamic theory which would indicate that adoption of a completely scientific picture of the world is neither possible desirable. This problem has also been discussed by Freud in *The Future of an Illusion* (1928). Freud looks forward to the gradual falling away of religion as an important social institution. But other analysts like Ives Hendrick consider this one example of wishful thinking on Freud's part.

This leads us to fifth problem which remains to be solved before modern systematized psychopathology may really fulfil its promises. This problem lies in the relationship of socio-economic theory to psychological theory. The problems of reconstructing the individual are intimately related to those of reconstructing the society. This should be quite obvious from what we have already discussed concerning the relationship between medical psychology and medical sociology. Some psychologists believe that the deep-seated biological urges of an aggressive sort makes a complete reorganization of society impossible. Freud (1936b) and his more orthodox followers take this viewpoint. Others like Kardiner, Frankwood Williams, Karen Horney (1939), and Faris and Dunham believe that so much in the psychology of the individual is sociologically determined that little psychological improvement in the individual is possible without rather drastic changes in the social order. At all events, the problem of just how much in the behaviour of the individual is sociologically determined and just how much psychologically, remains at the present time unsettled. The tendency at the present time is for the individuals who have previously insisted on psychological determination to admit many sociological facts, and vice versa. We have good reasons for believing that the basic science of human relationships of the future will be a socio-psychology-biology. Space does not permit us to deal with the important problems of the relationships between sociology and psychology in this book. We must, however, point out that it is highly likely that, for the really successful application of the new psychological principles, the development of a science of medical sociology will be necessary. At the present time the application of medical psychology is being held up through lack of a knowledge of sociological laws very much in the same way that, a very few years ago, the application of internal medicine suffered from a lack of the knowledge of psychological laws. We cannot consider in this text the social psychological aspects of the application of modern psychopathology, nor can we discuss the relationships between psychology and economics.[1] The rest of this chapter will be concerned with how we may best further our knowledge in the field of psychology and psychopathology.

We may ask, how may shortcomings of contemporary psychopathology be overcome? We may hope for continued and more detailed case studies by the psychoanalytical method. The central nucleus of what we know about psychopathology comes primarily from the psychoanalytical investigations of Freud and his followers. The case studies of the future, however, may well be undertaken simultaneously with characterological investigations, experimental psychopathological investigations, and pharmacological investigations. The detailed psychoanalytical case studies alone cannot hope to show us a great deal more than we have already learned from them. The range of case studies should also be considerably enlarged, and we need detailed psychoanalytical studies on many categories of behaviour disorder where at the present time we have only a few. Studies in the field of organic diseases, in the field of senility, in the field of character disorders, should thus prove very valuable.[2] Alexander has pointed out the necessity for psychoanalysis to become less secular in his paper "Psychoanalysis Comes of Age."

We must hope in the second place for increased knowledge through the more precise development of techniques for investigating constitution and character. The characterological studies and techniques of investigation, it is hoped, will cast considerable light on the choice between psychosis, neurosis, perversion, and character disorder. It is the author's belief that the characterologists, like the analysts, cannot much longer work profitably without the suggestive controls of each other. It is hoped particularly that more definite studies of body build like those of Kretschmer and personality types like those of Jung and others will be coordinated with psychoanalytical studies.

In the third place, considerable knowledge of the psychopathology of humans may undoubtedly be gained by the study of comparative psychopathology. We shall see that there are definite limitations to the implications of the psychology of the infraprimates for human psychology. Most notable of these are the limitations from the lack of social organization similar to that of the humans among the infraprimates. Since it is now admitted that so much of the mental disorders of humans are socially conditioned, and since rats, for instance, have neither society nor superego in the human sense of the word, these limitations will be apparent. On the other hand, it is quite possible to develop artificial situations in which animals will meet frustrations of a definite sort and in which the "animal equivalent" of behaviour disorders undoubtedly develops. We shall return to this problem shortly.

The most hopeful mode of attack on the problems lies in the development of an experimental psychopathology. By experimental psychopathology is meant actual experiments in definitely and carefully controlled situations in which both abnormal subjects and normal controls take part. Work on experimental psychopathology has developed very rapidly during the last decade. Development of experimental psychopathology was suggested by both Wundt and Kraepelin in the closing decades of the nineteenth century. Both psychiatrists and psychologists have done experiments in this field but only recently has there been the necessary cooperation between them. The earlier experiments were quite sterile compared with the fruitful discoveries made by the clinical method and the earlier clinical methods lacked precise experimental criticism. Today we have the definite beginnings of a science of experimental psychopathology in that several university laboratories and hospitals are devoting themselves to such studies. In the rest of this chapter, we shall outline the chief fields in which such work has been undertaken.

2. PREREQUISITES TO AN EXPERIMENTAL PSYCHOPATHOLOGY

Experimental psychopathology should proceed along the lines of investigation, which have been proved most successful in the older, better established sciences. In other words, it should utilize so far as possible a hypothetico-deductive method. The hypothetico-deductive method is of course basic to a field-theoretical attack, and so the theory should be based on field theory. This is particularly necessary because the theory of modern psychiatry tends more and more to be concerned with underlying dynamic and genotypic process. Since we have already seen that psychoanalytic theory both utilizes the hypothetico-deductive method and is a field theory, a very good starting point would be the experimental investigation of psychoanalytic concepts. In this chapter, we shall point out that this is possible in several experimental fields, most notably that of topological psychology. The earlier experimental work, for instance, that which came from the collaboration of Wundt and Kraepelin, was largely concerned with the exact measurement and description of symptoms. It is certainly true that the measurement of symptoms by the exact methods of the psychological laboratory is important and in actual psychiatric practice is not done nearly so much as it should be. Despite the widespread use of intelligence tests, memory tests, and devices for investigating the associations, it is only at the exceptional mental hospital that the patient is investigated by a trained laboratory psychologist. But while the experimental investigation of symptoms is important and the lack of its proper development is to be deplored, the development of experimental procedures which will investigate underlying dynamic processes may be much more fruitful. As we go on in this chapter, we shall see something of the work which has been accomplished along these lines. Here, let it be said that most of the work reported falls far short of being field-theoretical in its scientific stringency. While descriptive classification must always precede systematic explanation and while the exact and meticulous description of the symptomatic surface behaviours is necessary, the time seems ripe for attempting to introduce experimental methods for measuring and describing the dynamic structure of personality.

Field theory demands that the theoretical constructs be brought to the test of critical experiment. One of the chief reasons why experimental psychopathology has been so slow to develop adequate methods is that, in the interests of precision, psychologists have investigated only the very superficial aspects of emotional processes. We have many experimental techniques which may be utilized in recording the bodily changes associated with emotion, but on the whole these have been applied only in very artificial situations. Thus the results have been precise but sterile. As important as adequate theories are, their use in adequate experimental situations is even more important. The situations chosen must be close enough to real life situations that actual or real emotions rather than simulated or play emotions are brought into being. This does not mean that the intensity of the emotional situation in the laboratory has to equal the intensity of real life situations, as Lewin (1935) and Dembo have shown that it is quite easy to create emotional situations in the laboratory. The importance of utilizing real life situations can readily be demonstrated by reference to some of the existing literature. Thus, in early studies of hypnosis, it was found that hypnotized subjects behaved quite differently with play objects than they did with real objects. Most of the laboratory studies of emotion have been inadequate because the subjects knew they were expected to develop emotional behaviour. A similar shortcoming is found in the attempted introspective studies of emotional status. When the individual is behaving rationally enough to introspect on his emotions, there is usually little emotion to introspect on. Various devices are now available for raising real emotional responses within the laboratory situation. This usually done by frustrating the individual with regard to some goal so that emotion develops without his knowing that the experiment is primarily concerned with emotion. The pioneer work with this type of situation was done by Lewin and his students.

The results gained through experimentation must be interpreted with regard to the *transference situation*. Actually this is important with every experiment on human subjects in which the experimenter comes in face-to-face contact with the experimental subject and in this way applies to all or to practically all psychological work on humans. It is particularly important in working on psychopathological subjects, however, because the patient always comes to the experimenter as to a new physician. The experimenter has considerable positive or negative transference value for the subject and so from the beginning a specific factor enters into the patient's psychological field. This factor of transference undoubtedly makes it more difficult to evaluate the results of the experiment but by no means does it invalidate the possibility of an experimental psychopathology. Failure to take the transference situation into consideration, however, often makes the interpretation of results quite invalid.

In addition to considering the transference, the immediate past history of the subject's disease must be taken into consideration and the acuteness or chronicity of the disease picture carefully noted. Undoubtedly one of the chief reasons why so few experiments on abnormal patients have turned out successfully is that there is a tendency on the part of the experimental psychologist to group all the members diagnosed in any particular category together. Anyone with the slightest clinical psychiatric experience should realize the dangers in so doing. If one simply takes the one disease schizophrenia and compares the preschizoid personality with the acute manifestations of the disease, with the chronic manifestations of the disease, and with the recovery period, one sees a tremendous variation in symptoms and behaviour traits. Lumping these groups together and averaging the results of experiments on them will never give a true picture of any underlying dynamic process. Similarly, if one compares the manic and depressive phases of the manic-depressive psychosis without separating them in the tabulation of results, many of the individual behaviour traits and symptom descriptions will undoubtedly appear quite normal. Thus, one can say that one of the chief defects of the class-theoretical approach to the problems of experimental psychopathology is that of neglecting the precise momentary structure of the personality. Further, complications arise from the fact that most experiments done on psychiatric patients are done in an institution. One must remember that we are dealing with individuals in a particular environment. This means that the field of free action of these individuals is much more limited than the so-called normal groups outside institutions. It is necessary often to consider the individual's reaction with regard to the institution.[3] Furthermore, the individual is leading a life of very ordered routine and the requirement of taking part in special tests may be much more traumatic an experience than such a procedure would be in the normal subject. Whether the individual comes to the experimental situation voluntarily or involuntarily is of importance. Many patients look on taking part in a psychological experiment as a possible examination concerning their present mental status which may be used for them or against them. This also complicates the picture. All these complications necessitate the development of special controls. When these complicating factors are controlled, however, there is no reason why the institutionalized patient should not be experimented upon. Since we realize that the institutionalized patient shows particular disbalance of human personality structure, we have good reason for believing that the time spent in undertaking such special controls will be eminently worth while. In summary, then, experimental psychopathology should take account of all the factors we have just mentioned. It should be based on the hypothetico-deductive method and utilize field theoretical conceptions. The critical experimental situations utilized should be real life situations and concerned with integrated total behaviours. The transference situations should be taken into consideration and the complications, which come from the patients' institutionalization must be kept in mind.

In the following sections of this chapter, we shall present very briefly the experimental methods which hold promise for the development of experimental psychopathology. The experimental techniques are often so complicated and the factual results so extended that adequate presentation of either is impossible in the limits set for this book. Our survey will hence consist in a methodological introduction to the field rather than either a manual of laboratory instructions or an abstract summary of the results already obtained. Each mode of attack will be valued with regard to its possible contribution to psychodynamic theory and references to more detailed technical and factual accounts will be given. Only techniques which are psychological in nature can be presented. This means that a fairly large literature based on physiological and pharmacological research will have to be omitted. The only purpose of the following sections is to give the students of both psychology and psychiatry a survey of the possible modes of attack and so possible stimulate them to further investigations in this important field.

Throughout our discussion of the various methods, references to specific studies will be given. Some of the publications, however, cover the general field of experimental psychology and we must refer to them first. There are several books which deal with experimental psychopathology and which give abstracts of the detailed literature. Gregor's *Experimentelle Psychopathologie*, published in 1910, is the first on the topic and gives an excellent resume of all the work done in German laboratories and clinics up to that date. The reader will remember that this work was largely concerned with the measurement and precise description of symptoms. Hamilton's *Objective Psychiatry* is a later work which attempts to reduce psychiatry to objective and experimental methods. This book has been very influential in stimulating recent experiments in this country. D.E. Cameron's *Experimental and Objective Psychiatry* develops some of the psychological as well as physiological and pharmacological work. The work on schizophrenia is summarized in N.D.C. Lewis's book on the subject. J.McV. Hunt (1936) has summarized all the experiment reported in English on disordered patients through 1936 in an excellent abstract. Murray's *Explorations in Personality* is very important in that the most varying techniques are used to experiment on personality and the results are reported. The work of Dollard and his colleagues (1936) combines theoretical and experimental approaches to the general problem of *Frustration and Aggression*. Bentley's essay "General and Experimental Psychology" in Bentley and Cowdry gives a carefully selected account of researches which he thinks will be useful in this field. The role of the psychologist in psychiatric research has been the subject of essays by Cameron (1937), Lewin (1937), and the author (1937b)

3. THE RECORDING OF BODILY CHANGES IN EMOTION

The organismic solution of the psychosomatic problems makes the investigation of bodily changes in emotional behaviour very important. The origin of many physical diseases is realized today to lie first in functional and then, later, sometimes in structural changes in underlying physiology brought about by prolonged emotional states. Since all behaviour originates in the emotions, the bodily concomitants of emotional behaviour are imporant even in the primarily psychogenic disorders. The thalamus and the autonomic nervous system are always involved behaviour. There is always visceral and glandular response. Registration of this response by various psychological techniques gives us methods of objectifying and so measuring emotional states. It also gives us methods of relating somatic change to psychic change and studying these interrelationship. There is a vast accumulated literature on this problem. This has been recently summarized by Dunbar (1935). Menninger (1938) and Alexander (1936) furnish less complete but very readable summaries. Some of the chief findings and problems are touched on in the following lines.

Blood Pressure—Since the invention of the sphygmanometer[4] and the possibility of registering systolic, diastolic, and pulse pressure, there has been the growing realization that these figures fluctuate widely and fluctuate with emotion. No good physician is satisfied with a single determination of blood pressure these days and the so-called "norms" are known to fluctuate widely. There are many studies in the field which indicate blood pressure rises in emotion, particularly in fear and rage. Alexander and his colleagues in the most recent studies of blood-pressure reading during the course of psychoanalysis have shown the intimate correlation between height of the readings in millimeters of mercury and frustration and unconscious hostility. Studies by Menninger (1938a) report similar finding. For this reason, we may believe that so-called "essential hypertension" has a large psychogenic component.

Although there is some fluctuation in the manemotric readings for all subjects, some subjects not only have higher average readings but also fluctuate more greatly in their readings than others. The exact nature of this is not yet determined and is under investigation.

One of the chief technical problems requiring solution is the continuous registration of blood pressure. At the present time, except in techniques such as those of Darrow and Keeler, it is possible only to check the blood pressure immediately before or after some emotional experience. The devices for continuous readings are themselves cumbersome and require that the subject remain at rest or in a quiet position. The invention of some sort of sphygmanometer which would allow continuous recordings of relative systolic pressure over periods of comparatively free activity on the subjects's part is highly to desired.

Respiration—Through the pneumograph it is possible to measure the most important facts about respiration. The breathing curve gives us amounts breathed, frequency of respiration, course of respiration, and the relationship of the expiration-inspiration index to the basal metabolic rate. Like blood pressure, it has long been known that respiration varies with emotion. Respiration has been particularly important in connection with a problem of psychosomatic medicine, namely, asthma. That there is a strong psychogenic factor in asthma has been well known for some time. Alexander

French (1939), and the staff of the Chicago Institute for Psychoanalysis have been investigating this problem. Alexander has also made some characterological speculations concerning breathing curves. The technical problem of recording continuous breathing curves while the subject has some freedom is another one which should be worked out.

The Psychogalvanic Reflex—Since its discovery by Fere and Tarchanoff in 1888, the psychogalvanic reflex has interested psychologists as an indicator of emotion and as a possible lie detector. There is a vast literature on it. The deflections of the galvanometer with changes in skin resistance during emotion have been investigated with somewhat varying results. The instrument, on the whole, is "too sensitive" rather than not sensitive enough and extraneous physiological conditions probably upset some of the readings. The psychogalvanic reflex has been used along with reaction time and other physiological indexes in investigation of associations, both free and controlled. A good resume of this work is to be found in dunbar. The psychological literature is also summarized by Landis and Landis and DeWick (1932).

The Luria Technique—Perhaps of the greatest possible psychological significance in techniques of this general nature is that recently developed by the Russian psychologist, A.R. Luria. Luria's investigation of the disruption of behaviour in emotion stands out because it is based on an attempt to investigate psychodynamic theory experimentally. The theory is closely related to psychoanalytic theory and leads Luria to demonstrate the presence of the unconscious or semiconscious conflicts by disruption of simultaneously performed voluntary motor activity. In his technique, the involuntary movements of the left hand are recorded when voluntary movements of the right hand are inhibited. The subject is requested to press a key with the right hand on giving his association to a stimulus word. If for either conscious or unconscious motives the first association is repressed, this repression or inhibition is indicated in an involuntary movement of the left hand. Use is also made of reaction time, form of the right-hand response tremors. The Luria device combined with blood-pressure readings, pneumographic records, and the psychogalvanic reflex make probably the best indicator or emotional states we have today. Luria was able to show that stimulus words which arouse unconscious or conscious conflicts always could be ascertained from the record of the two hands with certain secondary records such as respiration. He thus confirms experimentally the effect of conflict on motor response and some of the basic formulations of Freudian theory. Luria's basic findings have been repeated by Barnacle, Ebaugh, and Leinere and by Huston, Shakow, Erickson, Trovillo, and Shuey. The last two investigators were particularly concerned with pointing out the possible use of Luria records in determining personality types and in psychiatric diagnosis. Certainly experimental psychopathology could make much use of the Luria technique. Like the other techniques, however, it is impossible to get continuous recordings without greatly limiting the freedom of the subject.

From blood-pressure records, respiration records, and the two hand records from the Luria technique, it is possible to get reactions at various levels of consciousness and various degrees of volition in investigating the response to certain stimuli. The relative systolic blood pressure gives us an unconscious involuntary response, the respiratory record gives us an unconscious but voluntary response, the Luria left-hand record gives us a conscious involuntary response, and the Luria right-hand a conscious voluntary response. Such a technique is useful in detecting unconscious emotional conflicts in the possible validation Rorschach records and in the experimental criticism of Freudian concepts. Experiments along this line have been started at the Menninger Clinic and the State Hospital at Osawatomie, Kansas. Preliminary reports have been made by Varvel and Brown and Orbison.

4. THE STANDARD TESTS

Intelligence Tests—Intelligence tests' may be used in development of experimental psychopathology. In connection with our discussion of hypophrenia, we have already touched on the problem of the I.Q. and intelligence testing. There we saw that this was such a large field of psychology as to preclude any detailed discussion of it in this book. The I.Q. test, however, has a certain role in experimental psychopathology and is a valuable device to get insight into the patient's adaptation to problems in the immediate environment. Recently it has become obvious to psychologists that the I.Q. fluctuates widely and the test reading of a psychotic patient must not be taken to mean that his intelligence was always or is permanently so depressed. The new Bellevue Adult Intelligence Scale which was developed by D. Wechsler (1939) is well adapted to work with clinical patients. Wechsler is working on the problem of deterioration. A special mental test for deterioration has been standardized by Babcock. Discussions on intelligence testing and its use in psychiatry will be found in D.E. Cameron, Pintner, and Garrett and Schneck. A complete up-to-date bibliography of tests is that of Hildreth; Buros's *Yearbook* summarizes the older work and gives the new work in the field of testing.

Character and Social Attitude Tests—There is also large number of tests for various personality types and social attitudes. This literature has been reviewed in Symonds. Buros's *Yearbook* brings the list up to date. Most of these tests require the answering of questionnaires printed on paper by use of a pencil and they are consequently called "paper-and-pencil tests." Although some of them may have some significance in experimental psychopathology, most of them are rather useless. In many of the older ones the purpose of the test was frankly stated and this led to weighting of the answers so that a great deal of unreliability was introduced. For instance nearly everyone has heard something about introversion and extraversion and has his own idea of whether he is an introvert or extravert. He thus will answer the questions in line with his preconceptions. Recently most tests have overcome this source of error by disguising the purpose of the test. It is doubtful, however, if these paper-

and-pencil tests give us any information which cannot be gotten in a careful clinical examination and such an examination will bring out facts about personality structure which the tests do not. They are useful for surveys of a total population when individual clinical examinations are impossible. Among the better known of these paper-and-pencil tests which have some psychiatric significance are the Neymann-Kohlstedt test for introversion-extraversion, the Bernreuter personality tests, the Thurstone Personality Inventory, and the Terman-Miles Masculinity-Femininity Test.

Social Intelligence Tests—It is well known that an individual's I.Q. may be exceptionally high, but that he may be socially maladjusted. This has led to the creation of tests based on the general pattern of the intelligence test, where social rather than intellectual maturity forms the standard for comparison. These tests have about the same applicability in experimental psychopathology as the intelligence tests. Outstanding examples are the Vineland Social Maturity Scale, the Haggerty-Olson-Wickman Behaviour Rating Scale, and Bleuler Maturation Test.

Free and Controlled Association Tests—The method of free and unhampered association is, as we have seen, basic to psychoanalysis. Some insight into the patient's associative processes can be gained in less time by use of the various association tests. These may be used alone or in connection with recording of the physiological concomitants of emotional behaviour. Free association tests allow the subject to give all his verbal associations to one stimulus word such as "mother" or "love" or "whisky." Controlled association tests allow one response to each stimulus word. These association tests are undoubtedly useful in uncovering conscious and semiconscious conflicts, particularly when they are associated with physiological recordings. The method was introduce by Jung (1919) and has been standardized by Kent and Rosanoff for the American public. The interested reader will find instructions for giving the tests with frequency tables and suggestions toward evaluating results in Rosanoff's *Manual of Psychiatry.* The free and controlled association tests like the paper-and-pencil tests seldom give any information not available from detailed clinical study, but they represent a possible timesaving device.

The Rorschach Test—Related to the association tests is the special procedure of the Swiss psychiatrist Rorschach. Rorschach constructed a series of ten ink blots which are ambiguous as to meaning but which suggest certain pictures to the average individual. The test is administered by allowing the patient to observe the cards in order and having him report everything he sees in them or that he is reminded of. The test is a semicontrolled association test, where the stimulus material has no objective meaning. Of all the tests so far reported, only the Rorschach will sometimes give information about the personality structure which cannot be elicited by clinical interviews. Some of the ink blots are coloured; they vary greatly in form and shading and complexity. A method is thus given for testing perceptual and cognitional integrations and comparing these with the emotional background. A highly complex method of scoring has been worked out. Separately scored are: the part of the card the subject looks at, what he sees on the card, and how he sees it. The result is given in a psychogram which is a configuration in which the important values are the interrelations between the variables. The Rorschach test is becoming a very specialized field of personality study and the administration of the test requires special training. The test undoubtedly needs objectification and some fruther standardization. Of all the tests we have discussed, however, this is undoubtedly the one which properly administered gives us the best information in the relatively shortest time. The most inclusive works in English on the Rorschach test are those of Beck (1937, 1938). Hertz (1935a) and Rickers-Ovsiankina have also published scoring schemes. The literature on the test is very voluminous and has been summarized through 1935 by Hertz (1935b). The Rorschach test is useful clinically in diagnosis and prognosis. It is possible that its application will have nosological significance. In the experimental field, it can well be used to evaluate various therapies.

With the possible exception of the Rorschach test, no one of the standard tests is in itself an experimental device. They are rather measuring instruments of varying validity and reliability, which give us a more or less objective picture of personality. They may have their definite uses in experimental psychopathology but comparative psychopathology and the topological approach offer more promise:

5. COMPARATIVE PSYCHOPATHOLOGY

Much of modern medicine is based on the comparative method. Comparative anatomy and comparative physiology are two of the cornerstones on which modern physiology and pathology are built. In the field of normal psychology, our knowledge of learning and perception has been definitely furthered by the comparative approach. Certain psychologists like Tolman and Yerkes have argued quite persuasively for the use of animals for experimental purposes in psychology. Their argument is based on a series of facts which are indeed impressive. (1) Since the Darwinian theory has demonstrated the continuity of all life, animals represent organisms much less complex than humans and consequently easier to study. Modern physics is based on the simplest laws of motion; perhaps behaviour theory can be based on the simplest laws of behaviour. (2) The animal may lead a comparatively standardized life except in the experimental situation. Thus extraneous environmental factors are completely controlled. (3) Experimental animals may—unless the stupid behaviour of antivivisectionists prevents it—be subjected to changes in environment and to psychological and medical treatments which are not permitted with human subjects. (4) Surgical techniques which may even lead to the death of animals allow more intimate study of the psychosomatic relationship than is possible with humans. (5) Control of breeding and reproduction and rapidity of reproduction permit a more accurate study of the hereditary and constitutional factors involved. These are very telling points and it is only natural that psychopathologists have been recently somewhat concerned with the problem of comparative psychopathology and particularly experimental neurosis in animals.

There are, however, severe limitations in the comparative approach which must also be mentioned. (1) The mere simplicity of behaviour is itself a limitation. Psychopathology is concerned with disorders of complex functions like reasoning and belief and, although animals show the nuclear forms of both, these probably differ in animals. It is hard to imagine paranoid delusions in the laboratory rat or dog. (2) The lack of language in animals is an even more severe limitation. A guinea pig has no "free associations." (3) The animals with the exception of a few species show only rudimentary social organization. Functional mental disorder is largely socially conditioned. (4) Most important psychological conflicts are concerned with the frustration of instinctual urges by "civilization". Although the physical forces of nature frustrate animals and perhaps some species have the beginnings of civilization, such beginnings are scarcely comparable to human culture. (5) Following on this, animals have probably little ego and practically no superego. Whereas these disadvantages make us less enthusiastic about the potentialities of a comparative psychopathology, they by no means make experiments on animal subjects useless.

Observation of the social life and sexual life of the higher apes has shown the beginnings of social and sexual mores and the undoubted frustration of certain of these by other members of the community. Koehler (1920b) points this out quite clearly at the end of his monumental experiments on chimpanzees and Zuckerman gives many examples of it. In a single observation, Tinklepaugh has reported a case of self-mutilation in a *Macaca rhesus* monkey who was separated from his mate and forced to live in an adjoining cage to the mate and another male. The behaviour reported was definitely "psychotic" with a complete change in the character of the animal. Pavlov reports the disruption or habitual responses in all his experimental animals following extreme fright situations. The author had a dachshund which from puppyhood grew up in a city apartment and was only taken out muzzled and leashed and had only sporadic contacts with dogs. This animal became undoubtedly a severe "neurotic" with libidinal fixations to humans much stronger than those to other dogs. Various observations by veterinaries and others report unquestionable evidence that "psychoses" and "neuroses" in animals do exist, particularly in domesticated animals. H. Dexler has given us the most thorough summary of the observations of Continental authors. Briefer summaries are to be found in the texts of Hempelmann and Maier and Schneirla.

Of probably greater importance are the attempts to study the development of abnormal behaviour experimentally in animals in the so-called "experimental neuroses." Pavlov first noted that an animal which was being differentially conditioned to a stimulus developed "neuroses" when the differentiation was no longer possible to the animal. This was indicated not only by gross behavioural changes but by disruption of previously learned habitual responses. Thus, in a conflict sutuation which is strongly motivated (the animals are hungry), neurosis develops when no solution to the problem is possible. This is so similar to our ideas of frustration and the development of neurotic symptoms in humans as to be highly suggestive. That such experimental neuroses occur in other forms has been demonstrated by Liddell for pigs, by Gannt for other dogs, and by Cook and by Maier, for the laboratory rat. Maier's work is particularly important because he investigates not only the disruption of behaviour but also the reintegration of behaviour.

Recently from the Yale laboratories have come experiments in which the presence of mechanisms very similar to those uncovered by psychoanalysis is shown in the rat. A good popular report of this work is given in the article by Miller and his associates in the *Yale Scientific Magazine.* Thus, N, Miller (1940) has investigated "emotional displacement" and Mowrer (1940) "regression" and "reaction formation" in rats. Such studies may be very important for two reasons. They allow the mechanisms to function under strict control and allow the investigation of the role of the nervous system in them.

Future research along these lines may throw considerable light on constitutional and hereditary factors, the amount of frustration possible under certain conditions, and the role of various therapies. Of extreme interest would be experiments on domesticated animals because of the social factors involved. Every dog lover knows that dogs show social emotions to a great extent. "Depressions" sometimes ending in death through grief are very frequent in dogs on being deserted by their masters. Anxiety and fear and jealousy also occur. The puppy goes through a series of frustrations very similar to those of the baby. He becomes weaned and thereafter fed at only certain times, he also becomes housebroken, his sexual life is regulated. Consequently, the rudimentary forms of oral, anal, and genital frustration are present in the process of domestication. Experiments with dogs or domesticated monkeys may well do a great deal in clarifying psychodynamic theroy in the future. To date, despite the interest in the comparative approach, our knowledge of human neurosis does more to elucidate the nature of animal neurosis than the knowledge of animal neurosis shows us about humans.

6. THE TOPOLOGICAL APPROACH

Of all the various approaches to experimental psychapothology, the author believes that the topological approach promises most. This viewpoint was presented in a recent paper (1937b). The following lines, taken from this paper, give the chief points of agreement and disagreement between topological psychology and psychoanalytic psychiatry. They also may be taken as a useful summary of the contemporary relationships between experimental psychology and psychopathology and psychiatry.

Topological psychology has developed independently or taken over from psychoanalysis certain basic methodological postulates which give the two systems much in common. A listing of these should make clear the possibility of cooperative research.

1. Critical philosophy is able to reduce all the various schools and *isms* of modern biological thought to two basic philosophies of biology. These may be called *organismic* and the *atomistic-mechanistic.* The organismic philosophy of biology stresses the wholeness of the organism and the priority of wholes over parts. Organismic thinking looks on the individual as a self-regulating energy system. It should be obvious that psychoanalysis adheres to this philosophy of biology, which is also basic to topological psychology. Opposed to this is atomistic-mechanism which stresses the priority of parts and looks on the organism as a machine. Atomistic-mechanism is, of course, basic to behaviourism.

2. The psychoanalyst has long stressed the fact that there is the most intimate connection between psychological mechanisms and the social anthropological culture in which the individual finds himself. Indeed the implications of the Freudian theory for anthropology are second only to those for medicine. The application of topological principles to social psychology also stresses this point. The social anthropological, economical, and political characteristics of the environment must all be characterized in determining the structure of the social field. Behaviourism, on the other hand, has been inclined to study the organism in isolation from its culture.

3. There is a close general agreement between the two theories with regard to the structure of the personality and to the nature of personality genesis. The multiple-structured self of the psychoanalyst, with its division into conscious, unconscious, foreconscious, and ego, superego, and id is closely paralleled by the regions in the person structure as described by Lewin. Furthermore both schools agree that this differentiation comes out of more unitary primitive wholes, the id or the analyst and the undifferentiated child person of the topologist. Both schools see this differentiation as arising in the process of growth, where the organism in an

environment of varying structure meets barriers to basic instincts or vectors.

Methodological studies have indicated that the most fruitful method of scientific advancement is the hypotheticodeductive or constructive method. This method allows the use of theoretical constructs like the libido, the ego, and the unconscious of the Freudians, and the vector, person, and reality dimension of life space of the topologist. Behaviour alone is observed, but this behaviour is coordinated with theory in order to integrate the various facts and to point to implications for further research. The whole growth of psychoanalysis is one in which facts were integrated into theories, which in turn were adapted to new facts. A similar process of growth has occurred in topological psychology. The purely inductive method which attempts a statistical accumulation of facts without theoretical coordination has been recently abandoned even by some of the behaviourists.

Both psychoanalysis and topological psychology believe in psychic determinism and in the uniformity and continuity in psychological nature. Basic laws are sought which must account for both normal and abnormal behaviour. All psychic phenomena, including symptoms, have a cause, a meaning or significance, and an economical function with regard to the psychobiology of the whole organism.

Despite such close agreement on such basic postulates, there are *differences* between the two schools. These differences are luckily of a nature, however, that they might be decided either clinically or experimentally. They may again be listed:

1. It is the nature of the theoretical constructions of the two types of psychology wherein the chief difference lies. The constructs of psychoanalysis have arisen in a rather haphazard manner in the course of the clinical practice of a few medical men of unquestioned genius. The psychoanalytic method has been so very fruitful in uncovering the most important and sometimes amazing correlations in the psychodynamics of the individual that the clinicians have

had little opportunity to criticize these concepts methodologically. The topologists, on the other hand, have attempted the most stringent, where possible even mathematical, definition of their concepts. Every behavioural event is to be ordered to theory, which is so constructed that experimental verification is possible. Where the concepts of psychoanalysis are seldom precisely enough defined to allow the critical experiment, those of topological psychology always are. If I seem here unduly to favour topological psychology, let me say I do so only from the standpoint of method. There are many problems raised by psychoanalysis, perhaps most notably that of symbolism, where the topological attack falls down completely. But those problems which topological psychology may attack are to be given a definite answer.

2. Present behaviour in topological psychology is always derived from the existing structure of the psychological field. In this, topological psychology may be said to be an ahistorical science. Ahistorical sciences like physics do not need to know the past history of events studies, because they are able to give a complete dynamic description of the momentary situation. It is freely to be admitted that few problems exist where at the present time we do not need to know something of the history. Psychoanalysis is a historical science, i.e., it is concerned with the effect of past emotional experience on present behaviour. Topological psychology does not deny that historical sequences have great present importance. It attempts, however, to derive present behaviour from the precise momentary situation. How far such deduction may be carried out, time alone will tell. All systematic sciences tend to be ahistorical.

3. I believe that there is to be found a slight difference in emphasis on the efficacy of the various factors of what both recognize to be a socio-psychobiological problem. The psychoanalyst is forced from his instinct theory of the basic urges to stress the psychobiological aspect of the problem. As an example of this let us consider the frequent argument of the psychoanalyst that war is inevitable and that socialism is

impossible, because of the aggressive urges or the Freudian death instinct. The motivating forces according to psychoanalysts are innate instincts or urges. The motivating forces according to the topological psychologist are functions of the organism *in* the environment. Although psychologists consider the environment, they attempt to deduce behaviour almost solely from the person. To put this difference in emphasis rather bluntly, the psychoanalysts assume considerably more immutability of human nature than do the topological psychologists. Both agree that biological mechanisms are subject to environmental manipulation. The topologists, however, would consider the potentialities of manipulation greater than do the psychoanalysts.

4. Finally, the data of psychoanalysis come chiefly from clinical practice, while those of topological psychology come from the experimental situation. This accounts, I believe, for the strong and the weak points of each. Clinical practice gives the problems of the psychoanalysts their great vitality and undoubted significance. Clinical practice, however, is fraught with sources of error. In every medical specialty exactness and precision have followed the introduction of experimental procedures. If the experimental method is applicable to neuroanatomy and physiology, why should it not be applicable to psychology? That it will be is the hope of the topological psychologist. [From J.F. Brown, "Psychoanalysis, topological psychology and experimental psychopathology," *Psychoan. Quart.*, 6: 227-237, 1937.]

From the earlier papers by topological psychologists, certain experimental verifications of psychodynamic theory are possible. In the famous experiments on the memory value of completed and of interrupted tasks Zeigarnik gives support to the psychoanalytic contention that unresolved psychic tension persists and influences future behaviour. This has been adequately demonstrated clinically many times, but its experimental demonstration makes it even more convincing. Ovsiankina's work on resumption of interrupted tasks brings us to the same conclusion. Hoppe's experiments on level of aspiration show the importance of social and hence psychodynamic factors in aspiration, performance, the effect of competition, and the experiences of success and failure. Mahler's experiments on the compensatory value of fulfilment of tensions at various levels of aspiration give us a possible wedge with which to study sublimation. The author's study (1933) of the dynamic properties of various levels of reality gives us a tool for investigating conflict at different levels of emotional urgency. Dembo's work on rage is of exceptional importance in that complete frustration of humans was observed by her for the first time. The above lines simply indicate some of the interrelations between topological experimental psychology and psychoanalytic theory. There are many other papers and the serious student of psychopathology should avail himself of the original papers or at least read the extended summaries given in Lewin (1935), Hartmann, or by the author (1936c).

The direct application of topological psychology to psychiatric problems has been the most recent development. Rickers-Ovsiankina (1937) has reported work with schizophrenics, Escalona has made an analysis of manic-depressives with topological techniques. Lewin, Barker, and Dembo have studied regression on frustration in children. The author (1936b) has made survey of the behaviour of all the psychiatric categories in a frustrating situation. On the basis of this study, he made the following conclusions, which are reprinted in order to give the reader some idea of the possible value of this type of work.

The results of the observations reported allow us to formulate the following tentative conclusions which are of general psychiatric interest.

1. The behaviour of psychotic and psychoneurotic individuals in a frustrating situation is much more variable and unpredictable than is similar behaviour by normals. Schizophrenic behaviour is most variable of all in this respect. Furthermore, the behaviours shown by the variously diagnosed groups show so much overlap that diagnostic categories cannot be said to represent discrete disease entities but rather

simply convenient points on some continuum such as regression or retreat from reality. That is not to be taken to mean that the various psychiatric categories vary *only* in this respect. There are undoubtedly other "dimensions" of personality than regressions. This conception of mental disease categories is becoming more and more generally accepted and may be said to be a basic concept of psychoanalytic and organismic psychiatry.

2. If the behaviour demonstrated by our control group may be looked on as normal or adjusted, the various psychiatric categories may be ordered with regard to deviation from the normal. With regard to the functional psychoses the most deviate group is certainly the schizophrenic, the next most deviate the manic-depressive psychotic, and least deviate the paranoid psychotic. The obsessional-compulsion neuroses are most clearly distinguished from the control group among the psychoneuroses. This order follows almost exactly that first conceived by Abraham (1927) and later developed by many psychoanalysts to describe the depth of libidinal regression in the various mental diseases. Our results thus confirm the psychoanalytic classificatory psychiatry.
3. From the observations reported here there is developed the possibility of the approximate description of personality structure in the various psychoses through use of dynamic conceptions. In nearly every case, we have been able to characterize the ease of building and discharge of segregated tension systems, the level of aspiration, and the effect of social pressure upon it. These represent only first approximations and further refinements on technique must be found to objectify our rating scales. We have thus far developed only a semiobjective procedure whereby rough index figures may be assigned. From such indexes, which are of only topological

> significance at the present time, we may hope to proceed to real measurements in time. We believe that our observations indicate the validity of this type of approach in psychopathology and our next step must be further to validate and objectify the methods of observation. [From J.F. Brown, "Reactions of psychiatric patients in a frustrating situation," *Bull. Menninger Clin.*, 3: 60-61, 1939.]

At the present time, studies of this nature are being continued at the Meaninger Clinic and work of a similar nature is being continued at the Menninger Clinic and work of a similar nature is being under taken by Dr. Adler at the Chicago Institute for Psychoanalysis.

7. OTHER APPROACHES

Besides the attack on problems of experimental psychopathology from the standpoint of topological psychology, other attacks by experimental methods are possible and may become very useful. Space permits only the listing of these methods and a few bibliographical references.

Questionnaire Studies—The psychoanalytic theory has been "tested" in a series of questionnaires. The earlier ones of these proved little because the questions pertained directly to mechanisms which were unconscious. More recently questionnaires have been devised to check whether the attitudinal results of unconscious motives and infantile experiences are what the psychoanalytic theory demands. In general, these studies have supported the theory. Examples may be found in the work of Stagner (1938), Stagner and Katzoff, and Krout.

Experiments with Hypnosis—Hypnosis can uncover the unconscious much more rapidly than psychoanalysis. Its therapeutic value is more questionable. There is no doubt that hypnosis has been held in disfavour and even disrepute by medical and psychological scientists in recent times. In a recent paper Erickson and Kubie point out how this lack of investigation of hypnosis is holding up experimental psychopathology. Hull's (1933) book summarizes the experiments of others and his own important ones in hypnosis. Dr. Milton Erickson (1937a, b, 1938, 1939a, b), in a long and impressive series of papers, shows the utility of hypnosis in experimental situations. Particularly interesting is his use of hypnosis to test psychoanalytic concepts. Freud (1933b) himself suggested the use of hypnosis and reports several experiments which corroborate his method.

Conditioned-reflex Methods—French (1933) pointed out that certain of concepts of conditioned reflexology could be translated into psychoanalytic terms. Hull and his students have attempted the translation of psychonalytic concepts into conditioned reflexology. Reference has already been made to the use of animals in such experiments. Miller, Sears, and Mowrer of Yale University have also done interesting work with humans in attempting to criticize psychoanalytic concepts experimentally with conditioned-reflex techniques.

Experiments on Human Frustration—Besides the experiments reported from the topological standpoint,several interesting experiments on aggression and frustration have been undertaken. These are discussed in Rosenzweig (1935) and the symposium on frustration edited by Rosenzweig (1938). A series of papers entitled "Minor Studies in Aggression" and another entitled "Analysis of Approach and Avoidance Contacts" are currently appearing from the Yale University Laboratories. Many specific psychological researches on the nature of thought processes in the various psychoses have been undertaken. The work of Hanfmann and Kasanin, and N. Cameron (1938, 1939) is worthy of study here.

8. THE FUTURE OUTLOOK FOR PSYCHODYNAMIC THEORY

We are living in a period of cultural crisis. What its outcome will be, no one knows. Many pessimists believe we are entering into a period of chaos, a new "dark age." Some optimists foresee a new and brighter culture as an inevitable outcome from the present confused world scene. This much is certain. Humanity has weathered crises in the past and has weathered them by inventing new adjustments and adaptations to the changing cultural environment. The crisis at the break up of feudalism was resolved through the application of the new physical science to problems of economic production and distribution. The present crisis is not due to the failure of physical science but to the lack of an applicable psychological and social science. It is hoped this book bears a great deal of evidence that in psychodynamic theory the groundwork for such a science has been accomplished. In the great discoveries of modern psychopathology we have perhaps found the tools which will enable the man of tomorrow to lead a fuller, happier life than does the man of today. As physical science removes the necessity of economic hardships from the world, psychological science may give us the insights necessary to love more greatly and to hate more wisely. If we learn to control our basic urges with greater wisdom we may create a world in which aggressivity and hostility are consturctively displaced to the extent that our vast knowledge of the physical laws may be applied to making the world a place for constructive, adaptive living.

NOTES

1. The author has already discussed the socio-psychological aspects in his *Psychology and the Social Order.*
2. At the Chicago Institute for Psychoanalysis, the Presbyterian Hospital in New York City, and the Menninger Clinic in Topeka, such studies are being undertaken. Cf. Alexander (1936), Dunbar (1935), and Menninger (1938).
3. Cf. the interesting paper of Dembo and Hanfmann, "The Patient's Psychological Situation on Entering a Mental Hospital."
4. It is assumed that the student is familiar with the nature of these registration techniques from other courses. Those who are not will find them in most standard works on experimental psychology or physiology.

REFERENCES

Abraham, K.: Selected Papers, Hogarth Press, London, 1927.

——"The history of an impostor in the light of psychoanalytic knowledge," *Psychoanal. Quart.*, 4: 570-87, 1935a.

—— "Amenhotep IV (Ikhnaton): A psychoanalytic contribution to the understanding of his personality and the monotheistic cult of Aton," *Psychoanal. Quart.*, 4: 537-69, 1935b.

Adler, A.: *Oragan Inferiority,* Nervous and Mental Diseases Publishing Company, Washington, 1917a.
—— *The Neurotic Constitution,* Moffat, Yard & Company, New York, 1917b.
—— *Individual Psychology,* Harcourt, Brace & Company, Inc,. New York, 1924.
—— *Understanding Human Nature,* Greenberg, Publisher, Inc., New York, 1929a.
—— *Science of Living,* Greenberg, Publisher, Inc., New York, 1929b.
—— *What Life Should Mean to You,* Little, Brown & company, Boston, 1931.
Alexander, F.: *Psychoanalysis and the Total Personality,* Nervous and Mental Diseases Publishing Company, Washington, 1930a.
—— "The neurotic character," *Int. J.Psycho-Anal,.* II: 292-311, 1930b.
—— "On Falstafi," *Psychoanal. Quart.,* 2: 592-606, 1933.
—— "Concerning the genesis of the castration complex," *Psychoanal. Rev.,* 22: 49-52, 1935.
—— *The Medical Value of Psychoanalysis* (rev. ed.), W.W. Norton & Company, Inc., New York, 1936.
—— "Psychoanalysis comes of age," Psychoanal. Quart., 7: 299-306, 1938.
—— "Psychoanalysis revised," *Psychoanal. Quart.,* 9: 1-36, 1940.
Alexander, F., C. Bacon, G.W. Wilson, H.B. Levey and M. Levine: "The influence of psychologic factors upon gastro-intestinal disturbances: a symposium," *Psychoanal. Quart.,* 3: 501-88, 1934.
Alexander, F., and W. Healy: *Roots of Crime,* Alfred A. Knopf, Inc., New York, 1935.
Alexander, F., and H. Staub: *The Criminal, the Judge, and the Public,* the Macmillan company, New York, 1931.
Alexander, F., et al.: "Emotional factors in essential hypertension," Psychosom. Med., 1: 93—198, 1939.
Allport, F. A.: *Social Psychology,* Houghton Mifflin Company, Boston, 1924.
——"Rule and custom as individual variations of behaviour distributed upon a continuum of conformity," *Amer. J.Social.,* 44: 897-921, 1939.
Allport, G.W.: Personality, Henry & company, Inc., New York, 1937.
Anderson, J.E.: *Happy Childhood,* D. Appleton-Century Company, Inc., New York, 1933.
Association for Research in the Nervous and Mental Diseases: *Localization of Function in the Cerebral Cortex,* The Williams & Wilkins Company, Baltimore, 1904.

9

PSYCHOANALYSIS: BASIC POSTULATES; THEORY OF PERSONALITY STRUCTURE

I. THE HISTORY OF PSYCHOANALYSIS

Sigmund Freud developed a dynamic theory to account for the interrelationships between hysteria and hypnosis late in the nineteenth century. He developed this theory on the basis of a therapeutic technique. He found that, if he could get the conscious part of the personality of the hysteric to accept the conflict which had led to the repression into uncosciousness of one of the conflicting urges, the symptoms of hysteria disappeared. Psychoanalysis, which this method was called, started as a specific technique for the treatment of one of the psychoneuroses. From this very modest beginning psychoanalysis has developed into the most systematized theory of psychological behaviour which we possess and undoubtedly into the most successful therapy which we have for some of the basic mental disorders. The idea of the relationship between hysteria and hypnosis had been established by Charcot and Bernheim. Freud had the early collaboration Joseph Breuer and knew his cathartic theory. But the important initial researches in psychoanalysis proper were all done by Freud alone. It soon became obvious that the Freudian psychoanalysis had very important implications not only for psychopathology but for the most varied medical problems on the one hand and for sociological and anthropological problems on the other. Freud soon found himself the center of an earnest group of researchers who were destined to develop modern psychoanalysis. After the psychoanalysts had found that some of the psychoneuroses were amenable to psychoanalytical treatment and had developed an etiological theory to account for them, they found that psychoneuroses, the psychoses, the so-called "psychopathic character disorders," and the sexual perversions were related phenomena. They further found that these various behaviour maladjustments resulted chiefly from experiences in the earliest years of life. They were also able to show that all these maladjustments were simply exaggerations or perversions of the so-called "normal" mental mechanisms. Finally, they were able to demonstrate that phenomena which all of us experience, such as dreams and the mistakes of everyday life, were related to more severe forms of behaviour maladjustment.

All these discoveries did not happen overnight, of course. The first communication on hysteria which Freud did in collaboration with Joseph Breuer was published in 1893. Freud was still publishing in the year of his death, 1939. His major contributions thus cover a period of close to fifty years. In the following lines a few of the landmarks in the history of Freud's scientific career are outlined. Those technical terms which are still strange to the reader will be developed in detail in this and the following chapters.

1856. Freud was born of Jewish parentage in Freiberg, Moravia. The family moved to Vienna in 1860, where Freud spent his childhood, was educated, and lived most of his life.

1873. Freud entered the University of Vienna, where he studied medicine and worked as an assistant to the great physiologist Brücke.

1881. Freud was graduated from the university and entered the general hospital in Vienna, where he worked chiefly in neurology and published many valuable neurological papers.

1885. He studied neurology with Charcot in Paris, returning to private practice Vienna in 1886.

1893. Preliminary publication of the *Psychic Mechanisms of Hysterical Phenomena*, with Joseph Breuer.

1895. *Studies in Hysteria* with Breuer. In the period from 1890-95 Freud had seen and treated many hysterics. In this period he gave up the traumata theory and the cathartic therapy which had originated with Breuer and developed the basis for psychoanalysis proper. Breuer ceased collaboration with Freud shortly after this time but they remained on friendly terms until Breuer's death.

1900. Publication of *The Inter pretation of dreams,* in which the psychoanalytic theory of dreams was elucidated.

1904. Publication of *Psychopathology of Everyday Life,* which elucidates the psychoanalytic theory of lapses.

1905. Publication of *Three Contributions to the Theory of Sex,* the expposition of the theory of psychosexual genesis, which will concern us in Chap. X.

1905-09. Various technical medical papers on psychoanalytic theory and the neuroses.

1909. Visit to Clark University and introduction of psychoanalysis to America. These lectures were the first popular presentations of psychoanalytic theory.

1910. The first International Psychoanalytic Congress was held in Nuremberg.

1915. Publication of *The Unconscious,* containing the most important discussion of the nature of the unconscious, which will concern us in this chapter.

1918. Publication of *Introduction to Psychoanalysis* in German.

1920. Publication of *Beyond the Pleasure Principle* which introduces the idea of the death instinct and will concern us in this chapter.

1923. Publication of *The Ego and the Id,* which gives the psychoanalytic theory of the structure of the personality and which will concern us in this chapter, and of *The Problem of Anxiety,* which gives his final theory of the role of anxiety in the neuroses.

1925-39. Freud continued many publications in the field of medical psychology but his most important works, *The Future of an Illusion, Civilization and Its Discontents, Moses and Monotheism,* were concerned with sociology philosophy. He died in London in 1939.

Through this whole period, like any healthy, growing science, the basic framework of Freudian psychoanalysis has changed several times. One of the chief defects of most textbook presentations is that usually only the earlier and less complete forms are given. We shall attempt in this book to present the theory as it is today.

After 1900, Freud had many disciples scattered through Central Europe and, after 1911, disciples throughout the world. Among these were the psychoanalysts C.G. Jung and Alfred Adler, who later introduced decided modifications into the psychoanalytic theory and left the main movement. It has gradually established itself all over the civilized world. Among others who discovered important psychoanalytic facts and introduced new theoretical constructions we may mention Abraham, Ferenczi, Alexander, Deutsch, and Reik. Freud's psychoanalysis was brought to the United States by G. Stanley Hall and Professor Putnam of Harvard. It was also furthered in this country by the New York physician A.A. Brill. Ernest Jones was most important in establishing the theory in England.

Today we have some hundreds of qualified psychoanalysts in the world, an International Psychoanalytical Society with its own press, national psychoanalytical societies in all the chief civilized countries, and a considerable number of journals devoted solely to the publication of psychoanalytical articles.[1]

Psychoanalysis today may be said to be the leading theoretical school of personality research in both its normal and abnormal phases. The term "psychoanalysis" today has at least three meaning. It is, in the first place, a technique which investigates the dynamics of the unconscious and conscious mental life of the individual. By dynamics in this sense we mean the distribution and change in distribution of psychic forces. Through an investigation of the mental life of the individual it is often possible to manipulate the psychic forces so that a restructurization of the personality ensues. So psychoanalysis is, secondly, a form of psychotherapy which attempts to restructure the neurotic or psychotic or perverse or psychopathic character so that he may make a better and happier adjustment to his life's problems. From the use of the technique of psychoanalysis as a therapy has grown a series of important and systematized theoretical constructions. Psychoanalysis is thus, in the third place, a system or school of psychology. It is in this third sense that we shall be chiefly concerned with psychoanalysis in these chapters. As a systematic psychology, psychoanalysis has implications not only for the "abnormal" but also for the "normal" adult of our society. The psychoanalysts have also investigated the psychology of primitive peoples, the psychology of aesthetics, the psychology of religion, and many problems in child psychology and social psychology. In this book we shall have but little to say about such investigations and shall be concerned with the technique and therapeutic aspects of psychoanalysis only incidentally. The technique of psychoanalysis and its application to therapy cannot be taught in a book. To attain proficiency in these matters requires years of specialized training by recognized teachers. We shall return to the problem of psychoanalysis as a technique in Part IV and have something to say about the implications of psychoanalysis for social sciences in chapter XI. Our central problem now will be the elucidation of psychoanalysis as a system of psychology.

2. BASIC POSTULATES OF PSYCHOANALYSIS

Theory of the Basic Urges—By the basic postulates of a science we mean the theoretical constructs which are the starting points of the systematic ordering of the facts of a science. In a healthy systematic science fact or data and theory or construct are integrated in a hand-in-glove fashion. A few factual observations become accounted for by a theory or hypothesis, and this theory in turn suggests where new facts may be gathered. Psychoanalysis has always shown such a close coordination of theory and fact. It has uncovered a vast array of facts which are quite valid independent of the fate of its theories. These facts, however, would scarcely have been discovered without the theories. In this chapter we shall present the basic postulates which will be used to account for the facts of personality genesis to be presented in the next chapter. The reader is warned, however, that certain facts will also be found in this chapter and certain theories in the next.

Since Freud was a biological scientist writing at the end of the nineteenth century, it was natural for him to take over some of the instinct biology of his times. The first important psychoanalytic postulation is that of biologically conditioned instincts, drives, or urges. It is necessary to mention instinct, drive, and urges because the Freudian conception of "instinct" *i.e., Trieb,* falls somewhere between the English "instinct" and "drive" and is probably best translated by the word "urge." Since Freud himself usually uses the term "instinct" and since his usage has been followed, we must also use the term. The reader is asked to keep in mind the exact connotation. We shall see later that the postulation of such instincts can be criticized on methodological grounds, but for the present let us see what Freud said about them. According to him, man has acquired, somewhere in his phylogenetic history, certain innate unlearned strivings or urges or instincts. Freud's instincts are not synonymous with the specific instincts of the animal psychologists in that they are not connected with specific environmental goals. They are rather postulated basic psychic energies which are innate and unlearned. Whatever the individual is or does at any particular time is determined by these urges working through the existing structure of his personality in his environment. The only reason that we behave at all is because of the motivating force of urges. These urges are modified, to be sure, by the life experiences of the individual, particularly those of the earliest years of life, but in their essence they remain biologically determined. Since these urges of a biological nature underlie all that an individual does and thinks about, *biological and psychological development are inseparably interconnected.* The force and direction of the urge are modified by experience, but in their simplest form they are a part of the herditary constitution. Consequently, psychoanalysis believes in variance in the biological constitution of individuals. This is mentioned because critics from the somatogenic school have falsely attributed to psychoanalysts acceptance of a naïve psychogenic standpoint. The modifications in the force and direction of the instinctual urges are, to be sure, brought about in a social environment. But Freud has never considered all behaviour to be psychologically conditioned. Rather, from the first, he has always spoken in terms of what might be called socio-psycho-biology.

According to Freud, there are two basic instincts or urges. In his earlier work, he made most of the instinct of Eros,[2] the life instinct, or love instinct, as he also calls it. Consequently, his earlier writings gave rise to the widespread conception that Freud said everything was due to sex. It is true that the *eros*, or life instinct, is the source of sexual behaviour in the wide meaning which Freud gave to the bringing people into close physical contact is called the *libido*. The libido often is, but should not be, confused with the life instinct of which it is a part. The life instinct is also the source of all the forces which impel us to build up, to construct, to preserve ourselves and the species. Thus the building of houses or the taking of nourishment are as much to be derived from the instinct of Eros as is the sexual life. By the sexual life as we shall see in the next chapter, Freud means not only what is popularly defined as sex, i.e., adult normal heterosexual relationship, but all the behaviour between human beings in which they come in close physical contact. Hence, under the concept of the life instinct, Freud subsumes the chief instincts of the nineteenth century biologists, namely, the instincts for self and for race preservation. Physiologically, the life instinct may be thought of as the fundamental tendency to maintain the individual organism and cause it to grow. Psychologically, it leads to the sexual impulses and the preservative impulses, which include besides food taking all the activities which we perform to preserve our bodies from the physical environment, such as building houses and making clothes. It also is the psychological source of all creative intellectual activity.

In his later investigations (after 1919), Freud discovered that human beings were not only basically constructive, preservative, and motivated by the life instinct, but that, under some circumstances at least, men hated as well as loved, destroyed as well as constructed, tore down as well as built up. He discovered this chiefly from the observation that individuals hated and wished to destroy other individuals at least almost as frequently as they loves them and wished to make them happy. He further found out that individuals entertain not only homicidal wishes but quite often suicidal wishes. Finally, he was forced to raise the question of why men die at all. And so he posited the instinct of Thanatos,[3] the death instinct, or the hate instinct, as it is also called. Physiologically this instinct represents the force which tends to destroy organic life and, hence, to lead organic matter back to the inorganic state. Psychologically, the death instinct gives rise to hostile and aggressive behaviour, to aggressive sexual activity, to self and race destruction. It also makes itself felt in destructive intellectual activity such as criticism, satire, or polemics.

As Freud was previously condemned for "attributing everything to sex," some more recent critics have condemned him for "attributing everything to aggression." However, in adopting the death instinct, Freud by no means gave up the life instinct. Since life goes on we must account for it. Furthermore, the instinct theory is the *starting point* but not the *cornerstone* of psychoanalysis. The facts to be explained in this and the next chapter can be just as well accounted for by supposing that aggression is early acquired in the lifetime of the individual and is generated out of the frustration of constructive urges. Thus, as Alexander has pointed out,[4] fear of the consequences of losing love because of jealousy gives rise to aggression without positing the death instinct at all. No matter whether love and hate are instinctual or early acquired, they are always with us. The "facts" of love and hate are psychological data independent of the theory.

The two instincts are not to be looked on as opposed and mutually independent forces. Behaviour primarily motivated by the life instincts may have strong components of the death instinct, and behaviour primarily motivated by the death instinct may have strong components of the erotic instinct. It is only through the neutralization of destructive urges by constructive ones that we are able to keep going at all. Finally, old age and death occur when the life instinct is no longer strong enough to neutralize the death instinct. This intermixture of the two instincts leads to the Freudian principle of *ambivalence*. Not even the most passionate love of a man for a woman is free from a certain amount of hate or aggressivity. The old proverb "True love never runs smoothly" may be a popular realization of this. One has only to realize the popularity of "caveman tactics" with most women, the undoubted pleasure with which movie audiences see some heroes strike the popularity of "caveman tactics" with most women, the undoubted pleasure with which movie audiences see some heroes strike the heroines, to realize the aggressive elements in the loving of human beings. Even in the act of love-making itself, a certain amount of aggressive pain is often inflicted. One speaks of an embrace "so passionate it was painful," and the like. In extreme cases we know of sadistic murders, which psychopathologists have realized for some time to be perversions of the erotic tendency. Thus the aggressive urges are usually present in erotic behaviour. On the other side, it is only through the neutralization of the aggressive urge by the erotic urge that we write polemics against our critics rather than directly attacking them with the pistol or horsewhip. Ambivalence is a phenomenon found not only in direct personal, interrelationships but also in most social attitudes.

These basic urges, then, fuse and blend and sometimes diffuse. All life is to be looked on as a conflict or a compromise between them. While the life or love instinct is predominant, life goes on. When the life instinct is not strong enough to neutralize the death instinct, death ensues. The personality is the result of the struggle between the forces of hate and love. This side of psychoanalytic theory, as Freud himself points out, is not so precise as we would like it. It has many poetical and some almost mystical aspects. But these constructs provide psychological tools to account for the basic facts of birth, growth, procreation, and, finally, death. From such crude general concepts, other more precise concepts are readily developed.

The instincts then are the basic sources of energy which give rise to the most various constructive behaviours on the one hand and the most various destructive behaviours on the other. From the time of birth (and according to some analysts even before birth), these behaviours come into conflict with the world about us. We can neither love everyone we wish to love, nor create all the things we wish. Nor can we destroy everyone we hate, nor burn their houses down. In orther words, both the hate and the love instincts become attached to both persons and objects. Society is so constituted as to prevent the fulfilment of many of our wishes. The process through which the love instinct or the hate instinct becomes attached outwardly to objects in the environment or inwardly to the self is called the process of *cathexis*.

We thus speak of *objective* and *narcissistic* cathexis. The individual both loves and hates other individuals and objects and he loves and hates himself (narcissistic love and hate).[5] Although there is no way of actually measuring psychic energy one can schematize the relationships so far discussed in a series of equations.[6] If *L* equals the sum of the forces of the death instincts and B equals behaviour, we may say that $B = f(L.D)$.

B will be primarily constructive when $L>D$ and primarily destructive when $L<D$. When $L<<D$, death ensues.

Similarly if O refers to object libido and N to narcissistic or self libido and C means constant, it is a good working hypothesis to suppose that $O.L. + N.L. = C.$ and also that $O.D. + N.D = C.$

Thus individuals extremely in love think but little of themselves, whereas on falling out of love they become extremely narcissistic. Similarly, although this may be hard to understand at this point, individuals who can no longer hate others tend to hate themselves, and we find the development of guilt feelings and depressions.

From birth, then, we are cathecting ourselves or others with the love instinct or with the hate instinct. In only some of these cases may we possess the individuals we love and destroy those we hate. It is through the frustration of some of these wishes that the personality has its growth and its genesis. Some frustration comes about through constitutional inadequacy of the organism and through the limitations imposed by the physical environment. The most important frustrations psychologically come about through our social institutions, familial, political, and economic. It is through these frustrations particularly that personality develops its structure.

Some Other Polarities—Besides the basic polarity between the life instinct and the death instinct, Freud has posited certain other bipolar tendencies. There is a decided polarity between *activity* and *passivity*. This in general we shall see is derived from the role the individual plays in the sexual relationship. On the whole it belongs to masculinity to be active, femininity to be passive. According to Freud, since all males have aspects of femininity and all females aspects of masculinity, this difference between activity and passivity is also fused in the personality. *Femininity-masculinity* represents another polarity. In the psychological sense the sex of the individual becomes determined only in the process of his life history. Consequently, individuals who may be predominantly masculine may have feminine traits and vice versa. Our activities are directed by the pleasure which we gain from them but must constantly be modified by our ideas of reality. This leads to the antithesis between the *pleasure principle* and the *reality principle*. We strive toward goals which give us pleasure. Very often, however, the realization of the consequences in reality of such behaviour forces us to inhibit it, and thus the antithesis between the pleasure principle and the reality principle develops. The infant, as we shall see, starts out primarily motivated by pleasure, but through the frustrations of the life situation is forced to develop a sense of reality.

The Freudians speak also of the polarities *objectivity-subjectivity, pleasure-pain,* and *love-hate.* These various reaction tendencies develop during the lifetime of the individual largely on the basis of the antithesis between the life and the death instincts. By *objectivity-subjectivity* is meant the difference between the physical and the psychological world, or the difference between the other world and the self, which all of us recognize. This development comes about, as we shall see, with the development of the ego and the growth of the reality principle. It is an important polarity, because in some cases of abnormal behaviour self and outer world are not clearly distinguished, in that the self is sometimes considered as part of the outer world or the outer world is sometimes considered as part of the self.

The polarity *pleasure-pain* is directly connected with the working out of the pleasure principle and directly derived, again, from the antithesis between the life urges and the death urges. The pleasure principle is based on the polarity of pleasure-pain, and, according to the Freudians, one of the chief motivating factors in all activity is the seeking of pleasure and the avoiding of pain. The *love* and *hate* polarity is essentially the same as the polarity between the aggressive and erotic urges and belongs to the general problems of ambivalence, which we discussed on page 206-207.

Conflict—All the polarities may become the sources of *conflict.* By conflict the psychoanalysts mean a situation in which two wishes are so incompatible that the fulfilment of one would preclude the fulfilment of the other. According to Freud, life is made up of a series of conflict situations. The baby wishes to remain in passive dependence on his mother, but, through the frustration of his nursing habits, he is forced to become active and feed himself. Passivity versus activity, the pleasure-principle versus the reality principle, love versus hate are all involved in this conflict. The young child wishes to retain only the emotional attachments within his own family, but the incest taboo and social frustration make him find friends outside it. The student wishes to marry his best girl, but society pushes him to go on and complete his professional training. All such are *conflict situations*. It is out of these conflict situations that the personality develops. That conflict situations occur in everyone's life needs no demonstration. It is a fact. The psychoanalysts have developed detailed theories to show how growth comes from conflict. In the next chapter we shall see how the complex, differentiated adult personality develops out of the simple, undifferentiated personality of the child, but we shall understand this development much better if we first see how psychoanalysis describes the structure of the adult personality and accounts for the ways in which conflicts may be resolved. The reason that we can follow the psychoanalytic theory of the structure of the normal adult personality and the theory of normal behaviour mechanisms better than the theories of personality genesis at this point is simple. This book is addressed to normal adults and we all know something of our own psychology.

3. THE STRUCTURE OF THE PERSONALITY

The Dynamic Aspects—In several places in the foregoing chapters we have seen that personality structure is complex. It is true that we should like to think of ourselves as having a soul, a self, a psyche, a person, or personality—our idea of the inner I—something that exists unchanged from birth to death. Religious people even think of the soul as going on after death. But whenever we fall into conflict situations we realize that the self may be divided into at least two parts. Whenever there is struggle between two equally attractive but mutually opposed goals, the apparent unity of the self must be questioned. Such conflicts occur throughout life and in their milder forms are of daily frequency. The student wishes to marry his sweetheart and continue his medical studies at the same time, but this he realizes to be a financial impossibility. The religious fanatic wishes to remain totally pure, but he is constantly bothered by lascivious ideas. In extreme cases of conflict, the self may become divided into two or three or even more distinct parts and we have developed the well-known multiple personalities.

Not only does the personality become involved in conflict but it undergoes constant dynamic change. In the psychoses and the psychoneuroses and the psychopathic character disorders, we have what amounts to a complete restructurization of the personality. Philosophers from the time of the ancient Greeks have realized that the personality was perhaps not constant, unitary, and active. Both Plato and Aristotle spoke of a tripartite division of the personality. Throughout history poets and literary men made much of the conflicts between various parts of the psyche. Freud, however, was the first modern psychologist to attempt a scientific description of the parts of the self or personality and to relate these to both normal and pathologic behaviour. Freud realized that to account for all forms of human behaviour in terms of systematized theory we would have to think of the self as divided.

Consequently, he speaks of the normal adult as being composed of the *id*, the *ego*, and the *superego*. The id is the main reservior of both the life and the death instincts. It is the source of most psychobiologic energy. The id is concerned purely with striving after pleasure and with the basic aggressive strivings. It has no idea of time, nor of reality. Consequently it is concerned only with arriving at the goals set up by our loves and our hates. If the strivings originating in the id were not controlled by reality and society we should become neither adults nor civilized, but rather live in a timeless world of immediate sensory satisfaction or discomfort. As we shall see, the child at birth dynamically is almost wholly id. The ego and superego, of which we shall speak next, are developed out of it in the process of meeting reality or growing up.

By the *ego*, Freud means what we ordinarily call the self or the conscious intelligence. The ego is the part of the self in closest contact with physical reality. The ego directs behaviour toward a maximal satisfaction of the individual's urges *consistent* with its knowledge of social and physical reality. It is thus the adjustor between the wishes of the id and the demands of physical reality. It realizes the consequences of its own activity and when able establishes balance between the environment and the organism. It is not in itself concerned with morality, with remorse, or with feelings of guilt, which, as we shall see, originate in the superego.

The *superego* is the chief force making for the socialization of the individual. We can suppose both id and ego to be present in individuals who theoretically grew to maturity outside a social group. Of course, such a growth is psychobiologically impossible, but for purposes of illustration let us suppose it is possible. Such an individual would have to adjust his id urges to the reality of the physical environment. But he would have no social conscience, no competitive ideal because he would be a member of no social group and would have no fellow members to compete with. The id is primarily biologically conditioned, the ego primarily conditioned by the physical environment, but the superego is primarily sociologically or culturally conditioned. Since this is so, psychoanalysis from the first has had to consider the effects of culture on personality just as it had to consider the effects of the biological heritage. The superego is appended to the personality relatively late in life. In practice it becomes almost synonymous with the idea of conscience, in that in it originate feelings of remorse and feelings of guilt. In it is what Freud called the *ego ideal*. In other words, it contains the ideal which we set for our own behaviour but to which we seldom arrive. The superego is morally superior. When the forces of the id lead the individual into behaviour which does not come up to its demands it seeks revenge and retribution. Dynamically there is a constant struggle between the forces of the id, which is solely directed toward libidinal and aggressive satisfaction, the superego, which is the voice of societal responsibility developed in the process of growing up and becoming civilized, and the ego, which is the most directly known part of ourselves —what we usually think of as the self or the conscious intelligence. For instance, when we speak of falling into temptation, having a struggle with it, and finally overcoming it, we have a situation in which the ego adjusts the forces of the id to those of the superego. For example, the feeling, "I should like to kiss that girl" is the conscious expression of an id impulse while, "But I won't do it now because she would rebuff me with so many people around" is the adjustment from the ego, and, finally, "But I must not do it at all, because kissing is not nice" comes from the superego. Similarly, "I should like to beat up my critic" comes from the id, "but he is larger than I and might beat me up" comes from the ego, while "you (as the voice of conscience) should turn the other cheek" comes from the superego. These examples are of conscious conflict. Probably even more frequent are unconscious conflicts which we can only speak of after we have introduced the concept of the unconscious.

Thus, by the dynamic aspects of the self, Freud means the agents through which conflicts arising in the instincts are worked out. In the normal adult personality there is a fairly harmonious balance maintained between the id, the ego, and the superego, and external reality. This balance is, of course, being constantly upset, and our actual behaviour, social, psychological, and to a large extent even physiological, is the resultant of the resolutions of these conflicts. We shall later see how the normal adult develops ego and superego out of id through earlier conflicts in the life situation. We shall also see that the various psychopathological phenomena represent economic restructurization or resolutions of conflict situations.

The Topographical Aspects of the Self—Conflict between the ego, superego, and id may occur in the conscious, foreconscious, or unconscious levels of the psyche. Freud refers to the unconscious, the foreconscious, the conscious as the topographical aspects of the self. Freud has done more than any other individual to popularize the term "unconscious." The author has elsewhere described what Freud means by the topographical aspects of the self, and this will be quoted.

The idea of the unconscious as a necessary supplement to the conscious is again not an original idea of Freud's. The idea of unconscious mental phenomena had been used by many speculative philosophers for almost two centuries before Freud's original researches. Leibnitz used it, as did E. von Hartmann, and shortly before Freud the concept played an integral part in Schopenhauer's philosophy, which through Nietzsche had influenced Freud's thinking considerably. That the psychological phenomena of temporary forgetting with subsequent recall, habituation, hypnosis, and multiple personality required the postulation of mental processes other than those of the stream of consciousness had been realized by most psychologists for some time. Freud's accomplishment here was similar to his achievement in setting up the theory of the dynamic aspects of the personality. He made the concept more fruitful and workable by relating it to the findings both of himself and of other in psychopathology.

The Conscious, Foreconscious, Unconscious—We all know what we mean by consciousness and by the *conscious* Freud means that segment of the mind which is concerned with immediate awareness. Most of us can summon into the conscious a great many other things, such as names, dates arguments, reminiscences of past experience, and the like, which are not constantly present. That segment of the mind where the readily recallable is to be located is called by Freud the *foreconscious*. But we all have experienced material which we cannot recall at will, but which may occur to us automatically and which we know is present in our minds through hypnosis and other experimental procedures. This segment of the mind is the Freudian *unconscious*. In it are to be found the ideas and wishes and strivings which were once in the conscious, but which have been forced into the unconscious. Also here are to be located many strivings and desires which originate from the energy of the id and have never been conscious. All behaviour is the resultant of the dynamical conflicts between the forces of the id, the superego, and the ego. These conflicts and their resolution take place either in the conscious, the foreconscious, or the unconscious. The beginning student is sometimes apt to confuse the dynamical aspects of the personality with the topographical situations of the mind. While the ego forces are chiefly resident in the conscious and id forces chiefly resident in the unconscious, there is a considerable overlap. The superego, for instance, has conscious, unconscious, and foreconscious parts, and large segments of the ego lie in the foreconscious and the unconscious. This is quite clearly demonstrated in the following diagram made from Healy, Bronner, and Bowers (Fig. 9.1). It is this discovery which has made Freud say that besides the dynamical problem in all human behaviour there is a topographical problem, i.e., where in the mind does the dynamics of the conflict situation occur? [From J.F. Brown, *Psychology and the Social Order,* McGraw-Hill Book Company, Inc., New York, 1936, pp. 314-316.]

The Economical Aspects of Behaviour—Behaviour is accounted for by the psychological struggles between ego, superego, and id, taking place in the unconscious, conscious, and foreconscious. The resolution most frequently and normally consists in the restitution of normal equilibrium and personality growth. Sometimes the resolution consists in the development of mental illness or of character defects and sometimes in the works of the genius. It occurs, however, and this was one of the greatest insights of Freud, always as the dynamics of the total situation demand. This dynamical resolution of conflict is the *economical* aspect of behaviour according to the Freudians. Thus, although the development of a major mental illness may be looked on as a terrible thing, it is still economical, because often only by so doing may the individual be maintained as an intact organism at all. It is well-known that life often becomes so unbearable that only through the development of a psychosis may we evade suicide. Similarly, although the works of the genius are to be looked on as socially much more desirable than the productions of the psychotics, we know today that genius arises only in conflict situations of extreme severity. We have already seen many examples of the economical aspects of symptom formation. Symptoms are economical, however, only in the sense that all behaviour is economical; namely, that conflict situations are resolved in accordance with the least expenditure of energy possible in one existing total situation. This proposition cannot at the present time be proved but it is an invaluable working hypothesis for psychology. Through accepting it we are able to see order in behaviours which were previously thought of as accidental and chaotic.[7]

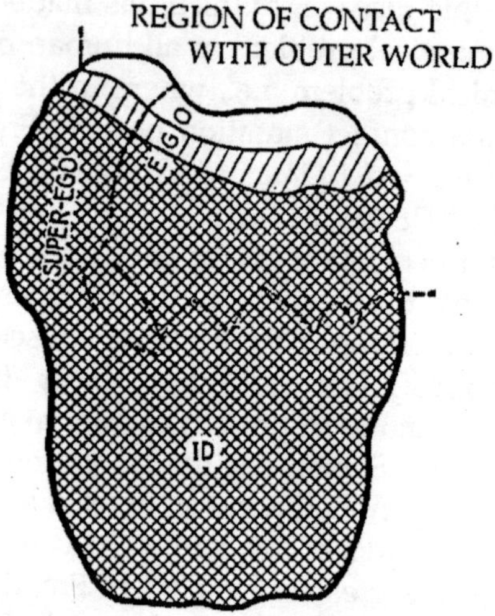

Fig.9.1. : Showing the topographical relationships of the conscious, unconscious, foreconscious and ego, superego, and id. Heavy shading =unconscious; light shading = foreconscious; unshades= conscious. (Redrawn by permission from Healy, Bronner and Bowers, The Structure and Meaning of Psychoanalyses, New York, Alfred A. Knopf, Inc., 1931.)

4. MECHANISMS

Conflicts between ego, superego, and id in the conscious or unconscious are resolved in an economical fashion in various manners through the so-called "mechanisms." These mechanisms are various unconscious or conscious processes whereby the inner conflict situation is eliminated or reduced in its severity. They have thus an economical function. There are many ways in which conflicts may be resolved. Outlets for the conflict situation which are socially acceptable may be provided. Deflected discharge of the energy in behaviour consistent with the standards of the ego and superego may be brought about. Barriers or defenses may be raised against the discharge of the conflict energy and thus preserve the integrity of the organism. For instance, the student who cannot afford to marry his sweetheart may utilize the libidinal energy previously directed toward her in writing love sonnets. He does this by the mechanism known as *sublimation*. A young man who hates his rich uncle and wishes for his death may overcome the conflict so aroused by developing hates for his boss through the mechanism of *displacement*. The old maid who suffers from the conflict which is aroused by the wish for a lover may protect against it by developing a fear that someone is under her bed; she is thus utilizing the mechanism of *reaction formation*.

It is difficult to give an orderly description of the psychoanalytic mechanisms for several reasons. Freud started with only a few, and as occasion demanded with the growth of the theory both he and his followers added others. There has been no attempt so far as the author knows to give them a schematic and orderly classification. Some of the later described mechanisms are more basic than the earlier and there is considerable overlap between many of them. Some of them are active throughout the whole field of behavioural problems and others refer to very specific mental activities in but a limited sphere. In the following paragraphs we shall attempt to introduce only the most basic mechanisms, in as orderly a fashion as possible. The various minor mechanisms will be introduced in the text as occasion demands.

We have already dealt with the conflict situation. All the mechanisms essentially derive from this since they are ways of resolving conflict. Not all conflicts are or need to be resolved. Many students finished their profession training and only years later marry their sweethearts. Many would be musicians go into business and always consciously hanker after a musical career. In this case we speak of the *continuation* of the conflict. Such continuation may be dangerous to the personality in some cases, but all of us are quite conscious of the continuation of many conflicts.

In normal adults very frequently and in children considerably less frequently, conflicts are resolved by *discriminatory decision and renunciation*. The young man may take a fond and sentimental farewell of his sweetheart and continue his studies successfully and remain quite conscious of a mild nostalgia for the girl throughout his life. The embryo musician may decide business has more to offer and give up an ambition to play and later get great pleasure out of going to concerts. The gay young blade may intelligently decide that alcohol and the fleshpots are really less desirable than a respectable position in society and give them up with only an occasional regret. In discriminatory decision the ego consciously weight the pros and cons in the conflict situation and renounces one of the opposed tendencies. Such discriminatory decision is always an advisable mechanism for solving conflicts at the conscious level. But not all conflicts are conscious and even conscious conflicts are not always so to be resolved. In general discriminatory decision may be applied when the ego is strong and the conflict relatively mild. In the next chapter we shall see that this is not the case in childhood, where the ego is weak and the conflicts particularly severe.

Continuation and discriminatory decision are of no great significance for personality genesis. *Repression,* however, is of the greatest significance. That part of a conflict situation which is most unacceptable to the ego and superego may be forced into the unconscious by the ego. When this occurs the mechanism is called "repression." Repression is often confused with *inhibition,* where the individual consciously and purposely refrains from an activity, as in cases where there is a continuation of the conflict and cases of discriminatory decision. It is also sometimes confused with *suppression,* where the individual consciously forces an unacceptable idea out of his mind successfully for a period of time. Repression forces the idea deep into the unconscious, is not discriminatively decided on by the ego, and only occurs in a situation where intense fear develops with regard to the consequences of carrying out some wish. It is frequent in childhood, where the weak ego the child is unable to cope with the real or imagined consequence of some of his loves and hates. In the next chapter we shall see how the sequence, love—jealousy— hostility toward object of jealousy—fear of the consequences of this hostility, leads to childhood repression. Some repressions are undoubtedly successful in that the repressed remains fairly dormant in the unconscious. In most cases, however, the conflict continues as an *unconscious* conflict and from this secondary conflict the need for further mechanisms to resolve conflict arises.

The resolution of conscious conflict need not concern us much more. Many times every day we make more or less satisfactory decisions as to courses of action in conflict situations. The most important discovery of modern psychodynamic theory is that of unconscious conflict and the mechanisms of its resolution. The wish which as we have seen is the father of both thought and deed is often an unconscious wish which was originally conscious and has been repressed. In this way the existence of unconscious conflict has a demonstrable effect on even our conscious resolutions of conflict. The young man who discriminately decided to part with his sweetheart in order to finish his professional training makes this decision as an apparent free agent. A psychoanalysis would show us that unconscious conflicts and repressed wishes have a great deal to do with his conscious decisions. He may, for instance, have an unconscious fear of the consequences of sexual relations and an unconscious wish to exhibit himself which are actually far more important in making up his mind to leave the girl and become a lawyer than are the reasons he gives to himself.

Unconscious conflict is resolved by the most varying types of mechanisms. The way in which it is resolved (either fully or partially, according to the economics of the total situation) is the most important determinant of personality. The determination of personality is not, of course, by the resolution of a single conflict but by the resolution of the series of conflicts which make up a life history. Unconscious conflict plays an important role in the growth of the "normal" personality. This will be our topic in the next chapter. In fact, much of the behaviour of the "normal" adult is determined by unconscious conflict and this will concern us. Finally, we shall be concerned with the ways in which the resolution of unconscious conflict leads to abnormal or psycho-pathological adjustment.

Before we classify the mechanisms utilized for the resolution of unconscious conflict we must point out that the transition from fully conscious conflict to deeply unconscious conflict is a continuous one. Consequently, the mechanisms of resolution of unconscious conflicts are also to be observed at the preconscious and at times conscious level. This is fortunate because the psychoanalysts would scarcely have discovered the mechanisms of the deep unconscious had they not been able to observe the working of similar mechanisms on a preconscious level in themselves and their patients. So, although the most important workings of the mechanisms are unconscious, we can still find suitable conscious mechanisms to illustrate them.

The mechanisms may be roughly classified into two groups, those which in themselves resolve or reduce a conflict in a rather specific fashion, which we shall call the "major mechanisms," and the mechanisms which are used as supplementary tools by the major mechanisms, which we shall call "minor mechanisms." The distinction is not a completely clear-cut logical dichotomy because in some cases minor mechanisms take over the function of major mechanisms and vice versa.

Repression is the major mechanism for the situation of conscious conflict. Conversion, regression, sublimation, reaction formation, and rationalization are the major mechanisms for the resolution of unconscious conflict.

Conversion is the mechanism through which repressed energy connected with the frustration of basic drives is changed (converted) into the functional symptoms of bodily disease. This is a particularly important mechanism in psychoanalytic theory because through it the analysts are able to account for all of the phenomena of hysteria and many of the phenomena of what are ordinarily considered organic diseases and problems for internal medicine. Of the specific mechanisms connected with mental disease, conversion is probably the most thoroughly understood. We have already studied in some detail a case of conversion hysteria. This case, that of the girl with the anaesthetic thigh, showed us how repressed libidinal energy was allowed a perverse outlet through the development of a hysterical anaesthesia. In this case, as in all cases of conversion, we have first the repression of an emotional conflict, followed by the failure of the complete repression and the return of the energy to consciousness in a disguised form. That the symptoms of conversion hysteria take the form they do can only be completely understood after we have learned about the development of the personality (in the next chapter). At a conscious level we all have wished to be ill to avoid some painful situation. Some people actually become ill under these circumstances. One of the ways in which conflict may be avoided is a conscious or unconscious "flight into sickness."

By *regression* we mean the reversal of the ordinarily progressive sequence of development and hence the return to more primitive forms of personality structure. Psychoanalysis is concerned with two forms of regression: *ego regression and libido regression*. These may occur together or we may have libido regression without ego regression. On the other hand, we seldom find ego regression without libido regression. By libido regression we mean the return to earlier forms of outlet of the libidinal impulses. Thus an adult may resolve an unconscious conflict by adopting the form of love relations of the child. We shall see many examples of this in our discussion of the psychoses. Similarly an individual who has developed a fair amount of superego may completely lose this when he loses social responsibility and conscience. As conversion was the most important mechanism in accounting for hysterical phenomena and relating the problems of medical psychology, regression is the basic concept in accounting for the development of the major functional psychoses. The psychoanalysts also use regression, however, to account for very much milder symptoms, so that one can speak of childish behaviour in the adult as being regressive, or the primitivization and disruption of normal child behaviour in temper tantrums as regression, or the temporary development of a previous form of sexual behaviour in an otherwise normally adjusted individual as regression. Conflict may thus be resolved by "flight into childhood."

By *sublimation* we mean the resolution of the basic urge frustrations through the substitution of a socially acceptable goal. Sublimation is a difficult term to use scientifically, however, because of its definitely evaluative connotation. Conversion, as we have already seen, means the substitution of behaviours which are socially acceptable but at the same time individually incapacitating. By sublimation we mean behaviours which in the eyes of society are not only acceptable but also have definite social values. According to the psychoanalysts, all forms of creative intellectual endeavor represent sublimations of the underlying basic urges. Sublimitation thus becomes a very important mechanism because through it we are able to account for the behaviour of the genius and consequently relate the genius to the normal and to the psychotic, neurotic, and perverse. We may best avoid the evaluative connotation of sublimation by thinking of sublimation as the redirection of basic urges into socially approved channels whereby the individual develops neither incapacitating physiological nor incapacitating psychological symptons. Through sublimation not only the creation of works of art and great scientific discoveries but also a great deal of moderately constructive normal behaviour is to be understood. Thus unconscious conflict may be resolved by a "flight into creative work."

The above mechanisms allow perverse or vicarious discharge of the repressed wish. We come now to a mechanism which is efficient in that it strengthens repression by denying the conflict. By *reaction formation* or *overcompensation* we mean the development of behaviours which are diametrically opposed to the unconscious wish.

Doing the opposite of some wish gives us outlet for repressed energy and is economical in the psychological sense in that by so doing we deny thoroughly and absolutely the original wish and so strengthen its repression. Consequently, according to the psychoanalysts, many of the positive things which we do are reaction formations against wishes which we cannot admit but are quite opposed in direction. We have already seen one example of this in our discussion of the well-known "old maid's neurosis." The old maid who constantly is afraid of finding a possible seducer under her bed is protecting herself from the admission of the wish to find one by developing fear, a reaction formation against the wish. A great deal of extreme "overmorality"and most prudishness probably arises on the basis of reaction formations. From analysis of actual cases psychoanalysts have discovered that many vegetarians are afraid of their oral-sadistic impulses and strengthen the repression of these by not eating meant in any form. Many vice crusaders and searchers after prurient literature are protecting themselves against their own libidinal impulses, which their superegos cannot admit.

Reaction formation is thus a very important mechanism in the psychoanalytic psychology because it allows us to derive many of the characteristics of the so-called "normal" personality and is one of the chief mechanisms for giving us a basis for understanding character disorders. We may thus resolve or rather reduce unconscious conflict by "behavioural denial of it."

By ......we mean the invention of consciously acceptable motives by the ego to cover up those unconscious motives which it cannot accept. The process of rationalization occurs along with various other mechanisms. Rationalization means "to make rational." It refers to the causes which the individual consciously assigns for his behaviour. Thus in conversion the individual rationalizes the sickness by attributing it to accident or germs; in regression the individual excuses his childishness because others are cruel or do not understand him; in sublimation art becomes "art-for-its-own-sake" or "olnly science is pure"; and in reaction formation the interest in prurient literature is rationalized by excusing it on the basis of protecting others. In many cases, however, rationalization is the chief mechanism for resolving unconscious conflict. Thus "guilt feelings" and love of display of many great philanthropists are rationalized in "philanthropy"; the bitter, even sadistic, polemical denunciations of rivals by scientists are rationalized as interest in the purity of science. We may thus resolve unconscious conflicts by "assigning spurious but consciously acceptable reasons for following out a repressed wish."

These major mechanisms utilize a whole host of minor mechanisms. Space allows only the presentation of the most important of these.

Transference signifies the shifting of the feelings of love—the erotic cathexis—from one object or person to another. We may also speak of transference of aggressive urges. Transference becomes very important at various stages in the indivdual's life, particularly when the family or society frustrates the existing libidinal cathexis. Examples of transference occur in the libidinal attachments to the parents, which are forced elsewhere in adolescence. We shall also see that transference is very important in the process of psychoanalysis.

Identification refers to the mechanism through which a person attempts to mold his own ego or self after that of someone else or believes himself to have some other person's personality. It has often been observed that children imitate the mannerisms of their parents. Superiors in all the professions are imitated by inferiors. The adoption of all sorts of characteristics of other individuals belongs to the identification process. Identifications may be made unconscious by repression. They also play an active role in many of the major mechanisms. The young man leaving his fiancee may, for instance, identify himself with an admired bachelor professor and so gain the necessary strength to give up his love affair.

Introjection refers to the incorporation by the ego into itself of the outside environment or of other individuals.

Introjection is like identification except that in identification the individual wants to be like the object, while in introjection he considers the object a part of himself. In extreme cases, as schizophrenia, the individual believes that he has the characteristics or abilities of others. In this way delusions of mistaken identity are examples of introjections. In a milder form all of us indulge in introjection through the phenomenon known to psychologists for some time as empathy. The great popularity of the success movie with the happy ending is only understood through the unconscious introjection of the hero and heroine by members of the audience. Identified individuals like the parents may be unconsciously introjected so that they become considered part of the person. We shall see the origin of the superego in this process. In normal life we tend to introject admired and loved objects and through this process strengthen the power of the love instinct. "I shall carry you forever in my heart," You are always with me," and like statements are popular examples of how introjection works. Introjection plays a role in most of the major mechanisms.

Projection may be considered as the inverse of introjection in that the ego attributes to environmental objects or other persons characteristics of their own personalities which are unacceptable to the ego. In at least semiconscious form, projection is the tendency in all of us to seek our faults in others. The "tu quoque" argument (i.e., the argument "you also are weak") is the standard example of this. Projection may also be unconscious. The vice crusader projects the prurience of his own mind on others in the process of his reaction formation. Projection protects us from the results of our own aggeressivity by attributing it to others. In extreme forms it becomes the basic mechanism in the paranoid psychoses.

Displacement refers to the transference of emotion from one object to another. Certain emotional reactions like hate for the parents or genital strivings for the siblings cannot be accepted by the ego. When we hate someone society demands we must love or love somebody whom society will not permit us to love, a conflict is, of course, engendered. By displacing the emotion to some other object, this conflict is resolved. When we are angry with our wives and take it out on the cat or dog (or sometimes vice versa, of course), we do this in a semiconscious fashion. But displacement works also unconsciously. The aggression we may feel for a parent is often displaced to social movements or other individuals. The young man who cannot admit hatred of his father may become a revolutionary or hate his boss. The child who cannot admit a real libidinal attachment to the mother may get a crush on a teacher.

The mechanisms of transference, identification, introjection, and displacement are of the very greatest importance for the role which they play not only in the major mechanisms but in the process of personality development. In presenting the mechanisms we have had to simplify them and remove them from the real life situations in which they occur. In actual behaviour we do not have simple conflicts being directly repressed and leading to the immediate resolution of the unconscious conflict by means of a simple mechanism.

Actually there are usually many conflicting impulses in the conflict situation. There is always ambivalence. The unconscious conflict usually is resolved by the interplay of several major mechanisms through utilization of several minor ones. Actual behaviour is what Freud has called "overdetermined." There are conscious determining factors which may be quite rational; there are the rationalizations; and finally there are unconscious mechanisms at work. The young man who chooses to study for a profession rather than to go on with marriage decides, perhaps quite rationally, that he cannot marry at this particular time. But his decision may be based on a rationalization of an unconscious fear of women. And this unconscious fear may be based on a whole series of early conflict situations, repressions, and subsequent reductions and partial resolutions by the most varying major and minor mechanisms.

The theories of basic urges, of conflict, of personality structure, and of mechanisms are the cornerstones on which psychoanalysis is constructed. They have been invented as constructs to account for the facts which have been uncovered by psychoanalysis. They help us understand the facts of personality development which will be given in the next chapter.

SUMMARY

1. Psychoanalysis was founded by Freud as a therapeutic method for handling neuroses. From this modest start it has become the most systematic school of psychology during the last fifty years. The chief events in Freud's professional career and in the growth of psychoanalysis were given.
2. The psychoanalytic theory starts with the postulation of basic life and death urges. These give rise to other polarities, such as activity versus passivity and pleasure principle versus reality principle. Frustration of basic urges gives rise to conflicts.
3. The normal adult personality has three dynamic constituent parts: id, ego, superego; three topographical locations; conscious, foreconscious, unconscious. Conflicts between basic urges and the environment are resolved by the dynamic parts working in the topographical regions in an economic fashion.
4. Conflicts are resolved by mechanisms. The major mechanisms are discriminatory decision, repression, conversion, regression, sublimation, reaction formation, and rationalization. The minor mechanisms are transference, identification, introjection, projection, and displacement.

NOTES

1. The rise of fascism has unfortunately hindered the development of the psychoanalytic movement in Central Europe. Particularly since the death of Freud, America has become the center of psychoanalysis. Cf. Alexander (1938).
2. Poetically so-called after the Greek god of love.
3. Poetically so-called after the god of death.

4. In his lectures at the Chicago Institute for Psychoanalysis.
5. Narcissistic from the Greek Narcissus, who fell in love with his own image. All of us are more or less narcissistic.
6. I am indebted to Dr. Franz Alexander's lectures for the idea of these "equations."
7. This proposition of economy has also found adherents in academic psychology. Cf. Wheeler (1932) and Lewin (1935).

10

PSYCHOANALYSIS: THEORY OF PSYCHOSEXUAL GENESIS

1. EVIDENCE FOR THE PSYCHOANALYTIC THEORY

In the last chapter, we saw how the "normal" adult personality was structured and how the various psychological mechanisms brought about resolution of conflicts arising between its different parts. In this chapter, we shall see how the structure of the "normal" adult personality arises. In the technique of psychoanalysis, Freud early came to the conclusion that the symptoms which his neurotic patients showed were related to events from the earliest years of the individual's life. He found first that the symptoms of the adult neurotic were related to frustrations of the libidinal part the erotic instinct. These frustrations occurred as early as the first year and continued through childhood. He was thus led to believe that children showed manifestations of the sexual urges and that any theory of personality genesis must take infantile sexuality into account. After accepting infantile sexuality, Freud gradually developed his theory of psychosexual genesis. By calling the theory that of *psychosexual genesis*, he emphasized the fact that sex has both an organic biological and a psychological aspect. When later he discovered the importance of the destructive urges, he was able to point out how their frustration played an equally important role in personality development. Although the theory is still usually referred to as the theory of psychosexual genesis, the destructive urges and their frustration play such a very great role that it might well be named the theory of psychosexual-aggressivity genesis. The theory of psychosexual genesis is concerned with the frustrations which the basic instincts undergo in childhood.

On the basis of the frustration of the biologically conditioned behaviours of childhood develop not only the psychological characteristics of the mentally ill, but also many of the traits of the "normal" personality. In this chapter, we shall discuss the development of the average individual. Since it will be impossible to give all the evidence on which our findings are based, the nature and the breadth of this evidence should first be outlined. This is particularly important because the belief is still widespread in some circles that psychoanalysis is pretty much a figment of Freud's imagination.

Freud was a great intuitive genius. The original evidence for his theory was based on but a handful of cases analyzed by himself. Freud set up almost all the basic postulates of his theory alone. He soon found adherents, however, and many other individuals were thus analyzed. Today, many thousands have been analyzed, and in the analysis of them certain regularities have been found. The theory originally was based on memories of childhood recovered by neurotic individuals in the course of psychoanalytic treatment. This evidence considered by itself, while very suggestive, cannot be conclusive for two reasons. There is, first, the possibility which critics of psychoanalysis always mention, that suggestion on the part of the psychoanalyst causes the patient to "remember" things which really exist only in the analyst's mind. Secondly, although all modern theories, including the Freudian, suppose that the same mechanisms are at work in the "normal" and "neurotic" mind, it could be that neurotic minds show differences in kind from the normal. Such criticisms were undoubtedly to be taken seriously in the early days of psychoanalysis. Today they are no longer so to be taken because they have been met by many other forms of evidence. We list some of these.

1. Analysis of "Normals"—Besides the neurotics, today hundreds of normals have been analyzed. Most of these are psychiatrists who have undergone an analysis in order to become trained psychoanalysts. (in chapter 3 to 7 we have seen why it is necessary for psychoanalysts themselves to become psychoanalyzed.) The findings in the psychoanalyses of such "normals," although differing somewhat in respect to content, completely confirm the general theory of psychosexual genesis. This overcomes the objection that neurotic development varies essentially in kind from normal development.

2. Observation of the Behaviour of Normal and Neurotic Children—After the theory of psychosexual genesis had been set up, observations of children by psychologists (many of whom were unfavourable to the theory) all pointed to the basic correctness of the theory. It would be misleading to state that all observers are in complete agreement on the detailed points, but the consensus of opinion supports the broad outlines of the theory. Certainly very young babies (under one year of age) show marked libidinal and aggressive attachments to the parents and siblings. That sexual "perversion" is normal in children and is a frequent phenomenon in adults is known to all psychologists. That the vast majority live for a period of time in a family is not debatable. With these facts in mind, the psychoanalytic postulate of infantile sexuality becomes an indispensable one for genetic psychology.[1] Not only professional psychologists but educated lay parents have noticed signs of infantile sexuality. Some of these have been noted by Ieves Hendrick:

Mothers who are not too slavish adherents of the "innocence" myths more often recognize the factuality of Freud's pronouncements than do scientists. They have seen the erections of babies, have noticed the infant's masturbation, have perhaps been amused that when a little girl's hand was removed from her genitals, she put it in her mouth. They have seen the intense curiosity of the child in its excrement, have perhaps felt normal adult disgust at the undeniable fact that a two-year-old would even touch faeces with apparent pleasure. They have observed a boy's pride in a stream of urine. Pediatricians have noted that suckling will often urinate when their most constant attendant picks them up, but not when someone else is holding them. If the mother has not shown too intense displeasure, questions as to sexual differences and reproduction by the infant will be persistent. To those who claim that direct observation of children discloses no curisosity in sexual topics and no pleasure in the body orifices, the analyst can only answer: None so blind as they who will not see," or, because of their own modesty, deny what they do see. And he will realize that child is extraordinarily intuitive, compared with the adult, recognizes immediately a momentary frown, the slightest sign of displeasure, and very rapidly learns to keep his sexuality secret from parents who abhor the notion that it may be manifest in a child.[2]

Such observations overcome the criticism that the results are due to suggestion.

3. Observations in the Field of psychopathology—The study, quite independent of psychoanalysis, of psychotic, sexually perverse, and characterologically disordered individuals has shown quite clearly that by accepting the main outlines of the theory of psychosexual genesis we may best relate these phenomena to each other and to normal behaviour. This aspect of psychoanalysis have already been discussed in in chapter 3 to 7. This observation alone would be only suggestive were it not for the more deeply founded direct psychoanalytic studies. With them it furnishes rather conclusive evidence.

4. Studies of Genius; Studies in the Field of Cultural Anthropology; Studies in the Field of Psychosomatic Medicine—Studies in all these fields show that in its broadest outlines the theory of psychosexual genesis, which was developed by Freud from the personal analysis of a few neurotic patients, is correct. Many modifications have, of course, been made in it in the course of time and there is still some debate about specific points. A vast accumulation of data, however, supports the essential contentions of psychoanalysis.

2. WHY THE "NORMAL" ADULT FINDS PSYCHOANALYSIS HARD TO ACCEPT

Despite the great amount of evidence on which the psychoanalytic theory now rests, the well-adjusted adult on first hearing is still inclined to look on the Freudian theory of psychosexual genesis as somewhat preposterous. This original reaction is a healthy one and quite understandable. It will increase our insight into the theory if we take time to see why this is so.

At the time of its original enunciation the layman's distrust of Freudian psychology was shared by the vast majority of medical men. Freud was considered a rather dirty-minded individual belonging to a decadent and corrupt culture. The chief disturbing factor at this time was the attribution of sexuality to children. In Victorian times even adult sexuality was misunderstood, and with the exception of a few pioneer sexologists like Krafft-Ebing and Havelock Ellis, no one even studied it. Undoubtedly to people then, as now, sex was of the very greatest interest. But it was considered a part of our lower natures, somewhat nasty, and however fascinating a topic for private discussion, not a publicly discussible human function. The heterosexual marriage relationship could be tolerated with reservations, but any other forms of sexual relationship were extremely wicked. Above everything, children were innocent and sexless. Now we have already seen how Freud considered heterosexual attachments between adults as only one specific instance of the general workings of the libidinal element of the life instinct. Libido, let us be reminded, refers to that very general urge to come into close physical contact with other individuals. Not only is the adult heterosexual love relationship libidinal in nature but also parental love, sibling love, and the love of close friendships in the heterosexual as well as the homosexual sense.

We arrive at normal adulthood only through overcoming the infantile sex urges. In the course of normal development, the infant must become weaned, he must be brought to habits of personal cleanliness, he must be broken of the universal habit of infantile masturbation. In the process of weaning, he must renounce his oral sexuality, that is, he must give up his desire for libidinal satisfaction through sucking at his mother's breast. In the process of toilet training, he must learn to control his urethral and anal expulsions. In breaking the habit of infantile masturbation, he must renounce all sexuality for the long period of latency, i.e., from about seven to fourteen. The details of all this follow in the next paragraphs. All these renunciations and subsequent repressions are brought about through conflict and very often are psychologically traunmatic experiences in the life of the child. Once these conflicts are satisfactorily solved, the individual can keep them solved only through complete repression, that is, denial of them. Consequently, it is easy to see that the average normal adult should erect defenses against the reawakening of these severe psychological conflicts. In this, the normal adult is behaving economically just as the abnormal individual is protecting himself from his conflicts by the development of his symptoms. To take but one example: the average adult would be inclined to deny vehemently any pleasurable. Interest in the act of defecation. We shall later see that defecation plays a very important role in some of the psychoses. The mere prevalence of bathroom humor is an indication, however, that the average individual has anal interests. Occasionally, even in the normal individual, attenuated forms of interest in anal behaviour are permitted. In burlesque shows and in chorus dances, the region of the buttocks is exploited on the stage. Children and primitives, like psychotics, to a certain extent are quite willing to admit an interest in the anal regions and in the process of defecation.

Today we find two types of individuals who are inclined vehemently to reject the Freudian theory of psychosexual genesis. The first group includes all those who know nothing about it, and their rejection is quite normal and easily understood. On the other hand, many psychologists and even some psychiatrists are still denouncing the Freudian theory in a polemical fashion. They are exhibiting the well-known factor of "resistance." Even those psychiatrists who are quite ready to attribute infantile sexuality to others usually show resistance when they undergo psychoanalysis themselves.

The layman, and until very recently even the psychologist, is inclined to consider the child only as an incomplete adult. He is inclined to think that the child perceives the world as the adult perceives it, only not so completely, without its finer nuances, and reacts to the world as the adult reacts to it, only less efficiently. This leads to difficulties in understanding child psychology. When psychoanalysis says that the child identifies himself with one of the parents and later introjects the image of his parents as a part of his own personality and identifies this image as a part of himself, the average individual believes this impossible because he himself would not be so confused. All the more recent researches into child psychology not only by the Freudians but also by academic psychologists lead us to believe that the psychobiological organization of the child is quite different from that of the adult. For a long time, we have realized that children are anatomically quite different from adults. Now we realize that these anatomical differences are probably slight compared with the psychological differences. The child is very much less differentiated than the adult and much more of a psychobiological unit. Furthermore, the child does not differentiate the inside world of imagination and the outside world of reality as does the adult. These differences between adults and children fit in well with the Freudian ideas of psychosexual genesis. Knowledge of them makes the theory much more plausible to the average layman. When our modern psychological ideas of the child's personality are better known, one of the chief stumbling block in the way of acceptance of Freud's theory will be removed.[3]

The theory of psychosexual genesis is based not only on the psychoanalysis of adults but on the observations of the simplest and most homely human relationships of childhood. It is an attempt to account for personality as something which develops out of the biological constitution of the newborn child as that child is forced to grow up and meet the reality of the world in which we live and the responsibilities which accrue with increasing independence previous theories all conceived of growth and development as the unwinding of hidden springs within the organism. Freud's theory is field-theoretical because it always considers the interaction of the forces within the organism and the forces of the environment. When the ovum is fertilized by the sperm, an individual is created. To begin with, he is completely dependent on the mother organism. He does not even breathe for himself. At birth he begins to breathe, but all through the nursing stage the mother organism provides him with food. He must learn to eat for himself, to walk, to talk, to control his sphincter muscles, to read and write, and finally to leave the parental home and set up one of his own. Each one of these stages makes him more independent. There are undoubtedly factors of physiological and psychological maturation which "push" him on in this process but there seems also to be some principle of physiological and psychological intertia which makes individuals satisfied with the *status quo* when this is pleasant. Thus growth, both psychological and physiological, is a process which does not unwind automatically but which is brought about by upsetting the equilibrium of the established *status quo*.

Sometimes the duties and responsibilities of the growing-up process are more unpleasant than the pleasures of independence given by growing up and all of us at one time or another long for our childhood. When we are comfortable and satisfied, we are inclined to let things ride. And children are like us in this. Freud showed that we only grow up (i.e., allow ourselves to be "weaned" from dependence on the mother organism first and then on the familial environment) because we are forced to (i.e., our *status quo* is upset). Freud studied objectively and scientifically how we react to the process of being "weaned" not only in the direct and important sense of being weaned from the mother, but in all the other "weanings" we have to go through.

It is amazing that the dynamics of these "weanings" were never studied before. They are the universally homely facts of childhood, but adults still find them hard to accept because the memory of them has been repressed in most of us. The process of personality development in the child is divided by the psychoanalysts into five relatively separate but temporally overlapping stages. These are called the *oral stage*, which is subdivided into the *oral sucking* and *oral biting*. Here the chief psychological frustrations of the child are those of weaning. This is followed by the *anal stage*, again subdivided into *anal expulsive* and *anal retentive*. Here the chief frustrations are those concerned with toilet training. This is followed by the *phallic stage*, where the chief frustrations are those concerned with infantile masturbation. In the *latency period*, which follows, the experiences of psychosexuality are largely repressed. At puberty, psychosexuality again emerges at the *genital stage* and from this time psychosexuality remains conscious.

Many students on first learning that the oral and anal stages are called "psychosexual stages" react with disgust. Many critics including the author feel that he names for these stages were ill-chosen. But here again the student and critic must remember the broad way in which Freud uses "sexuality" and his definition of "libido" in terms of all close human love relationships. With this in mind there should surely be no offense taken when it is pointed out that weaning and toilet training have "libidinal" and "sexual" components. Alexander (1940) has recently suggested that a complete revaluation of the concept of sexuality be attempted, reserving sexual to refer only to the genital aspects of behaviour. Until this is done the widely used terms of "oral" and "anal" must be retained. Once again the reader is asked to keep the very special meanings of these terms in mind during this and the following chapters.

In the following sections, we shall outline the detailed development of these five stages. For each of them, we shall give (1) the name of the stage of development; (2) the approximate age and duration; (3) the libidinal localization,[4] i.e., the bodily organ where most of the libido is located; (4) the libidinal mode, i.e., the manner in which the libido is expended; (5) the libidinal object, i.e., the object on which the libido is cathexized; (6) the frustration which gives rise to conflict; (7) the conflict complex or nature of this conflict; (8) the changes in behaviour resulting from the resolution of this conflict; and (9) the changes in personality resulting from this development. This sequence of data is given schematically in Table 10.1, which is to be found at the end of this chapter. The reader is asked not to refer to this chart, however, until he has followed the development of the oral sucking stage which immediately follows.

3. THE ORAL STAGE

Oral Sucking—The first "weaning" occurs at birth. The newborn child reacts to the frustration of being born with the development of the "independence" of breathing and the "responsibility" of having to do so. Otto Rank (1929) considers birth itself the first and greatest universal human frustration. Most psychoanalysts think that Rank considerably overemphasized the importance of birth but all admit that it may have psychological significance. The nervous system of the child is so relatively undeveloped that it probably has less effect than Rank believes. The psychoanalysts have very much evidence, however, that the behaviour of the child in nursing and in weaning is of the greatest significance for his personality.

The newborn child is a completely helpless individual. We have reasons to believe him to be very undifferentiated as a person. He is largely *id* in the sense used in the last chapter, and has no idea of the *self*, or *ego*, or *conscience*; or *superego*. His wants are few. He wants to be fed when he is hungry, to be kept dry and warm; and approximately the first eight months[5] of his life are concerned with caring for these needs. He is usually fed at the mother's breast, but even in these modern day when breast feeding is becoming more rare, he is generally fed with warm milk and in close physical contact with the mother. The young child probably does not differentiate clearly between breast and artificial feeding. To begin with, he is primarily a physiological organism. When his stomach is empty or when he is cold or when he is uncomfortable from defecation or urination, this physiological status is translated into the first psychological unpleasantness. Feeding at the mother's breast is the most important activity, both physiologically and psychologically, for young child. For this reason, psychoanalysts refer to the period from birth to about eight months as the oral sucking period. The libido is located chiefly in the mouth and oral region: the mode of pleasure finding and hence tension relief is sucking and swallowing. The child has no conscious knowledge of his aggressive urges. He is motivated primarily by the erotic drive, which is localized in the mouth, and his first rather diffuse strivings are for oral satisfaction. For this reason, the child's instinctual life is said to be *preambivalent*. Nor does he distinguish clearly between himself and his mother. His libidinal satisfactions come from his skin and bodily musculature but he has no conscious knowledge of loving himself. His libidinal satisfactions are hence called autoerotic (as opposed to narcissistic). His total attitude is one of passive dependence.

Although some children (low-grade idiots) never progress beyond this stage, the average child is forced by the frustration of weaning to begin develop a differentiated person structure. About the age of eight months, weaning begins to play an important role in the child's life. He is taken from the breast and some, at least, of his food is gained by other methods than sucking. This is a traumatic experience for the child. He has to begin to develop some self-directed activity other than sucking to satisfy his needs. The first crude ideas of outside reality and the first diffuse ideas of himself as an individual develop at this time. At the same time, he develops his teeth and has for the first time an instrument with which he may exhibit aggressive behaviour. Most mother who nurse their children until the teeth are developed are well aware that at about this time the child shows his dissatisfaction at the frustrations of weaning by biting. In this conflict situation, we have the beginnings of what we shall later call the "Oedipus situation." The result of the resolution of the conflict created by the frustration of the purely passive oral sucking behaviour is the development of oral aggressiveness or the oral-sadistic period. This is accompanied by considerable repression. Throughout the oral sucking period, the child is predominatly dominated by the pleasure principle. His personality to begin with is all id in its dynamic aspects and chiefly unconscious in its topographical aspects. At the end of the oral sucking period, the ego begins to emerge and with it consciousness and an extended sense of reality. One must not get the idea that this emergence occurs at exactly eight months or any other definite time. Actually, this is a very gradual process of a dialectical nature.

The chief facts of the early oral period are shown schematically on the chart to be found at the end of this chapter pages (258-260). Column I through 9 give the steps of the psychosexual genesis so far discussed. The reader should next refer to column I of the row marked "oral sucking." Columns to through 12 will be used in connection with the next chapter and columns 13 through 15 in connection with Chapter 3 to 7. The author finds that he can follow the complexity of the psychosexual development as described by psychoanalysis more easily on such a chart. To a certain extent, charts such as this are misleading. The process of psychosexual genesis is a dynamic, dialectical one. It unrolls gradually. On the chart, we can only point out certain static situations at certain chosen times. If one keeps in mind the fact of the gradual transition between stages, however, this chart should be very helpful.

Oral Biting— With the development of teeth, the child can show aggressive behaviour and so enters into a new stage of his development. This lasts from around eight months to around eighteen months. Again, the time limitations vary greatly. One must not get the idea that all the behaviour of the oral sucking stage automatically disappears at eight months or is completely replaced by the oral biting behaviour up to eighteen months. On the contrary, much of oral sucking behaviour remains and certain aspects of even the grown personality and the adult character have already been determined at eight months. In the following chapters, we shall see what many of these traits are. For the present, to give only several examples, let us say that all our eating and drinking behaviour through life represents the continuation of the oral sucking stage, although its form becomes much changed through environmental influences. Thus, eating and interest in food represent oral characteristics. Likewise, the pleasure all of us get from kissing a loved one on the lips originates in the oral stage.

Although certain adaptations to the oral sucking period remain permanently in the personality, new traits emerge and the personality develops further differentiation with the frustration of weaning. In the oral biting stage, the aim or mode of pleasure finding is in biting as well as in sucking and swallowing. The child is motivated not only by the erotic urges of tender sucking but by the aggressive urges of destroying. He becomes ambivalent toward his mother. He loves her as the source of his satisfaction, but at the same time he hates her, because, to a certain extent, she has neglected him in that he is no longer completely dependent on her. We have seen that the oral sucking child was primarily autoerotic. This autoeroticism continues, but we find with the emergence of the ego the appearance of the early narcissism. A child not only loves his body and the comfortable feelings ensuing from it, but he begins to have an idea of himself as an object and part of the libido is directed to himself. Soon after the development of the oral biting stage, the child is finally weaned from the bottle and forced to play an active role in his own food-getting process. Besides this, he is being trained in habits of personal cleanliness throughout this period. Often, at around this time, a second child appears, and we know that the baby has enough of an idea of reality at this time to be jealous of this second child. The combination of the final weaning, the beginnings of training in habits of personal cleanliness, and the possible appearance of a new child represents the second major traumatic experience. The ego becomes even more differentiated from the id and the child is forced to begin to realize that he is not the center of the world, but that there is outside reality which he will have to meet. The effect of the resolution of this complex leads to the strengthening of the ego and further development of the reality principle as a motivating force, although the pleasure principle is still dominant. In many cases, the feeling of "being cheated" develops. The manner in which the child comes through the late oral period is of the greatest importance for his later personality structure and character. The ego in the development has become at least partially differentiated. More of the topography of the person is concerned with consciousness. The British school of psychoanalysis (for instance, M. Klein and E. Glover, 1928) believe that the beginnings of the superego are formed at this time.

In this way, psychoanalysts attribute much of our later character and personality structure to the frustrations of earliest childhood. We should now have a better idea of what is meant by infantile sexuality. Since our original eating behaviour starts out in connection with a libidinal gratification, Freud shows that there are sexual elements even in the process of food getting. From the beginning, the child is a socialized and sexual individual. The evidence, as we saw above, on which our brief outline of the oral stage is based comes from the detailed psychoanalysis of many individuals as well as the supporting observations in many other fields. Those readers who are still incredulous owe it to themselves to read some of the more detailed studies which are referred to in the bibliography appended to this chapter. Table 10.1 may again help the student to follow the intricacies of the oral biting period. Again, it must be emphasized that the chart is able only to pick out certain cross sections of a static nature.

4. THE ANAL STAGE

The Anal Expulsive Period[6]—The average student will find it easier to accept the correctness of the psychoanalysts' ideas about oral development that he will those concerning anal development. The oral period is largely concerned with food getting at the time when the infant is very undifferentiated and where the mode of food getting may be modified. The food getting itself may not be completely frustrated, however, Man must eat if he is to continue to live. Even the partial continuations of oral behaviour are socially more allowable than those of anal behaviour, which we are now about to discuss. Under the proper circumstances, we are all allowed to eat and kiss. Admiration for a pretty mouth is universally acceptable. Our toilet habits are, however, strictly regulated by society. To admit pleasure in defecation is not socially permissible. But we do know that many neurotic and psychotic individuals do get pleasure from the processes of defecation and urination. To admit publicly admiration for the buttocks and anal region is also rarely permissible in our society. Karin Stephen points out that such admiration is quite permissible in some primitive societies and that we have very good reason for believing that the average individual was interested in the buttocks and anal region and received pleasure from urination and defecation during his childhood.

But even the adult receives, under some circumstances, at least a feeling of quite comfortable relief from urination and defecation. All of us have experienced situations when we would like to go to the toilet but where, either through lack of facility or through embarassment, we cannot go immediately. Under such conditions a great deal of visceral tension arises, the relief of which may be actually pleasant. In connection with the oral stage, we saw that the growth of the teeth and the aggressive ability to bite differentiated out of the oral frustrations. The young child to begin with is without sphincter control. The musculature connected with evacuation of the bladder and bowels is at first undifferentiated. Probably the child only experiences evacuation when the visceral tension is very high, so that the normal act of evacuation may bring to the child feelings of relief similar to those which the adult experiences after extreme inhibition of anal function. Children are not by nature cleanly in their personal habits and must, like puppies, be "housebroken." The anal expulsive period *overlaps* with the oral period and occurs from about six months to three years. In the anal expulsive period the aim or mode of pleasure finding is the expulsion of the feces and urine. But the child comes to perceive that parents place great weight on the feces and urine being given to the parent under the proper social situation. The child is often told, "Do something now for mother," or "Make sure that you go to the toilet before we go out." Very early, then urine and feces are seen by the child as something dirty to be gotten rid of, on the one hand, and something valuable to be retained, on the other. Since the ego and sense of reality become well developed at this period, the child comes to feel very powerful in this respect. The morning going to the toilet is so emphasized by many parents that a good bowel movement appears to the child the most important thing in the day's work. It is also something for which he is given rewards. On the other hand, he soon realizes that besides the personal pleasure from urination and defecation and the rewards they bring under the right circumstances, under the wrong circumstances, he may use urination and defecation aggressively. All individuals who have children have noted the almost fiendish glee with which children begin to demand the "potty" under circumstances where a suitable place is not available. Many psychoanalytically wise parents realize that bedwetting is at the same time a pleasure and an aggression.

In the anal expulsive period, autoeroticism continues but becomes predominantly anal in its nature. The narcissism of the oral stage continues likewise. The social frustration is in personal habit training. During this period, the ego becomes well established and the pleasure principle activates only relatively little more of the child's behaviour than does the reality principle. The child has come to what psychoanalysts call "the level of reality testing." At the level of reality testing, the reality principle is strongly enough developed that the child perceives the consequences of giving into the pleasure principle under certain circumstances. From this time on in the normal development, pleasurable acts are generally carried out only insofar as they are not completely irreconcilable with reality. This is an important point to which we shall return later in connection with the distinction between psychotic and neurotic behaviour.

In this period come the beginnings of the formation of the superego, the exact details of which will concern us shortly. In this period there are also the beginnings of the formation of ideas of sex differentiation in the child's mind, the first realization that the child must turn into a person of a definite sex. The Oedipus situation continues to be the chief conflict situation. The little boy has the first beginnings of thinking of himself as a future man, the little girl has to realize that eventually she will have to turn from the mother to the father. The development of the Oedipus situation is so complicated that we shall deal with it separately after developing the rest of the theory of psychosexual genesis. The effect of the social frustration of personal habit training is the development of the anal retentive stage. In these anal frustrations, we have another experience which may be psychologically traumatic. Through anal frustration, we saw that the individual is forced more and more to face reality. He gets his first ideas of ego responsibility. He must stand as an individual in the family.

The Anal Retentive Period—Where the child previously gained pleasure from the expulsion of urine and feces, the child now realizes the social value of retaining, controlling, and possessing them. Furthermore, the child's reasoning is different from ours. A child comes to see the excreta as things of independent value. Although it is hard for us to realize it, there are at this time in the child's thinking certain confusions. Children must learn their own anatomies. Thus all the openings in the body are to a certain extent considered equal; the mouth, the anus, and the vagina are not clearly differentiated. All things extending from the body also become confused. Thus the penis, nipples, and feces are unconsciously equivalent. The feces themselves play a dual rule. They are valuable under certain conditions as gifts; under other conditions, they are dirty and may become insults.

Some of this childhood confusion continues into adulthood. The anal region becomes something valuable and beautiful or something repulsive and used to insult. Thus, the insulting factor of flatus in realized among all individuals. Everyone realizes what is meant by "giving the bird" or "bronx cheer." Practically every language has a colloquialism in which the insulted one is asked to kiss the anal region. On the other hand, if the child, feces properly given represent gifts. Thus, feelings of omnipotence and extraordinary power come from the time when the child first realizes that he can control this all-important process of urination and defecation.

In the period roughly from twelve months to four years, the child comes to personal cleanliness. The final frustration of his anal behaviour occurs at around the fourth year. At this time, still another type of psychosexuality is beginning to be active, namely, genitality. The conflict brought about by the giving up of anal pleasures leads to the resolution of the anal retentive period. In the jump from anal expulsive behaviour to anal retentive behaviour, we have the development of the period of reality testing. The child not only sees reality as something with which he has to meet and as something which is not always friendly, but he realizes that he has to stand alone in a family. He has the first vague realization that not only is he not the center of interest but that father and mother really are perhaps even more interested in each other than they are in him. This is a hard blow for the child to take. He develops into the phallic period, where the "Oedipus" and "castration" situations are worked out and where the child is forced to relinquish infantile sexuality completely. The development of the anal period may also be followed in Table 2 if one keeps the limitations in mind, which we have previously stressed.

5. THE PHALLIC STAGE

Just as the child has to be brought to personal cleanliness, he has to be brought to wear clothes. Nudism is quite a natural phenomenon with young children. Children learn about sex differences at a very early period. They practically always have occasion to see not only brothers and sisters naked, but also to see mother and father naked. Thus, they come to realize the difference between the sexes. Futhermore, often children see mother and father in sexual intercourse and even if they do not actually observe parental intercourse, they soon come to realize something about it. When they are out of the room or put to bed or forced to go and play, it is obvious that something very interesting occurs between the parents. In the early phallic period, the chief aim or mode of pleasure finding turns from the anal region to the genitalia. Just, however, as we saw that the oral period did not cease to exist at the emergence of the anal period, similarly, neither oral nor anal periods cease to exist with the development of the early genital period.

The early genital or phallic period develops dialectically out of the anal period. Some analysts even insert another period, the so-called "urethral period", before it. The process of urination is, under certain circumstances, a pleasant one. Furthermore, it is known that urinary visceral tension very often increases the pleasure of sexuality in adults. Consequently, there is probably a period in the life of both the little boy and the little girl where the pleasure of urination is partially anal (in the technical sense of the word) and partially genital.[7] We know from numerous observations by child psychologists that all children masturabate intermittently during early childhood and that masturbation becomes the most important source of psychosexual satisfaction in the fourth and fifth years the aim in which of pleasure making of the early genital or phallic period is through the touching, the rubbing, and the exhibiting of the genitalia. This phallic interest is primarily narcissistic in character. The child is interested in his own genitalia rather than in those of the opposite sex. Most adult males can remember a period in which they indulged in urination contests and were much concerned with the size of their own and their friends' penises. Similarly, most adult females remember interest in the genitalia of both sexes. Very often children of opposite sexes engage in mutual masturbation, where the little boy is concerned with his penis and the size of it and the little girls is concerned with her lack of a penis. All children know by this time that papa has a big penis and that mama has no penis at all. There is a great deal of confusion in the child's mind as to just how the sex organs function. It is, however, realized by normal children at the fourth or fifth year that the story about the stork is a monstrous lie. Children know that the new child comes out of mama, but how it gets in and how it gets out is another problem. In this period, the child begins to have ideas, however erroneous they may be, about sexuality. He masturbates frequently and begins to wonder what the consequences of sexuality are. For the first time, the child must choose an object for the sexual act and this choice naturally falls on the parents or, in some cases, the siblings. This is not because of any hereditary mechanism but because the parents and siblings are in the life situation of the child. Also, the parents are persons of great power and tremendous prestige to the child. The male child, interested in his penis, cannot help but think, "When I grow up, I shall have a penis like father." The female child very often thinks, "When I grow up, I shall have breasts like mother." In this way children overcome feelings of inferiority. Such solutions to the child's feelings of inferiority are not the only possible ones, however. Both little girls and boys wonder why mother has no penis, while father does have one, and the idea which most frequently occurs to them in connection with this is that originally mother did have one but she somehow lost it. Similarly, little girls often think that they at one time had penises but lost them. The male child tends to think of loss of the penis as a colossally unfortunate possibility; the female tends to think of her penis as already lost. This situation in the male leads to the Oedipus situation, the castration complex, and the repression of infantile sexuality. It leads to the same thing in the female but the sequence of events is somewhat different; we must therefore treat the phallic period of the male and the female separately.

The male has always been dependent on his mother and, when he develops his first ideas of sexuality and its significance, he chooses the mother as a love object. He realizes, however, that the mother is possessed by the father.

He sees the father not only as a potential rival for the mother's affection but also as the possible avenger of his desires on the mother. During this time, his masturbation fantasies often contain the mother as a sexual partner. One must not get the idea that the child necessarily has any precise and exact ideas of what coitus means. He does know, however, that the penis is connected with coitus and that coitus is a highly valued and pleasurable act to the parents. The parents feel they must prevent this infantile interest in genitalia and the ensuing masturbation. He is taught by both the mother and the father to stop masturbating, to "take his hands away from there," "not to play with himself." He is often told the horrible consequences of masturbation, that it is bad and nasty, and in some cases he is even threatened with castration. "If you do not stop playing with yourself, I shall cut it off," says either the father or the mother. The situation arises which is known as the Oedipus situation. The boy loves his mother, wants to possess himself of her, but realizes the consequences of becoming a real rival to his father. The fear of castration frustrates the infantile masturbation in connection with the Oedipus situation and leads to the repression of infantile sexuality. Since the oral and the anal components of sexuality are not completely clearly differentiated from the phallic in the child's mind, this repression of the Oedipus situation carries with it all ideas of infantile sexuality. The male child, however, not only loves the mother but identifies himself with the father. When he grows up, he will be like father; when he grows up, he will have a penis like father. Consequently, he *introjects* a part of the father, particularly that part of the father which tells him that he must give up his infantile sexuality. This becomes the *superego*. Actually, parts of the mother have also been introjected in connection with the prohibitions of anal behaviour. What we call our conscience is actually the voice of the parents saying, "You shall control you bowel movements"; in other words, "You shall do your duty". It is the voice of the parents saying, "You shall not indulge in masturbation"; in other words, "You shall deny sexuality".[8]

Such a solution to the Oedipus and castration complexes is called the *positive* solution of the problem This is the normal one and leaves the child in the so-called "latency period," where sexuality remains in the unconscious, so that he may grow up and become civilized and eventually take over the role of the father in his own family. Very often, however, we have the reverse of this process. The male child chooses the father as love object, considers the mother as rival, identifies himself with the mother. In such cases, we have the basis for the development of adult male homosexuality rather than adult male heterosexuality.

By the castration complex, psychoanalysts understand much more of infantile behaviour than is shown in the fear of actual castration. The castration complex covers the fears of all sorts of painful retaliation on the part of the parents because of the sexual and aggressive wishes of childhood. The male child, as well as the female, is always bisexual and fears the loss of his father's love as well as the actual punishment by the father for his attachment to the mother. Possessive love in the child leads to jealousy, which leads to imagined aggressions, which lead to the fear of punishment (castration as only one form) for imagined aggressions and fear of loss of the love of the one who is the object of the aggressions. The castration complex refers to this whole behaviour situation. Freud called it the castration complex because in its most severe pathological manifestations it is always actual castration which is feared. Although actual castration may rarely be threatened in our society, in some societies it is not only threatened but practised. That adult males place a higher value on their sexual organs than on any other is so obvious a fact to the honest individual that it needs no particular demonstration.[9]

The outcome of the Oedipus and castration situations in the female is of the same import as it is in the male but follows a slightly different sequence. The female also develops superego, which prevents her from continuing to indulge in infantile masturbation and which protects her against sexuality until society permits it after the period of adolescence. In general, we may say that the little girl reverses the procedure in that she has masturbatory fantasies about the father and considers the mother the potential rival. It is the mother's warning voice which is incorporated into the mind of the girl through the process of introjection and becomes her superego. The first libidinal cathexis, however, for the little girl is the same as for the little boy. In the oral and anal stages, it is the mother more than the father who is the source of all good things in her environment. Consequently, we see that the Oedipus situation in the female starts out with a love of the mother. The same interest is sexuality which characterizes the little boy, however, characterizes the little girl. She also wonders as to why she is different and why she has no penis. Adler has pointed out that it is normal for the little girl to have a *penis envy*. At the urethral period, she also gets sexual excitement through urination and begins infantile masturbation. Her growing knowledge of sexuality convinces her that she may no longer choose the mother as a sexual object, but now must choose her father. Unconsciously, a penis may have the same value as a child. Thus, the girl begins to see in the possibility of having a child a compensation for her loss of a penis. Her masturbatory fantasies, then, are concerned normally with imagined intercourse, but again one must not suppose that the child knows precisely what happens in intercourse with father or that as a result she will have children. Most little girls at this age not only want children, but if allowed to express their desire want many children. The repression of the Oedipus situation through the fear of its consequences occurs much more slowly in the girl child than in the boy. The girl child is also taught that she must give up her infantile masturbation because of threatened loss of love if she continues it. The superego in the girl in the normal outcome of the Oedipus situation, then, is the mother identification through introjection. The voice of the conscience is the carry-over of the voice of the parents saying," You must be clean anally; you must do your duty," and the voice of the parents saying, "You must stop your infantile masturbation, you must give up sexuality if later you are to have children." Thus, as the male conscience makes the individual active and dutiful and causes him to inhibit his sexual functions to fit into the rules of society, the female conscience does the same thing.

As the little boy may go through the Oedipus situation in a negative fashion, so may the little girl. In this case, the little girl wants to be like her father and identifies herself with her father in order that she may love or be loved by someone like her mother. This is important in the development of female homosexuality and we shall return to it later.

The Oedipus and castration complexes of girls are not nearly so well understood as those of boys. We have developed the theory along the lines that Freud, himself, adopted. Freud's theory of female sexuality has been widely and probably correctly criticized. There is probably more controversy as to the exact sequence of the development and resolution of the female Oedipus situation than on any other theoretical point in psychoanalytic literature. In a book of this nature, we cannot go into the details of these controversies. In the bibliographical note appended to this chapter, references to the literature are given.

As in the case of the oral and the anal periods, certain aspects of phallic genitality continue in the structure of the adult personality and the adult character. In the next chapter, we shall give many examples of these.

6. THE LATENCY PERIOD

From the fifth to the seventh year, because of the fear of the social consequences, infantile sexuality is gradually repressed, and for a period of about five or six years the individual is not consciously concerned with sexual matters. Such repression as occurs in the latency period is seldom complete and is never sudden. All of us can remember some interest in sexuality through this period. At the age of thirteen or fourteen, sexuality emerges again. Before psychoanalytic theory, it was considered that sexuality was a slowly maturing part of the personality and had its first emergence at this time. The period between five years and puberty is called the "latency period." In this period, the infantile sexuality is repressed and reaction formations strengthen this repression. The libidinal urges are sublimated in the process of education. This period is that of the most rapid formal learning. Most children undergo all the schooling they are to receive in this time. But, perhaps of even more importance, they learn how to behave in society and to have ideals. Eroticism and narcissism decrease in the latency period, but libidinal attachments to parents, teachers, and friends continue although there is little overt libidinal striving toward them. The little boy rarely thinks during this period of kissing or playing affectionately with his schoolmates. Some disguised libidinal energy gains outlet through "roughhousing" and in all sorts of games. But the little boy is embarrassed by show of affection on the part of his parents, particularly in public places. He seems, on the surface, to be without heterosexual or homosexual libido. The same is true of the little girl, although she gets into the latency period at a later time and emerges from it earlier than boys do. Girls generally are more affectionate through this period than are boys. The psychoanalysts explain the reason for this in that the girl has accepted her castration whereas the boy still fears his. Some individuals never really give up their infantile masturbation. Some boys know all about sex and think about sex during this period. Some girls do likewise. Otherwise, we could not account for either the sexual perversions or the development of certain forms of erotic behaviour in adulthood. Studies of social anthropologists show us that this latency period is not inherent in biological nature, but is rather an artifact of our particular patriarchal civilization. In some cultures, there is no latency period. Our culture, in which the educational process is so important, requires it.[10]

The repressed libidinal urges remain sources of unconscious conflict. In order to prevent the strong libidinal urges from becoming conscious, it is necessary to develop reaction formations against them. Reaction formations occur in the development of what for lack of a better term may be called the "Sunday-school mind." Children through this age are very goody-goody, prudish, and apt to criticize any of the social "vices" of their parents, like smoking, drinking cocktails, and the use of make-up. They become girl and boy scouts, do a good deed everyday, and feel very superior morally.

In the story of Snow White we have a beautiful allegory about the latency period. Let us review the story briefly. Snow White is a beautiful child princess whose widowed father has taken a second wife. This second wife is the "fairest lady in the land" and is possessed of a magic mirror which convinces her of this. As Snow White grows a little older, however, the mirror warns the stepmother that Snow White will become more beautiful than she. This excites the queen's envy and she plans to have Snow White done away with. She gives Snow White into the hands of a huntsman, commanding him to kill the child. Snow White prevails upon the huntsman, however, to free her in the woods, where she is taken care of by seven little dwarfs who work underground. The stepmother learns from the mirror of Snow White's continued existence with the dwarfs and tries agains to kill her. After several unsuccessful attempts, she succeeds, not in killing Snow White, but in putting her into a comatose state. The dwarfs, however, keep Snow White in a beautiful coffin for seven years. She does not die but remains in a deep unconscious sleep. At the end of seven years, the wicked queen is dead and the fairy prince comes with a sword with which he opens the casket and takes Snow White to be his bride.

A complete analysis of the Snow White fantasy would take us rather far afield. We wish merely to concentrate on showing that the Snow White fantasy is simply a fairy story about the latency period. The central theme of the story is quite obvious. Snow White awakens after a long sleep and is free to marry the prince. In the long sleep, she is guarded by seven dwarfs. These seven dwarfs represents the seven years of the latency period. They are dwarfs, underground creatures, indicating that Snow White, i.e., female sexuality, is underground, in the background, or repressed for seven years. The actual awakening is brought about by a prince bearing a sword, with which he raps on the coffin. The prince is the symbol, of course, of masculine sexuality, the sword representing the penis. After the seven-year sleep, i.e., after the latency period, Snow White can be happy and marry the prince. After the latency period, sexuality is again permissible.

But what put Snow White to sleep? In this case, it was the jealous stepmother, the queen. Actually, of course, in psychoanalytical theory, it is the true mother, the rival for the father's affection. Undoubtedly in the original storyteller's mind, the reaction formation against attributing hostile influences toward the daughter by the real mother was so strong that a stepmother was chosen to play this role.[11] The situation is that of the normal married relationship of father, mother, and child. In dreams and in fairy stories, kings represent fathers, queens represent mothers, and princes or princesses represent the children. The jealousy of the stepmother represents the probably normal feeling in this story of an older woman approaching the period when she must renounce her own sexuality. At all events, mother-daughter jealousies occur quite as frequently in real life as they do in fairy stories. The huntsman who is commanded to cut out Snow White's heart represents the threat of castration in this story. This analysis is easy because the equivalent of heart and sexuality is one which occurs in practically every language in the world. The phrase," I give my heart to you," is a euphemism indicating a real or wished-for surrender in the sexual sphere. The pleading on Snow White's part with the huntsman represents the renunciation of sexuality in the face of the castration situation. "If I live with the dwarfs (i.e., if I give up sexuality) for this period of time, then I can still go on living (i.e., I can preserve my sexuality until later)." The subsequent visits of the queen in disguised form and the attempts on Snow White's life by the queen may be taken to represent the fact that the latency period, particularly in females, is not brought about by a single traumatic situation but rather occurs over a period of time.

If we attribute the symbolic value of the family in general to Snow White's family and the symbolic value of female sexuality to Snow White herself, the fantastic meaning of the tale is apparent. The immense popularity of fairy tales of this sort with children is due to the fact that the children, at least semiconsciously, make the symbolic identifications to which we refer. If Snow White were an isolated fairy story on this theme, one might think that the resemblance between the story and the actual events of the latency period was completely fortuitous. The same type of symbolism, however, with regard to the inner personal relations between members of the family and in the family situation is the basic structure of all fairy tales. A little consideration of various fairy tales in the light of what the reader now knows of psychoanalytic theory will convince him of the truth of this statement. The chief points about the latency period are summarized in Table 10.1. These may be again viewed only as a picture of the average static cross section at about nine years of age.

7. THE GENITAL STAGE

At the age of puberty one gets the gradual revival of all of the infantile sex stages. In the normal case, the revival of the phallic stage predominates but gradually this phallic interest turns into real genital interests, which are less infantile than those of the phallic stage. Revival of oral and anal interests also occurs. Children begin to show an interest in kissing and in games like post office. They have a decided revived interest in anal stories and anal behaviour. It is actually *in* the boy scout troop very often that the individual boy learns the four-letter Anglo-Saxon words. The threat of castration still lies heavily over the individual, however, and the first object choice is usually homosexual. Most boys at this age enagage either in mutual masturbation or in social masturbation. By social masturbation is meant masturbation in the company of others. The fact that attachments are homosexual at this time is not due to any inherent biological nature, but rather is due to our social mores in segregating our children at this age. At first, there usually develops a feeling of antagonism toward the opposite sex. All of us remember the disdain with which we viewed the first of our "gang" to become "girl crazy." All of us remember the embarrassment which we felt about our first puppy-love affairs. Gradually, however, society allows the outlet for sexual behaviour at the adult level. Such an outlet is not established at once. Kissing games and necking parties become quite permissible, provided they do not go too far. Interest in dirty jokes becomes part of the process of adolescence. The first love affairs remain phallic rather than truly genital in nature. In the phallic phase, as we saw, the narcissistic components are particularly strong. The individual is chiefly concerned with himself as lover. In the true genital phase, this narcissism is replaced by real object love: the individual is chiefly concerned with the love object. The adolescent individual is concerned with satisfying his own sexuality rather than with giving love. The boy wishes to convince himself that he is a man, or the girl wishes to convince herself that she is a woman. Gradually, however, around eighteen to twenty years, true adult normal heterosexuality emerges. The individual who arrives at this is allowed by society to start an actual sexual relationship and start the familial history over again. This development may, again, be followed in Table 10.1 if the limitations we have continually stressed are kept in mind.

8. SUMMARY: RESUME OF THE DEVELOPMENTAL PROCESS

The Freudian theory of psychosexual genesis is very complex. By the time we have discussed normal behaviours conditioned in the process of psychosexual genesis, which we do in the next chapter, and the light which this theory throw on the psychiatric syndromes, which we shall do in Chapter 3 to 7, the reader will undoubtedly understand it more clearly than he does now. At the present time, it may help to clarify the theory of psychosexual genesis to give a resume of the chief frustrations and their resultants in a somewhat condensed form.

In every normal life, there are four chief frustrating experiences, experiences in which the individual has to give up a mode of adjustment which was satisfactory to him and accept a new type of adjustment. In each such readjustment, the individual accepts more responsibility but he gains more independence. With the acceptance of reality and responsibility come privileges and rights and power, so that one must not look on frustration as a negative process. With these frustrations comes also the differentiation of the

TABLE 10.1*
THEORETICAL NORMAL DEVELOPMENT

Name	*Age*	*Libidinal Localization*	*Libidinal mode*	*Libidinal object*
1	2	3	4	5
Oral sucking	Birth to 8 mos.	Mouth, lips, tongue	Sucking, swallowing Introjection Preambivalent	Autoerotic Passive, dependent
Oral biting	6 to 18 mos.	Teeth, jaws	Biting, devouring, destroying Sadistic introjection Ambivalent	Autoerotic and narcissistic Oral-sadistic attachment to mother
Anal expulsive	8 mos. to 3 yrs.	Anus and buttocks	Expelling, rejecting, destroying Projection Ambivalent	Continued narcissism and attachment to parents
Anal retentive	12 mos. to 4 yrs.	Anus, buttocks sphincter control urethra	Retaining and controlling feces and urine Ambivalent	Continued narcissistic and anal-sadistic attachment to both parents
Phallic	3 to 7 yrs.	Urethra and outer genitalia Clitoris and penis	Urinating Infantile masturbation Ambivalent	Oedipus choice on ambivalent level
Latency	5 to 12 yrs.	No new zone Old zones denied	Repression and reaction formation	Decline of autoeroticism and development of social feelings
Genital	12 to 20 yrs.	Genitalia	Coitus Postambivalent	First homosexual crushes, hero worship, then heterosexual sex objects

* This table was combined with some modification from the similar ones of Abraham (1927), Healy, Bronner, and Bowers, Rickman (1928a), and an unpublished table of W.C. Menninger.

TABLE 10.1 (Continued)

Frustration conflict	*Complex*	*Behavioural results*	*Structural results*
6	7	8	9
Weaning	Beginnings of Oedipus complex Mother choice of both sexes	Development of oral aggressiveness Ambivalence	Pleasure principle overwhelmingly predominant Practically all id and unconscious
Final weaning New child	Continuation of ambivalent Oedipus complex Mother choice of both sexes	First consciousness of reality Feeling of being cheated Anal interest	First development of reality sense; emergence of ego and conscious
Necessity of sphincter control	Continuation of ambivalent Oedipus complex Realization of sexuality Both sexes conscious of father	Social reality Feeling of power Development of sphincter control	Reality of growing importance Ego definitely developed Beginnings of superego (level of reality testing)
Need to accept social reality and complete sphincter control	Castration in girl Beginnings of positive Oedipus in boy	Development of interest in genitalia	Reality overbears pleasure Ego development essentially complete Beginnings of identification and superego
Threat of castration for infantile masturbation	Castration in boy and renunciation in girl	Repression of infantile sexuality	Reality established Superego complete Id repressed into unconscious
Behavioural problems of late childhood	Superego conflicts of late childhood	"Boy and girl scout" behaviour	Establishment of superego
Puberty	Adolescent homosexuality	Adolescent masturbation Interest in opposite sex	Reemergence of pleasure principle and id drives Personality complete

TABLE 10.1. (Continued)

Normal behaviour formation			*Sysmptom formation*		
Continuations	*Sublimations*	*Reaction formations*	*Psychosis or neurosis*	*Perversion*	*Character defect*
10	*11*	*12*	*13*	*14*	*15*
Drinking Eating (chewing) Smoking Kissing Oral hygiene, etc.	Wine testing Epicureanism Oratory Wit Sarcasm, etc.	Food faddism Dislike of milk Prohibition enthusiasm Purism in speech continual visiting of dentists, etc.	Schizophrenia Manic-depressive	Passive oral-inversion Active oral-sadism	Schizoid Narcissistic Infantile Cycloid
Interest in daily bowel movement Constipation, diarrhoea Erotic pleasure in defecation "Chic Sale literature," anal stories, etc.	Painting Sculpture Philanthropy Statistical studies, etc.	Disgust with feces Excessive fear of dirt Prudishness Pedantry Parsimony Petulance, etc.	Paranola Compulsion neurosis	Passive anal-inversion Homosexuality Active anal-sadism	Paranoid Compulsive
Masturbation Narcissistic dating Petting Dirty jokes Dancing, etc.	Love poetry Acting Sacred love, etc.	Puritanism regarding sex Modesty, etc.	Anxiety hysteria Conversion hysteria	Phallic narcissism Exhibitionism, voyeurism Nymphomania Satyrisis	Neurotic Hysterical
The continuations, sublimations, and reaction formations of the latency period include all the others in a socially modified form.					
Normal sex life	Renunciation of sex for art, science, society Rejection of sexuality	Socially constructive work	At the gential level there are no symptoms found		

personality and the development of special abilities. The first great frustration is the frustration of the passive oral feeding habit. The infant is happy, the center of attention, taken care of, everything done for him: psychobiologically he is in a state of either continual equilibrium or easy return to equilibrium. The frustration of adjustment through weaning leads him to differentiate something of his ego and to realize that there is an outside world.

Even after he has developed his ego, however, he has no ego responsibility. He simply has to be more active and less passive. Finally, the frustrations at the anal level lead him to develop ego responsibility. This is perhaps even a greater frustrating experience than the first. The first leads him to realize that he has an ego, that he is someone. The frustration at the anal level forces him to realize that he has to do something about it, that he has ego responsibility, that he is not the center of the world but only a part of it, that he stands as an individual. He is forced to see that adjusting to social and physical reality is as important a part of the scheme of things as is the pursuit of pleasure. His ego is virtually completed at this time.

The next great shock is that of phallic frustration. The individual is already partially socially responsible but he still derives all his erotic satisfaction within the family. He only has to meet the reality of the family world until this time. Ego responsibility has been developed but not superego responsibility. We raise our children in the intimacy of the family situation and suddely tell them that they can have no real libidinal satisfaction in this. This is a colossal blow to the ego's self-regard and it requires a colossal expenditure of psychic energy to establish a new equilibrium. This new equilibrium is established through the resolution of the Oedipus and castration situations. As the oral stage led to the development of a sense of reality and the beginnings of the ego, and as the anal stage led to the development of ego responsibility and a more developed sense of reality, the phallic stage may be said to lead to the development of superego responsibility. The individual now must stand alone within society and the world at large rather than the immediate family.

The next great frustration is that of adolescence. Even before psychoanalytic theory was established, it was known how important adolescence was in developing the personality. The family circle and family ties must at this time be broken. The individual must accept complete sociosexual responsibility as well as ego and superego rsponsibility. Freud's great importance with regard to adolescence was in pointing out that the roots of adolescent conflict go back to the infantile period. Growth and education are the processes whereby the completely passively independent, undifferentiated, unconscious id of the baby grows to be the highly differentiated responsible, conscious personality structure which contains the ego, id, and superego of the adult. This growth is a gradually developing, dialectical process. An adjustment at any level is replaced by a new adjustment on repeated frustration. The four frustrations we have just described, namely, oral, anal, phallic, and genital, are not the only frustrations the individual has to meet. He must learn to walk, to talk, to do his schoolwork, and a host of other things, but they are, as should be clear now, of a peculiarly severe nature in our culture and occur at critical stages in the individual's life.

NOTES

1. *Cf.* the works of Klein, A. Freud (1928), and Isaacs.
2. Ives Hendrick, Facts and *Theories of Psychoanalysis,* Alfred A. Knopf, Inc., New York, 1939, pp. 62g-62h.
3. Concerning the differences in structure between the child and adult, compare the well-known treatises of child psychology by non-analytic psychologists like Lewin (1935), Anderson, Piaget (1926), as well as those of psychoanalysts.
4. Actually the designation "libido" should always be understood as referring to *libidinal and aggressive* impulses. The nomenclature of the psychosexual theory was pretty well established when Freud introduced the concept of the death instinct. Cf. p. 158.
5. Throughout this section, the time designations given are the average ones, and one must keep in mind that for the specific individual there is often considerable variation in these.
6. Dr. Franz Alexander (in his lectures at the Chicago Institute for Psychoanalysis) is inclined to place the anal retentive period before the anal expulsive period. We follow the designations of Abraham (1927), who first made the distinctions. The mere fact of this slight disagreement between two such eminent psychoanalysts indicates only the overlapping nature of these various periods and the dialectical nature of psychosexual genesis.

7. *Cf.* Ferenczi's fascinating, if highly speculative work, *Thalassa* (1938).
8. Actually the child is subjected to many other influences than the parental. Siblings, uncles and aunts, pre-school teachers, and playmates all play a role in the formation of the superego. The influence of the parents is so great, however, that Freud stressed it perhaps even too exclusively.
9. For a good review and somewhat different treatment of the castration complex, compare the paper of Alexander (1935).
10. Cf. Margaret Mead (1932) and Anna Freud (1929).
11. In the greatest English literary creation about the Oedipus situation, Shakespeare's *Hamlet*, the protagonist fights the stepfather, not the father. This is an example of artistic distortion through sublimation.

11

PSYCHOANALYSIS: SUMMARY, CRITICISM

1. SUMMARY OF THE PSYCHOANALYTIC THEORY

We have developed the psychoanalytic theory in its systematic aspects. In this chapter, we shall have something critical to say about it. Much may be said quite justifiably about the form in which the theory has been expressed; undoubtedly even some of the content of the theory stands in need of revision. But the fact remains that through the work of Freud and his chief followers, we have the only systematized theory of psychology which accounts for both the normal and the deviate forms of total human behaviour. Academic psychologists on the whole have dealt with problems which are, to be sure, psychological problems but still only part problems of the integrated behaviour of organisms. No matter how important for both physiology and neurophysiology the work in perception has been, or no matter how important for both pedagogy and theoretical biology the work on learning has been, the fields which have been most thoroughly investigated by the academic psychologists have little to do with the deep problem of personality structure and genesis. Recently, it is true, some of the experimental psychologists, most notably Lewin and his colleagues, have begun to concern themselves in this field, and their work, together with that of other academic psychologists which has implications for psychopathology, will be discussed in the final chapter of this book.

Psychoanalysis is a method of observation, a psychotherapy, and a system of psychology. We have so far presented in detail only its systematic aspects. This system may be divided into several parts and for review we can do no better than take up these parts separately and show how they are related. The *theory of the basic urges* is that part of the Freudian theory which deals with the dynamics underlying all human behaviour. The basic urges of a constructive sort (the erotic impulses, the tender impulses, the building-up impulses) and the basic urges of a destructive sort (aggressive impulses, hostile impulses, tearing-down impulses) are to be considered biologically determined and innate. They are present in man from birth and are probably never clearly differentiated. As long as there is enough constructive force to neutralize sufficiently the aggressive force, man goes on more or less well adjusted to his life situation. When the aggressive urges outweigh the erotic urges, sickness and maladjustment ensue. How this may occur is shown in the theory of *conflict*. According to the theory of conflict, from birth until death these basic urges must meet with blockage and frustration imposed partly by the real physical forces of nature, but even more drastically by the social structure. In order to preserve society, man must learn to curb both his erotic and his aggressive urges. In a dialectical fashion, this brings about changes in the structure of the personality, which is thus to be considered as conditioned by the way in which the organism meets frustration. If the basic urges are the *sources* of energy for human behaviour, the form of this behaviour is constantly modified by the conflict. Freud has some define ideas as to what happens in a conflict situation, that is, some ideas about the possible ways in which conflict may be resolved. The behaviour of resolution will have some significance with regard to the life history of the individual and the method of resolution will be economical when we consider the individual as a psychobiological unit.

A third great part of the psychoanalytical theory is concerned with the *structure of the normal adult personality*. It supposes that the normal adult individual furnishes w ai

Freud has called dynamic problems, topical problems, and economic problems. Nornal adult life is made up of the control of the basic dynamic urges by the dynamic aspects of the personality: the ego, the superego, and the id. These dynamic forces come to final economical reequilibration by working out conflicts in the various topographical parts of the self: the unconscious, the foreconscious, and the conscious. The next important subdivision of the Freudian theory is the *theory of psychosexual genesis*. It is concerned with the normal sequence of events through which, from the undifferentiated primitive organism of the infant, the normal adult emerges. It is also concerned with the possible development of abnormal personality traits. In general, this process of growth is a dialectical one, in which the frustration of some form of behaviour leads to growth and differentiation of the personality, so that succeeding frustrations are on a higher level. Thus, the frustration of passive oral behaviour in weaning leads to the development of aggressive oral behaviour. In turn, the two stages of anal behaviour are developed. The frustration of anal sexuality leads to the development of phallic genitality, the frustration of phallic genitality leads to the latency period, which is overcome by the reactivation of sexuality at puberty.

TABLE 11.1
SHOWING HOW VARIOUS BEHAVIOURAL CATEGORIES ARE EXPLAINED BY THE VARIOUS PSYCHOLOGICAL VIEWPOINTS

	Psychosis	*Neurosis*	*Perversion*	*Disordered Character*	*Genius*
Theological and unenlightened lay views	Punishment by God for sinning	Nervousness	Sinners	Sinners and ornery	Inspired by God
Lay-view point	Result of bad heredity and emtional strain	Nervousness	Sinners	Sinners and ornery	Poetic inspiration
Orthodox psychiatric viewpoint	Constitutional inferiority plus behavioural strain	Constitutional inferiority and nervous strain	Heredity or bad conditioning or not a problem	Heredity or bad conditioning or not a problem	Not a problem
Psychoanalytic viewpoint	All are explained as various ways in which internal conflict achieves economic resolution through personality restructurization.				

The theory of psychosexual genesis leads directly to the understanding of normal modes of behaviour and personality traits on the one hand and the theories of psychoanalytical psychiatry on the other. We have so far considered the normal personality and psychopathologies of everyday life and dreams. In Chapter 3 to 7, the theories of psychoanalytic psychiatry will be presented.

In general, with a good constitution and or not too adverse environmental of a normal adult personality, a moderately happy individual who lives the average span of years. Given a less favorable constitution and or a more unfavorable environment, we may have the development of a mentally ill individual, a sexual pervent, a disordered character, or a genius. Psychoanalysis thus presents a theory which deals with nearly all psychological problems of a vital sort. Only when we think of the popular and even of the older scientific psychiatric theories of all these behaviour forms can we realize what great advances the psychoanalytic theory has made. In table 11.1 we give briefly the explanations assigned to these various behaviour forms from the layman's view and in the older types of psychiatry.

From this table, we see how the mystical, prescientific ideas of personality structure are changed into the integrated, systematic presentation of Freud. The exact mechanisms through which these various types of mental abnormality develop may only be given in the following chapters. Although the framework for a completely integrated and systematized theory of normal and abnormal behaviour has been laid down by the works of Freud, many details remain to be clarified. We have, however, the basis for building a systematized science.

2. CRITICISM OF PSYCHOANALYSIS

Psychoanalysis has been criticized on the most varied grounds. Much of this criticism has been that of morally incensed individuals, who, without, understanding anything of what Freud means by sex, have attempted to show that psychoanalysis is "immoral," "wicked," "nasty." From our foregoing presentation, it should be quite obvious that the theory is none of these things. Consequently, we shall not deal with this type of criticism.

Another form of criticism, with which we shall also not deal in detail, comes from a basic misunderstanding of the role of biological factors in psychoanalysis. It is claimed that psychoanalysis has no place for physical, hereditary, or constitutional factors. Such a misunderstanding could only arise in the minds of individuals who have never read Freud. The theory is actually a *psychobiological* one and Freud stresses this in all his works. Other critics have censored Freud for not allowing sociological or cultural factors and role in his theory of personality determination. Since, however, the superego is almost completely sociologically determined, this type of criticism is also not to be taken seriously. The theory is thus actually a *socio-phycho-biological* one. Besides these popular misconceptions, many of the criticisms by academic psuchlogists and orthodox psychiatrists have been based on either an incomplete or a distorted understanding of some of the basic postulates. Psychoanalysis, like all healthy theories, has undergone continued change and modification in the last fifty years. It should be obvious that even today in some of its aspects it is more complete than in other aspects, that many loopholes remain, that many problems are only partially understood. We must say of the Freudian theory that even if it does not have all the answers, it does pose all the questions. Posing the questions in a scientific fashion represents a colossal advance over what nineteenth century psychology and psychiatry were able to do.

We believe that Freudian mechanisms function in contemporary society and in very much the way that Freud claims they do. Anyone who has had any extended experience with psychotic and psychoneurotic patients, anyone who has really talked with homosexuals, anyone who has known the criminal and other perverse character types after having obtained a good theoretical background in psychoanalysis will be convinced of the basic correctness of the content of Freudian theory. Some aspects are more easily understood and seen as correct than others. Perhaps to the average individual the psychology of the anal period is the hardest to understand. The normal, healthy individual, on first hearing about it, is inclined to say, "This is preposterous stuff and nonsense." Of course, psychoanalysts have pointed out why the normal individual finds this preposterous. The normal individual has in early childhood repressed his interest in anal sexuality. But anyone who has had close contact with an individual suffering from compulsion neurosis or one who is paranoiac or homosexual cannot fail to see the Freudian theory verified time and time again almost to its minutest details in the behaviour of the individual concerned. The mechanisms which Freud has uncovered undoubtedly occur not only in the mental patient, but in all of us.

If, then, we are in general agreement that the facts accounted for by the Freudian theory are in order, we must turn to the formal aspect of the Freudian theory and its underlying basic postulates. Many modern scientists who accept the facts and their interrelationships as uncovered by Freud are very critical of Freud as a methodologist. The whole Freudian theory is based on the theory of basic urges, and these urges are almost equuivalent to the instincts of the nineteenth century biologist. Freud, himself a medical man, naturally accepted the prevalent view of the nineteenth century that there were biologically founded innate reaction tendencies or instincts. Of course, he advanced considerably beyond usually accepted instinct theory. At the time of Freud's earliest papers everyone accepted without any question the existence of instincts for self- and race-preservation. Freud's own writings, perhaps more than those of any other modern scientist, have given us reasons for doubting the nineteenth century theory of human instincts. Freud early showed that besides the components of the libido which lead to heterosexual fixations, all of us have libidinal components which are homosexually directed. In cases of explicit homosexuality we find an individual whose sex behaviour completely invalidates the idea of an instinct for race preservation. Consequently, with regard to this aspect of nineteenth century biological theory, we may say, following Freud's theory, that individuals are instinctively race-preservative or instinctively race-destructive. Before Freud's time the biologist, insofar as he was concerned with homosexual behaviour at all, was inclined to consider it as a morally reprehensible perversion and an abnormality quite beyond the normal laws of development. Consequently, it was great methological advance when Freud insisted that the aberrant forms of sexual behaviour must be covered by the same basic principles which cover the normal forms. In so doing, he was himself beginning to dig the grave of biological-instinct theory. With the instinct for self-preservation, Freud and his followers early discovered the self-destructive and the aggressive aspects of behaviour, which even the most normal of us exhibit at some time of other Consequently, again we can only say that man is either self-preservative or self-destructive. The now widely acknowledged fact that there is no human behaviour trait which is solely biologically or hereditarily conditioned has led most modern biologists to give up instinct completely as an explanatory mechanism. Today we still use the term "instinct" to describe certain primarily biologically conditioned, innate, and teleological behaviour patterns. But we do this with the realization that whatever behaviour actually occurs is a function of the biological organism in an environment whose social, psychological, and political characteristics must also be taken into consideration.

The psychoanolytic theory of basic urges has never been thought through to its complete logical consequences by Freud or most of his followers. If we are tosay that behaviour is either self-preservative or self-destructive, or race-preservative, or race-distructive, we might as well say that there are no basic instincts which lead to definite behaviours quite independent of the existing environment. Freud, in accepting the best biological theory of his time, continued to build on this and modified it without definitely submitting it to a through methodological reconsideration. When we do this, we find that the theory of basic urges must be modified. Today most academic psychologists and even many of the psychoanalysts are inclined to accept the facts of erotic and aggressive behaviour but to attribute these behaviours to the total socio-psychobiological field. This is a matter of more than academic interest and has definite implications for psychotherapy, sociological theory, and social philosophy. To take only one example: If the theory of destructive instincts is correct in that one of the components of aggressivity is the wish to kill, the control of this instinct both in the individual and in society would be almost impossible. Some psychoanalysts have contended, basing their arguments on the instinct theory, that war is inevitable and socialism impossible. If on the other hand the wish to kill, which we must honestly admit as a real psychological fact, develops in the social field through frustration of constructive impulses, then change in the educational and social system might divert aggressivity into socially more acceptable forms. Actually, it is implicit in the hope of psychoanalysis that through individual therapy this can be done. Actually, the methodological shortcomings of the theory of basic urges are by no means insurmountable, and there is no reason why the acceptance of a field-theoretical interpretation of the behaviour covered by the concept of instincts in any way invalidates the correctness of the intercorrelations of behaviour which the psychoanalysts have observed.

Methodologically, it is also difficult to accept the theory of the double tripartite division in the structure of the normal adult personality. From all the more recent studies in genetic psychology, it is quite obvious that the process of growth does consist in the differentiation of more complex wholes out of more primitive units. The concept of the unconscious as opposed to that of the conscious results necessarily from what we know about not only psychopathology but normal psychology as well. But the idea of the strict division into conscious, foreconscious, and unconscious as definitely bounded topographical regions can only be looked on as a crude first approximation of reality. Although it is undoubtedly true that there is an underlying difference between the structure of immediate sensory perception and the structure of deeply repressed emotional experience, it is probably quite unlikely in reality that three definite regions of consciousness and only three are to be distinguished. So we see that, while theoretical constructions of some sort are necessary to account for psychopathological facts with regard to level of consciousness, first approximations. Similarly, with the concepts ego, superego, and id. We have already pointed out that this division of the psyche into three parts is necessitated by psychological facts which were roughly at least perceived by Plato and Aristotle. Undoubtedly some differentiation between the deep-lying dynamic forces of the mind (id), those connected with perceived reality (ego), and those connected with social responsibility (superego) is necessary. Psychoanalysis often speaks of ego and superego and id in the fashion in which medieval philosophers spoke of the Christian soul. The ego takes on all the properties of a selfish Homunculus who pulls the strings for what the psychoanalysts call ego functions: the superego is similarly thought of as a more or less conscious moral Homunculus controlling superego functions: and the id is an unconscious nasty little Homunculus controlling id functions. Freud probably more than any other modern psychologist has discredited the animistic prescientific psychology of the Christian theologians. But as he did the spade work for discrediting the instinct theory of the nineteenth-century biologists and then failed to throw it over completely, so also he prepared the way for a field theoretical psychology of personality dynamics without really ridding himself of all the characteristics of demonology. It is now probably possible to express the psychological interrelationships which Freud theoretically deduces from ego, superego, and id on the basis of field-theoretical constructs. We shall return to this problem in connection with our discussion of experimental psychopathology in Part V.

Many other concepts of the Freudian psychology are in definite need of clear and unambiguous definition. These concepts are undoubtedly dynamical and field-theoretical in nature without being as methodologically adequate as we could wish them to be. Here we shall take space to speak of only a few of these. The whole idea of libidinal progression and regression makes use of a dynamic concept of directional change without being based on any mathematically adequate conception of direction. Freud has been forced, in accounting for these things, to fall back upon mechanical and geological analogies which while pedagogically valuable as illustrations by no means clarify the real dynamic problem. Lewin (1937) has pointed this out in an excellent discussion of the relationship between topological psychology and psychoanalysis.

The whole problem of reversibility of psychological growth process is a very difficult one. That there can be psychological regression independent of physiological growth processes is, I think, an indisputable fact. On the other hand, the probability that in such cases physiological growth processes do not reverse themselves entirely makes it highly unlikely that we may consider regression as a direct reversal of a total process. The behaviour of an extremely regressed psychotic individual is not by any means the exact equivalent of the behaviour of a very young child. Quite frequently psychoanalysts speak as if it were, and this difficulty comes about through lack of any adequate definition of direction regression.

The idea of repression, which is so basic to psychoanalytic theory, is another concept which needs methodological clarification. Since Freud accepted inner biological urges and inner dynamic forces as a basis for developing his theory, repression becomes a matter of the ego forcing material unacceptable to the conscious into the unconscious. The only way we can really visualize this is that the ego is a small person within the psyche of the individual, who is able to get rid of unacceptable thoughts by dropping them into the unconscious. If it is true that psychological forces are forces within the psychological field rather than within the individual, then the theory of repression must be rewritten to take into account the structure of the environment. By so doing, it would be possible to bring the Freudian theory into good general agreement with the modern psychological theories of remembering and forgetting.

To mention only one other important need of clarification of Freudian concepts, let us take the idea of reaction formation. Reaction formation, as we have seen, consists in turning behaviour into its diametrically opposed form to protect oneself against anxiety and to strengthen repression. Squandering money is to be considered as a sublimated form of the spreading of faces, hoarding of money is called a reaction formation against this type of behaviour. It is easy to see that by allowing opposite behaviours to be accounted for as the continuation and reaction formation of the same basic mechanism there is little possibility of bringing Freudian theory to disproof. From the standpoint of modern operational logic, a theory must be expressed in such a way that it may be proved. This is surely the case with the Freudian theory. On the other hand, from the stand point of modern methodology, the evidence or experiment which is designed to prove the theory must be one which could have a possible negative outcome and so disprove the theory. At the present time, many of the concepts of psychoanalysis are undoubtedly developed in such a way that only proof and not disproof is possible. This is not to be take to mean that nothing like reaction formation occurs. As a matter of fact, anyone who has had clinical experience must realize the value of a concept like reaction formation. On the other hand, for both theoretical and practical reasons some more definite clarification of what causes the development of a symptom in one individual and a reaction formation in another is quite necessary. The criticism which we made of the concept of reaction formation is applicable to many of the other Freudian mechanisms. It is particularly applicable to the interpretation of symptoms in disease. The practicing analyst gets around this difficulty by speaking of over determination. When he speaks of over-determination, he means that, whenever there exists the possibility that different symptoms may develop, the one chosen has more causal factors in its favor than the others. Even so, most competent lay critics and many analysts themselves recognize the methodological shortcomings of Freudian theory in this respect.

All these conceptual, methodological difficulties of Freudian theory undoubtedly represent a transition from class-theoretical psychology to a field-theoretical psychology. Freud started his work when psychology was purely a class-theoretical science and ended it when psychology was becoming a field-theoretical science. In all fairness, we may say that this transition is being made more because of the efforts of Freud than because of the efforts of any other individual. It would be too much to expect that any one individual could complete such a transition. There is some danger that the great accomplishments of Freud will be taken as works of such genius that some individuals will hesitate before making changes in the methodological basis of Freudian theory. This is the danger of doctrine becoming rigid and inelastic out of respect to a very great human genius. Freud himself would certainly be the last man to encourage such procedure. From his first writings to his last, Freud introduced changes in the theory, and the great majority of these changes were toward making the theory more scientific. It is inevitable that sooner or later the last aspects of class-theoretical thinking in psychoanalysis will be overcome.

There are other aspects of psychoanalysis to be criticized beside the conceptual methodological ones. Psychoanalysis is the outcome of the clinical methodology. In this lies both its strength and its weakness: its strength, because in the clinic one meets really important psychodynamic problems face to face, in their raw form, often without the superficial veneer of socialization and civilization. From really talking to people about their troubles, from really asking them what they actually fear and hate and love, analysts are able to uncover the most vital information about underlying psychodynamics. Clinical research, however, is fraught with sources of error. In some of the older medical disciplines, like neurology, the sources of error of the clinical method have become notorious. Neurology today, despite the fact that originally our most valuable ideas concerning neural functioning came from the clinic, is chiefly furthered by experimental research. We believe that, just as experimental physiology developed systematic physiology as we have it today and experimental nerology developed systematic neurology as we have it today, experimental psychology may eventually put psychopathology on a more sound scientific basis. But no matter how much precise experimental investigation changes our opinions of psychodynamics, the human race will always be indebted to Sigmund Freud for the first great systematic pioneer research in this field.

3. OTHER PSYCHOANALYTIC LITERATURE OUTSIDE THE SCOPE OF THIS WORK

In our presentation of psychoanalysis, we had only space to deal with those aspects of the theory which are most important for problems of psychopathology and the normal personality. Freud and the psychoanalysts have dealt with many other topics from the general psychoanalytical position. The following paragraphs, which are little more than a bibliographical note, can only hope to give the reader some idea of the other fields investigated and to call his attention to the most important works in each of them.

Studies in Organic Medicine—The psychoanalytic theory, in accepting the organismic view in psychopathology (i.e., that there are psychological and physidogical problems in all mental diseases), also accepts that there are psychological factors in all physical diseases. With this postulate, the dichotomy between mental and physical disease disappears. The first important psychoanalyst to deal with this concept was Ferenczi (1928) in his theory of the pathoneuroses. By a pathoneurosis, Ferenczi referred to neurotic conditions which arise because the patient expends so much libido on a physically sick organ that neurosis in the ordinary sense ensues. Besides Ferenczi's pioneer studies, Felix Deutsch (1922) and Groddeck did important early work in the field of internal medicine. At the present time, the psychoanalytic factors in nearly every physical disease have been investigated and very detailed studies have been made of hypertension, asthma, certain cardiac disorders, and certain endocrinological disorders. This literature is admirably summarized in Menninger (1938) and in Dunbar (1935). Attention should also be called to the journal *Psychosomatic Medicine,* which specializes in this field. The paper of Benedik and Rubenstein is a good example of what can be done in this field. The medical student can certainly read some of this literature with profit.

Studies in Sociology and Anthropology—That psychoanalysis, which is concerned in such detail with the psychology of the family drama, should have implications for sociology and anthropology is easily understood. Freud himself has made important contributions to this field in his books, *Totem and Taboo* (1927) and *Group Psychology and The Analysis of the Ego* (1922). Today the importance of psychoanalysis for sociology and anthropology is widely recognized. Some other individuals who have dealt with these topics are Fromm, Horney (1937), Glover (1933), Hopkins, Dollard (1937), and Brown (1936c). The sociology student could certainly read all these works with profit.

Studies in the Field of Aesthetics—The artist and his audience are both psychological organisms and it would be strange if psychoanalysis had nothing to say about art. Certain literary artists, as will be clear from our discussion of genius, intuitively anticipated the findings of psychoanalysis and expressed them in a poetic fashion. We need merely to mention that the very name of the Oedipus situation is taken from the Greek tragedy and the whole of Shakespeare's *Hamlet* is concerned with the same famous theme. Actually, there are four distinct problems here; the form of the art, the psychological aspects of the content of the art, the psychology of the artist, and the psychology of the audience. Freud again made the most important first contributions to this field in his works on Michelangelo (1924a, Vol. IV), Leonardo da Vinci (1916), Keller (1924b Vol. IX), and Jensen (1924b,Vol. IX). Also important in this field are the studies of Bonaparte on Edgar Allan Poe, Reik on Goethe, and the woks of Sachs and Rank (1924) on problem of aesthetics. Students of art and literature will be well rewarded by reading some of them.

Studies in the Field of Philosophy—Our present understanding of the importance of the family drama has led to studies in social and speculative philosophy. Freud himself has published an important criticism of religion in his *The Future of an Illusion* (1928): his *Civilization and its Discontents* (1930) is probably one of the keenest essays in the analysis of modern culture.

12

OTHER THEORETICAL APPROACHES

1. THE SCOPE OF THIS CHAPTER

We have devoted the last three chapters to a rather complete presentation of psychoanalysis. We have attempted to present it in all its implications and to give at least the chief ramifications of the theory. We have chosen the psychoanalytic theory for the most complete presentation, because it is the most complete and systematic theory of personality genesis on a psychological basis. It would be misleading not to say something about other schools which attempt to develop psychodynamic theory but which deviate more or less widely from psychoanalysis, and something about other types of theoretical approach. In this chapter, we shall discuss certain theoretical positions in the field of psychopathology. Since the theory of psychoanalysis was presented in some detail, we may present the other theories in much less space. These theories deviate from psychoanalysis more or less widely, but psychoanalysis was the father of them all. In other words, all the theories agree that symptoms are caused, have significance, and are economical. They agree that certain basic urges meet frustration so that personality genesis becomes a matter of socio-psycho-biology. They disagree as to the nature of the basic urges, as to the nature of the chief frustrations, and as to the nature of person structure. Consequently, we shall not present these theories as completely independent systems, but only in the aspects in which they differ from psychoanalysis. The author believes this procedure is quite proper in its emphasis, because today it is increasingly realized that psychoanalysis is the most systematic and probably scientifically the best founded.

Besides the psychodynamic approaches, however, there are numerous other theoretical approaches in the field of psychopathology. None of these represent systematic schools, as the various systems of psychodynamics are rather theories with regard to certain aspects of personality structure or personality genesis. Among these are the mechanisms of repression and resistance, the nature of infantile psychosexual genesis, and the importance of the unconscious. He denies repression, rejects psychosexual genesis, and denies the validity of the distinction between conscious and unconscious. In the place of libidinal and aggressive urges, he posits a striving for prestige on the basis of masculine protest. Prestige is sought in three spheres—the economic, the sexual, and the social. The basic complex in determining personality genesis is the inferiority complex. Ideas from the conscious or unconscious are not differentiated.

Adler's chief criticism of Freud is that Freud overemphasized the role of the sexual in life, particularly the Oedipus situation and the castration complex. When Adler broke with Freud, Freud was chiefly concerned with libido theory and had not yet introduced the theory of the death instinct, so that to a certain extent the Adlerian criticism was justified. Adler, to be sure, stated that the sex elements in the psychological process of personality growth were of very great importance, but he said that sexual goals were part of the general goal of personal prestige. While Freud said the chief motivating force for human beings was the desire to love and be loved, Adler said the chief motivating force was the desire to stand out among one's fellow men. This desire he calls the prestige motive and says that the three chief forms of prestige for which individuals strive are social, sexual, and economic. By the drive to sexual prestige, Adler means more or less what Freud means by libido. By social prestige, Adler means the prestige gained by standing out among one's fellow men as a leader in social enterprise. By economic prestige, Adler means the prestige which comes from successfully making a living. Thus Adler accounts for our desire to belong to all sorts of exclusive groups, such as clubs, fraternities, societies, and the like, our desire to stand high in the various professional or occupational hierachies, our desire to belong to various groups in which the common herd does not have membership, as coming from the social aspects of the prestige motive. Our desire to get ahead economically, to make money, comes from the economic prestige motive. Adler considers sociological factors to be more important than Freud does. The motive force behind repression with him is the force of community feelings. Now it is quite true that Adler has given a very good description, in the sociopsychological sense, of most of the things we are concerned with in our contemporary industrialized civilization. It is certainly the ambition of most college students, for instance, to love and be loved in the sexual sense, to belong to the various clubs, fraternities, and societies, both professional and social, and to have enough money to dress well and go places. The college student further daydreams about himself as being the possessor of a beautiful wife and several handsome children, being a member of the exclusive clubs of his environment, and living in an expensive house in the best residential of his community. It is probably also true that most individuals who could arrive at this mode of life would do so. All of us are not attractive to the opposite sex, popular with our own sex, and successful in business. Failure to arrive at any one of these goals undoubtedly leads to change in our personality make-up. The Adlerian theory fits contemporary American social ideals so patly that it is small wonder that, some years ago, Adler was so much the vogue that the college student on first hearing it was inclined to think the Adlerian theory more adequate than the Freudian. We shall see later, however, that the Adlerian theory is superior to the Freudian only in a very superficial fashion.

Adler also bases much of his theory on infantile developments. Undoubtedly his best study is that of organic inferiority (1917a), in which he points out that all of us, or at least practically all of us, are actually inferior to certain others in their physiological organs. According to Adler, the child very early perceives that he is weaker both physically and mentally than the adult. Adler first pointed out that one of the ways in which the child realizes his organic inferiority is in the smallness of his penis. The girl child is particularly concerned with this because she has no penis at all. This gives rise to the rather well-known Adlerian theory of penis envy, which has been accepted in psychoanalysis. The realization of organic inferiority of the child causes the child to develop an inferiority complex. According to Freud, all children develop an Oedipus complex. According to Adler, all children develop these definite feelings of inferiority. The psychology of the inferiority complex is again undoubtedly a real one. All of us at one time or other doubt that we are as good as the next man, wish that we were stronger or more beautiful, or more popular, or more powerful. From these feelings of inferiority, the child develops the desire to become superior, to grow, and to meet the adult on an equal footing. Thus feelings of inferiority give rise to the masculine protest. The masculine protest against the inferiority complex plays very much the role in the Adlerain theory that overcoming the Oedipus complex through psychosexual genesis does in the Freudian theory. Struggle between the masculine protest and social reality thus goes one, and out of this struggle the personality has its growth and differentiation. Whether the individual develops into the normal adult or into the psychotic or neurotic personality, becomes sexually perverse, or develops a character defect depends on this conflict. Many of the points which Adler made against Freud had some slight value at the time he made them. The Freudian theory, however, has incorporated every valuable criticism from Adler without falling into the looseness of many Adlerian concepts and without sacrificing the undoubtedly valid concepts of repression, infantile sexuality, and the unconscious. If Adler's theory seems better to fit our conscious conflicts than does Freud's, it does so only by sacrificing the biologically well-founded ideas of Freud on the unconscious and sexuality.

Adlerian psychology fails to go far beyond the conscious conflicts between the ego and society, which are very superficial compared with the deeper ego-id conflicts.

Despite the fact that the emphasis on inferiority complex and the Adlerian idea of penis envy and masculine protest are valuable and original contributions of Adler to psychoanalytical literature, the status of the individual psychology as a science is not nearly so secure as that of psychoanalysis. Adlerian psychiatry is particularly unsystematic. The individual psychologists are unable to account for the interrelationships of psychoses, perversion, the normal adult personality, and character defects. In chapter 3, 4, 5, 6, 7 we have seen that orthodox descriptive psychiatry can very well be arranged on the framework of the psychoanalytical theory of psychosexual genesis. The Adlerians, on the other hand, are not able systematically to picture descriptive psychiatry in terms of infantile inferiority. Although Adler has made valuable contributions and although much of what he says shows keen insight into the superficial situation, his individual psychology cannot be considered as a rival theory having the same status as psychoanalysis. The author believes that the psychopathology of the future will assimilate the single valuable contributions of Adler, but that the school of individual psychology will soon be of only historical interest.

Adler has been a very productive writer, first of rather scholarly treatises on psychoanalysis and more recently of popular potboilers on the psychology of personality. The reader who wishes to familiarize himself further with the school of individual psychology is advised to read only the early books. Of these undoubtedly the best are *Organic Inferiority* (1917a) and *The Neurotic Constitution* (1917b). His later popular works have little to recommend them to the serious student of psychopathology (1929a, 1929b, 1931).

The Analytic Psychology of C.G. Jung—Another early follower of Freud and one who made decided contributions to the earlier psychoanalytical movement and later left it (in 1912) is the Zurich psychiatrist C.G. Jung. Jung was particularly important in the early days of psychoanalysis because he was one of the first to introduce psychoanalysis outside the limits of the Vienna medical center. Jung's career parallels Alder's. At first a staunch supporter of Freudian psychoanalysis and contributor to it, he was very highly esteemed in psychoanalytical circles. Later, like Adler, he found himself at odds with Freud concerning libido theory and later still he became the central figure of the second most important heretical school of psychoanalysis, that at Zurich. Jung's contributions to psychopathology, unlike Adler's, are not limited to the field of psychoanalytical investigation. The present paragraphs will be concerned only with his psychoanalytical position and later we shall say something about his contributions to characterology and psychiatry.

Like Adler, Jung found it necessary to quarrel with the Freudian libido theory before the Freudian theory of the death instinct had been adopted. Jung continues to use the concept libido but defines it in his own fashion. With Freud we saw that libido meant the urge which brings people into close physical contact. With Jung, libido becomes a rather generalized gregarious or social instinct, the general force which brings people together in any forms of social contact, *whether it be intimate or not.* Jung further developed his own ideas as to the role of the unconscious. We have seen that, according to Freud, the unconscious is, to be sure, biologically conditioned but develops separately in each individual. Adler denies its importance entirely. Jung, however, introduces the idea of the racial unconscious and so believes that not only the strivings of the individual but those of the whole race are represented in it. Thus, in dreams we have not only to interpret the personal unconscious motives but the racial unconscious motives. Dreams furthermore are not only the resolutions of conflict in sleep. They also are preparations for the future and as such have a prophetic significance. This part of the Jungian theory, dealihg with the racial unconscious and the prophetic nature of dreams, cannot be called scientific.

Jung, too, has advanced his own ideas on the structure of the personality. The conscious part which is in contact with reality is called the "persona." The central core of the conscious is the ego. There is also some personal unconscious. In the lower levels of unconsciousness, standing in the same relation to the unconscious as the ego does to the conscious, is the "anima" or unconscious femininity in the male and the "animus" or unconscious masculinity in the female. Inner subjective reality is mediated by them. Jung thus while accepting determinism and personality genesis almost completely rewrite the Freudian theory.

Furthermore, Jung's theory also lacks the systematic aspects of the Freudian theory. There is no clear picture as to how the various types of reaction to frustration become actualized, not is there any systematic theory of the psychoses. All these facts lead us to believe that, as with Adler, the many positive contributions of Jung will become assimilated into the regular psychoanalytic literature and the Jungian school will soon be only historical in importance. As this presentation of Jung is likewise very sketchy, the student who wishes to understand more about the Jungian psychology should read, besides *Psychological Types* (1923), the earlier studies on *Dementia Praecox* (1909), and his The *Theory of Psychoanalysis* (1915). Jung, too, in recent times has published a series of popular treatises on personality (1933, 1939). The author considers these later writings of Jung almost worthless.

Minor Variations in Psychoanalytical Theory— There are a considerable number of psychoanalysts, who, while accepting the Freudian theory in most of its important aspects, have introduced minor variations in it or have stressed certain points. Most of these individuals have not tried to set up separate schools and on the whole consider themselves as psychoanalysts. However, they are not orthodox psychoanalysts and are considered beyond the pale of orthodox psychoanalysis by the International Psychoanalytic Society. We shall have space only to mention several of these whose theories will be met by the reader who goes into psychodynamic theory at all extensively in the future.

Otto Rank accepts most Freudian theory, but wishes to begin the catalogue of important traumatic experiences earlier than Freud does. Rank says, and the idea is at least plausible, that the change from being fed through the umbilical cord to the process of being fed through the mouth is perhaps an even greater change than that brought about in the early oral period. Consequently, the first major traumatic experience is the trauma of birth. Rank claims this must always be taken into consideration not only in the therapeutic analysis but also in the building of theory. Rank has presented this aspect of his theory in great detail in the book, *The Trauma of Birth* (1929). Undoubtedly from a biological standpoint the act of being born represents a traumatic experience to the organism. The whole *modus vivendi* of the fetus is upset when it becomes the neonate. An adaptation which was wholly passive is upset and the first type of activity (breathing) is required from the newborn child. There is often, as indicated by dreams, folklore, poetry, and sometimes wishful thinking, a desire to return to the mother's womb.[1] Freud accepts the value of the birth trauma as a trauma on a biological level but because of the almost complete lack of psychic development at birth refuses to grant it the psychological importance which Rank claims for it. In this Freud is right. The interested reader will find Freud's criticism of Rank in *The Problem of Anxiety* (1936).

Stekel is another onetime prominent psychoanalyst who has suggested many innovations in the theory. He accepts certain positions of Adler and Jung and believes that by educating the patient the course of a psychoanalysis may be greatly shortened. His work is rather an eclectic hodgepodge and the author believes his position to be even more untenable than Jung's. Interested readers may wish, however, to look into his *Psychoanalysis and Suggestion Therapy* (1923) and decide for themselves.

3. THE CHARACTEROLOGICAL APPROACH

Besides the various psychodynamic theories, the most important psychological (as opposed to psysiological) approach to problems of personality is that of the characterologists. Since the time of Hippocrates, scientists have been attempting to find certain types of men, or subspecies of men, and trying to show that associated with these types there are certain psychological differences. Most of these theories suppose that these differences arise constitutionally and are hereditary. Undoubtedly there are outstanding constitutional and anatomical differences among the various races, and these differences have led to various theories of racial psychology. The whole problem of racial psychology cannot concern us here. We must, however, point out that practically all research in the field has pointed to the fact that no racial differences of a psychological sort have been found which may be attributed to biological facts alone. In other words, the real psychological differences between whites and Negroes, and gentiles and Jews, occur not on the basis of biological differences but on the basis of differences in culture patterns which are realized to be largely environmentally conditioned.

Besides interest in racial types, however, there has been interest in subspecies of *Homo sapiens* of a general psychological sort and of a more specific constitutional sort. Hippocrates, as is well-known, distinguished men into choleric, phlegmatic, melancholic, and sanguine types. He did this on the basis of the prevalent theory of bodily humors. *Phlegmatic* individuals were supposedly characterized by a superabundance of phlegm and because of this were supposed to be slow and easygoing psychologically. *Sanguine* individuals were characterized by a superabundance of blood and were for this reason supposed to be hopeful and confident psychologically. *Choleric* individuals had a superabundance of yellow bile, which led to the psychological characteristics of being quick to rage, changeable, and inclined to fly off the handle. *Melancholic* individuals had a superabundance of black bile and were inclined to be slow-moving, depressed, and sad for this reason. The realization of the complete inadequacy of Hippocrates' underlying physiological theory led to the abandonment of it as a serious theory in both psychology and medicine. The mere continuance of the characteristics of his theory, however, as names for existing personality types which everyone understands, shows that it may have some real significance.

Following Hippocrates, the great Roman physician Galen enlarged on his type-and-humor theory, and such characterologies were frequent through the Middle Ages. In general, as in the case of all Middle Age science, the theories became less and less scientific rather than more scientific and with the growth of modern science fell into disrepute. Again in the eighteenth century, however, characterology became of great popular vogue and gained again a certain amount of scientific interest.

Among the characterological schools of the eighteenth century, the physiognomists, of whom Lavater was the leader, were the most important. The physiognomists believed that psychological characteristics were associated with bodily build through the general contours of the body, particularly the contours of the face. These individuals were followed by the phrenologists in the nineteenth century, of whom the chief representatives were Gall and Spurzheim. They believed that the contours of the skull were indicative of certain psychological characteristics. One still sees evidence of the activities of the phrenologists in poorer sections of our great industrial cities, with the familiar charts showing areas of the skull marked "animativeness," "acquisitiveness," "philanthropy," etc. In the nineteenth century, the Italian criminologist Lombroso developed a theory that the characters of certain antisocial individuals, particularly criminals, were determined through a combination of physiognomic and phrenologic traits. Psychological degeneracy, then, was revealed in the presence of certain stigmata such as prominences on the skull, cauliflower ears, misshapen noses, and the like. Following the Lombroso school, there was a long interest in graphology or the science of distinguishing character through handwriting. Those constitutional differences which lead to differences in the handscript were supposed to create different character types.

By the turn of the twentieth century, the work of all these schools had fallen into practically complete disrepute among scientists. Carefully controlled experimental studies of estimating psychological character from photographs did much to discredit the physiognomists, as these experiments invariably turned out negative. The discovery of the chief areas of localization in the anatomy of the brain discredited the phrenologists by showing that there are no specific brain centers for the type of trait which the phrenologists attempted to correlate with bumps on the head. Investigations by later schools of criminologists put the Lombroso theory into disrepute. The fact that even experts in handwriting could do little to distinguish the psychological characteristics of handwriting of people unknown to them where the context of the writing was not personal also discredited the graphologists.

The mere fact that so many people for so many years have been intersted in trying to correlate psychological traits with physical characteristics or have been concerned with trying to isolate various psychological or physical types is evidence at least that such types may exist. In the twentieth century there has been a revived interest in typology and characterology. The modern typologists and characterologists are concerned with the possible correlations between psychological behaviour and underlying constitution. The scientific ones among them, however, are desirous to take into consideration what is known about both biological constitution on the one hand and modern psychological theory on the other. It may be that through modern characterology we shall develop the knowledge of certain specific problems of psychiatry, such as that of the choice of disease. Considering all we have learned in the last chapters about the effect of barriers in the psychological field upon the development of the personality, it scarcely seems possible that any psychological characteristics are for all time predetermined in the germ plasm or the constitution. Since, on the other hand, we believe that hereditary factors enter into all problems of behaviour along with environmental factors, it may be that constitutional factors, such as bodily build, or psychological type factors, like introversion and extraversion, are contributing factors to the finished personality. The work in the field of modern scientific characterology is so new and there so many rival schools that it would be simply confusing to attempt to cover the whole field in a book of this nature. We must content ourselves with giving a brief resume of the leasing characterological schools and some indication of the possible usefulness in each distinction.

The Concept of Introversion-Extraversion—The most widely known of the modern character types are those which C.G. Jung (1923) popularized as introverts and extraverts. According to Jung, the introverts have a subjective attitude; they tend to withdraw from the world of fact into the world of fantasy. They are chiefly affected by stimuli arising within the world of inner experience. In terms of his (not Freud's) libido theory, in the introvert the libido is turned inward. The extraverts, on the other hand, have realistic objective attitudes, they tend to react to the world of physical reality, and they are chiefly stimulated by the real world. Their libido is turned outward. Hence, the distinction *intro-* and *extravert*. Jung himself was concerned with the perceptual-cognition attitudes of individuals rather than with their social attitudes, and it is quite possible for introverts to have many social contacts and for extraverts to be socially withdrawn. The distinction as Jung originally used it was concerned with the way the individual perceived and thought about the real world. This is important to point out because, in the hands of some American social psychologists, introvert comes to mean a socially withdrawn and self-sufficient individual while an extravert is a "hail fellow well met." Undoubtedly social attitudes often follow modes of cognition and perception and in general the introvert is inclined to be more withdrawn than the extravert. Between the two and more balanced is the *ambivert*. Jung illustrates his characterological distinction with historical biographies and case histories. He goes on to make distinctions between extraverted thinking, feeling, intuitive, and sensational types. These finer distinctions cannot be enlarged upon here. Similar to Jung's two types but not identical to them are the distinctions of James, Rorschach, and Spranger. There has been considerable work by Americal experimentalists on the concepts of introversion-extraversion.

The idea of introversion-extraversion is undoubtedly of some significance in pschoapathology. Schizophrenics, as we shall see, may be looked on as extremely introverted and manic-depressives as extremely extraverted. No one today can seriously believe that the total personality is predetermined by a constitutional personality type, but constitution undoubtedly, as even Freud himself admits, may play a considerable part in the depth of regression and the choice of neurosis and may have something to do with fundamental modes of racting. It is not entirely clear to what extent either introversion or extraversion is constitutional.

Kretschmer's Characterology Based on Physique—According to Kretschmer, the various personality types have an affinity for a certain type of physique or bodily build and, when individuals having such physique become mentally ill, they tend to develop certain forms of mental illness. Thus, extraverts (or cyclothymic temperaments, as Kretschmer calls them) tend to have the pyknic body build and when psychotic to develop manic-depressive psychosis. The introverts (or schizoid group) on the other hand tend to have the asthenic[1] or athletic body build and when psychotic tend to develop schizophrenia. In addition, there is the dysplastic body type. The chief physical characteristics of the various Kretschmerian body types have been summarized nicely by Nicole as follows:

The grouping of physical types, according to Kretschmer, includes the following four main classes:

A. The Athletic Type—Strong skeleton, powerful musculature, fine chest, and free neck. Hands and feet large, at times even reminiscent of acromegaly. Biologically this type seems a milder form of the Afrecan Negro physique and—going farther back in the evolutionary scale—of the gorilla.

B. The Asthenic Type—The individuals are usually thin and long. The skin is dry, the shoulders are narrow, the arms lean and long, and the chest flat. Viewed historically, this type would seem to spring from the chimpanzee and the earlier Aryan races. It is a type frequent in dementia praecox.

C. The Pyknic Type—This one is very different. The body cavities (head, thorax, abdomen) are large, there is a marked tendency to deposition of fat, and the contours of the body are rounded and graceful. The face is soft and broad and the hands short and wide. In many ways, this make-up seems to hark back to the Mongol races and—in the animal series—to the orangoutan.

D. The Dysplastic Group—This is a mixed one, comprising mostly types that approximate mild forms of glandular syndromes. For example, we have the elongated eunuchoids with their deficient secondary sexual characteristics; the eunuchoid and polyglandular fat abnormalities, and infantile and hypoplastic varieties showing marked underdevelopment and disproportion. These types of Kretschmer have been added to by other writers, notably by Rodalie, while constitution has been studied by Willemse (in delinquency) and also by Stockard.

So much for the physical aspects of personality. The next step was to correlate it with the mental side, and this not only in respect of confirmed mental derangement, but of "normal" individuals also. First as regards psychoses. Once elimination has been made of those disorders directly attributable to accidental and physical causes, such as toxemia and exhaustion where the prominent clinical features are delirium and stupor, and epilepsy, and general paralysis, we have left the important class known as the biogenetic psychoses. These can be divided into two main groups:

1. The Cylothymic (or manic-depressive) Group—The disorder is principally in the emotional sphere and is remarkable for its tendency toward rapid though temporary recovery followed by relapses and recurrences. The personality, although deranged, is to a marked degree unified; there is no apparent disharmony between the different components of the patient's conduct; he is in fact what Bleuler calls "syntonic." He is, too, in good contact with his surroundings and he responds to environmental stimuli.

2. The Schizophrenic Group—This includes the dementia praecoxes, the paraphrenias, and paranoia's. They all evince to a varying extent a failure of synthesis; they appear to be divided within themselves; there is a lack of correspondence between ideas on the one hand and emotion on the other. Further, their may be expressed the phenomenon of antithesis known as ambivalence. In the milder forms, we recognize the "shut-in" personalities of Hoch, that are so reminiscent of Jung's introverts.

The factors of predisposed personality had already been stressed by Meyer and others, and Kretschmer enlarged his classification so as to include all types, normal as well as abnormal, thereby emphasizing the points of similarity between sanity and insanity, rather than those of dissimilarity. His two great groups became *Cycloid* and the *Schizoid*, and only the definitely abnormal among them were termed cyclothymics and schizophrenics. The former—the normal cycloids —were recognizable from their sociability, good nature, expression of emotion, and tendency to alternating modes. In contrast to these, the normal schizoids exhibit associability, dry and unsympathetic outlook, eccentricity and restlessness, perhaps coupled with a brilliant intellect. [From J.E. Nicole, *Psychopathology*, Bailliere, Tindall and Cox, London, 1934, pp. 98—100.]

The chief physical characteristics and the chief related mental characteristics of the asthenic and pyknic types are shown schematically in Fig. 12.1.

Although no one has found perfect correlation between mental disease, body build, and personality type, there is now abundant emphasis that there is some affinity between these things. A well trained clinical psychiatrist can walk through a ward of psychotic individuals and diagnose these much better on the basis of physique than chance alone would allow. The use of the Kretschmer types has some value in practical psychiatry.

Again many detailed questions remain to be solved. Is the basic body build really determined in the germ plasm? Can individuals whose basic personality changes show also such

ASTHENIC	PYKNIC
Tree Point Face	Five Point Face
Vertical Predominance	Horizontal Predominance
Hour Glass Figure	Beer Barrel Figure
Elongated Limbs	Shortened Limbs
Jerky	Smooth
Introverted	Extraverted
Shut-in, Asocial	Sociability
Emotionally Anaesthetic	Emotionally Cyclic
Schizoid	Cycloid
Schizophrenia	Manic-Depressive

Fig. 12.1. Showing the relationships between Kretschmer's body types, personality traits, and disease affinities.

striking changes in bodily build? All babies are pyknic. How do so many happen later to become asthenic, athletic, or dysplastic? Even in bodily build environmental influences play a role. Until more thorough studies have been made, we can with Kretschmer attribute some causal effect of the physique on total personality but cannot make it either basic or constitutional as he attempts to do.

Other Characterological Schools—There are many other approaches to personality from the standpoint of characterology. Roback has devoted a big book to abstracting the literature in this field alone. Interested readers may go to it. Besides the work of Jung and Kretschmer, the most interesting modern studies on types from the standpoint of psychodynamic theory are those of Rorschach, Saudek, and Terman and Miles. We shall have something to say about these in the final chapter.

4. THE SOCIOLOGICAL AND ETHNOLOGICAL APPROACH

It is undeniable that sociological factors have the greatest importance in building the personality. One of the chief shortcomings of psychodynamic theory in the past has been an overemphasis on the individual and familial psychological factors to the neglect of the larger sociological and cultural factors. We have already stressed the importance of the social factors in the psychological field. The author in his *Psychology and the Social Order* has given his views on the social determinants of personality at length. The fact remains that in practically all cultures, even the primitive ones, individuals show singn of personality maladjustments which arise on the basis of frustration of emotional urges. The occurrence of the chief psychopathic behaviour forms, although statistics vary as to incidence of types, in the various modern civilized cultures is also an undoubted fact. We must consequently conclude that, although cultural differences make for personality differences, much of the personality is laid down by psychobiological factors and that the cultural modifications are secondary.

The field of ethnology is a rich one in which to test the basic postulates of psychodynamic theory. Studies in this field already undertaken do much to contradict the instinctual basis of psychodynamic theory. We have already seen, however, that psychoanalytic theory does not depend for its systematic validity on a strict adherence to the instinctual basis of psychic urges. The attempt to deduce everything in the personality from the sociological and ethnological structure of a society is probably as much mistaken as the attempt to deduce everything in the structure of the society from the psychobiological aspects of the personality. To repeat the basic contention of organismic psychiatry, "The personality has its genesis in the way which individuals of specific biological constitution meet barriers in the psychological field." Most of these barriers are imposed by society and are hence cultural. The nature of a culture, however, is limited by psychological factors are influenced by the culture. The basic problem which we must investigate in thinking about societal change is just what in the personality may be changed with changes in culture and how far we may change culture without seriously complicating social adjustment because of psychobiological considerations. The author has considered this problem at a more advanced level in a series of papers (1937b, 1938, 1939a).

The work of coordinating psychodynamic theory with ethnology and sociology has begun from both sides. In the last chapter we referred to the psychoanalytic studies in sociology. Important works raising the problem of the effect of cultural factors on psychodynamics are those of Rivers (1921 to 1926), Malinowski (1927, 1929), Mead (1935), Williams (1934), Kardiner, and Faris and Dunham.

5. ENDOCRINOLOGICAL AND BIOCHEMICAL APPROACHES

The theoretical approaches so far mentioned have been from the standpoint of organismic or psychogenic theory. There are many valuable approaches from the standpoint of somatogenic theory. The reader will remember that this book is of necessity limited to the discussion of psychological factors. For the sake of completeness, we wish to mention something of the endocrinological and biochemical approaches.

The greatest advances in modern physiology have been in understanding the role of the autonomic nervous system and the endocrine glands. Since emotions (wishes) have been discovered to be the fathers of both thoughts and actions and since the energy of emotion is regulated chiefly by the autonomic nervous and endocrine systems, it is natural that psychopathologists should study endocrinology.

There is not space in this book to discuss either the anatomy or the physiology of the autonomic and endocrine systems. The average student will remember something at least about them from his elementary courses. The discovery that certain hormones serve as facilitators and regulators of all growth (particularly sexual growth and differentiation) and that certain others are correlated with define changes in emotion and mood at first led some writers like Berman to think of the endocrines as the final regulators of personality. Such overemphasis on the somatic factor has been more recently discarded, as is shown in Hoskins's more recent book.

The organismic solution to the psychosomatic problem is the only possible one from what we now know about the functionings of both the autonomic nervous system and the endocrine glands. It is as foolish to say that endocrine dysfunction causes emotional dysfunction as it is to say the inverse of this. What we know is the close correlation between these things, and we probably have more detailed knowledge of the emotions than we do of endocrinology. This does not mean that endocrinology should not be studied by psychopathologists. In many cases, endocrine therapy and endocrine surgery are more applicable to personality upsets than psychology. They are borderline subjects to psychopathology proper, however, so we shall have no more to say about them here. The interested reader is referred to the works of Berman and Hoskins.

Besides endocrinological studies, there has recently developed a series of hypotheses about the effect of disbalance in brain chemistry on personality. McDougalls's (1936) X-hormone theory speculates on the presence of an X-hormone which may lead to the inhibition of cortical control on thalamic function. McDougalls's speculative theory is given some support in the work of Bancroft (1931a) on the effect of sodium amytal and sodium rhodanate on the inhibition and facilitation of neural impulses in the cortico-thalamic tract. More recently Sakel and Meduna, who have introduced the insulin and metrazol shock therapies, have again shown the importance of biochemistry for the psychosomatic problem. The medical student might well look into these sources. In general, the biochemical approach has the same limitations and shortcomings as the endocrinological. This is not to say that it will not one day be of great importance to psychopathology.

SUMMARY

1. Since the psychoanalytic theory has been treated in such detail, the other theoretical modes of attack must be outlined more briefly.
2. Adler's indivdual psychology and Jung's analytic psychology are compared and contrasted with psychoanalysis.

3. The characterological approach has promise as an adjunctival theory to psychoanalysis. The inadequacies of classical characterology have been partially overcome in the work of Jung, Kretschmer, and others.
4. The sociological and ethnological approaches also show much promise. The relative weight of psychobiological and cultural factors in determining personality may be decided through ethnological study.
5. The endocrinological and biochemical approach have recently shown-much promise. These various approaches are not to be considered rival theories to psychoanalysis, but rather as approaches which may supplement psychoanalytic knowledge and refine it.